THE AMERICAN REVOLUTION AND THE PRESS

Medill School of Journalism
VISIONS *of the* AMERICAN PRESS

GENERAL EDITOR
David Abrahamson

*Selected titles in this series*

MAURINE H. BEASLEY
*First Ladies and the Press: The Unfinished Partnership of the Media Age*

PATRICIA BRADLEY
*Women and the Press: The Struggle for Equality*

DAVID A. COPELAND
*The Idea of a Free Press: The Enlightenment and Its Unruly Legacy*

HERBERT J. GANS
*Deciding What's News: A Study of "CBS Evening News," "NBC Nightly News," "Newsweek," and "Time"*

TOM GOLDSTEIN
*Journalism and Truth: Strange Bedfellows*

KARLA K. GOWER
*Public Relations and the Press: The Troubled Embrace*

MARK NEUZIL
*The Environment and the Press: From Adventure Writing to Advocacy*

NORMAN SIMS
*True Stories: A Century of Literary Journalism*

MICHAEL S. SWEENEY
*The Military and the Press: An Uneasy Truce*

PATRICK S. WASHBURN
*The African American Newspaper: Voice of Freedom*

# THE AMERICAN REVOLUTION AND THE PRESS

## THE PROMISE OF INDEPENDENCE

Carol Sue Humphrey

*Foreword by David A. Copeland*

MEDILL SCHOOL OF JOURNALISM

Northwestern University Press
Evanston, Illinois

Northwestern University Press
www.nupress.northwestern.edu



Printed in the United States of America
10 9 8 7 6 5 4 3 2 1

**Library of Congress Cataloging-in-Publication Data**

Humphrey, Carol Sue.
The American Revolution and the press: the promise of independence / Carol Sue Humphrey; foreword by David A. Copeland.
p. cm.—(Visions of the American press)
"Medill School of Journalism."
Includes bibliographical references and index.
ISBN-13: 978-0-8101-2650-3 (pbk. : alk. paper)
1. United States—History—Revolution, 1775–1783—Press coverage—United States. 2. American newspapers—History—18th century. 3. Journalism—United States—History—18th century. I. Medill School of Journalism. II. Title. III. Series: Visions of the American press.
E209.H86 2013
071.309033—dc23

2012051275

∞ The paper used in this publication meets the minimum requirements of the American National Standard for Information Sciences—Permanence of Paper for Printed Library Materials, ANSI Z39.48-1992.

*In Memory of Don Higginbotham,*
*an amazing adviser who both challenged and encouraged*
*his students*

# CONTENTS

# FOREWORD

*David A. Copeland*

When discussion turns to America's move toward independence from Great Britain and the role the press played in the process, quotations from those who were firsthand observers are truly powerful. "What do we mean by the Revolution? The war? That was no part of the Revolution," John Adams wrote to Thomas Jefferson in 1815. Instead, Adams said, one needed to consult newspapers and pamphlets in all the colonies to uncover the true Revolution. Historian David Ramsay's well-known statement from his 1789 history of the Revolution serves notice, too, that "the pen and the press had merit equal to that of the sword" in bringing about the separation of colonies from their colonial rulers. And New York printer John Holt wrote to master newspaper essayist Samuel Adams on January 26, 1776, with this observation: "It was by means of News papers that we receiv'd & spread the Notice of the tyrannical Designs formed against America and kindled a Spirit that has been sufficient to repel them." Bernard Bailyn probably best summed up the relationship between the Revolution and the press at the beginning of his 1967 *Ideological Origins of the American Revolution:* "Every medium of written expression was put to use" to ensure that all Americans received the message that the time had come to separate from Great Britain.

But the question that this insightful volume by Carol Sue Humphrey so ably asks and answers is: How was it possible for a relatively minuscule number of printing establishments, estimated at around forty, to provide thirteen colonies and a population of approximately 2.5 million with so much material for discussion and debate that those colonists were willing not only to defy British law and taxes but also to create a declaration for their independence and to fight to obtain self-rule? From a perspective in the twenty-first century—when information about almost any subject is passed on in seconds and it is nearly impossible to see anyone walking who is not looking down at some portable device to stay informed—it is hard to imagine that the speed of sharing information in the age of the Revolution was measured in days and weeks. It also becomes nearly impossible to believe that plodding paragraphs and pages of type—not photographs, nor images, nor voice transmissions, but paragraphs that required readers to sift through thousands of words sans headlines or story leads—could bring people to the point of declaring their independence from the most powerful nation in the world. But that is exactly what happened in what would become the United States in the second half of the eighteenth century.

Simply saying this is so and offering quotations from those involved in the Revolutionary era as support may be enough because the end results are observable. But in eighteenth-century America, a melding of ideas and events had to occur to make it possible for the press to become such a powerful tool.

First, there was the expansion of free speech and the press that, by the time of the Stamp Act in 1765, practically ensured that whatever someone wanted to say in a newspaper could be said. The trial of John Peter Zenger had not provided colonists with any laws to protect them, but, as a writer in the *Pennsylvania Gazette* noted three years after the trial, the results were better than law because they were written upon the hearts of the people. Truth as a defense against libel, a trial with a jury of peers of the accused, and the possibility of finding the defendant not guilty were seldom heard of prior to 1735. But by 1765 no other libel trials had occurred in America, and irate printers and citizens alike reacted to the Stamp Act with great fervor. In New York, Lieutenant Governor Cadwallader Colden said that colonial papers had violated every law of sedition and libel in their reaction to the Stamp Act with assorted lies aimed at arousing the populace. But, he noted, any attempt to seek prosecution would be worthless. In Massachusetts, Governor Thomas Hutchinson could not get a single grand jury to return a charge of libel in the colony even though the most virulent charges against the British government came out of the papers and essayists there. Writers, however, believed they had the right to attack the government, and they continued to do so for the next decade. "YOUR Press has spoken to us the words of truth," is how an essay in the *Boston Gazette* on March 14, 1768, described newspaper content. John Adams was certain by this time that government would never be able to silence the voices of the people no matter how oppressive laws and taxes became. Nothing, he said in the *Gazette* on September 30, 1765, was more cherished by Americans than a free press. And now—as should be—it was "easy and cheap and safe for any person to communicate his thought to the public."

Second, by the time that Americans had begun to think that separation from Britain was the recourse for unwise taxes and oppressive government, the colonies had grown away from thinking of themselves as thirteen separate entities and saw themselves more as people with a core of common interests and concerns. Benjamin Franklin and a few others had made a proposal for a converged and limited all-colonial government in 1754 at the Albany Congress. Franklin's iconic "JOIN, or DIE" woodcut was created to bolster support for his plan of union. Colonial legislatures were not ready for a union, but they still provided troops and finances to help one another during the French and Indian War. However, that severed rattlesnake in what would be the nation's first editorial cartoon would surface again in 1765 and yet again in the 1770s as the symbol for American unity. That it was so omnipresent says much about the change in point of view by colonials. One writer in the October 13, 1757, issue of the *Pennsylvania Journal* observed, "All the colonies have a natural Connection and Interest in one another, and in the same Places." Samuel Adams called all who opposed the Stamp Act "Saviours of the Country." He was not speaking solely to the readers of the *Boston Gazette;* the "Journal of Occurrences" that he and Benjamin Edes created may have described the horrors of the British occupation of Boston, but it speculated that it was only a matter of time before the same happened elsewhere in America. The "Journal" was not simply a series that described the woes of the people of Massachusetts. It was an account of an American problem. The fact that nearly every paper in colonial America eventually ran the "Journal of Occurrences" verifies that this mindset had infiltrated a majority of those living in the colonies.

Third, there was a desire on the part of nearly all those who lived in the colonies to be a part of the discussion. This public sphere was fueled, as Jürgen Habermas has demonstrated, by a rise of the middle class who wanted a say in what was taking place as much as the elites who had held both economic and political power for centuries. In America, though, those that wanted a voice—or at least wanted to know what was occurring—stretched from one end of the cultural spectrum to the other. The fact that lively debate was very much a pastime in the eighteenth century played perfectly into this desire to be included in the discussion. In taverns, in coffeehouses, on the streets, in homes, the public prints were read aloud, and that content was available to all who could hear. Although literacy rates were relatively high in colonial America, literacy was not essential to being engaged in what was taking place. If one could hear, one could contemplate and form an opinion. One could not offer a written reply if one could not write, but in America in the 1760s and 1770s thousands of people did. They kept the prints and the public sphere filled with ideas to debate, to discuss, and ultimately to sway public opinion. And even though everyone did not join in the written polemical debate, almost everyone existed within a sphere of influence—from lawyers to farmers, from women to merchants, and even slaves.

Debate continued within the oral tradition. Because the news from the press was shared in oral form, the written word was spread much deeper into society and was probably more powerful than any one form of media message today. This fact helps explain how approximately forty newspapers in 1775 could reach 2.5 million people. This is why timeliness measured in days and weeks was perhaps more powerful than updates of minute details found scrolling on all-news networks or on Twitter. In colonial America, the same stories were printed, read, and debated aloud, then reread and re-debated in practically every town and home. Political debate fed into the idea of being American, too. Lack of stature in a community did not necessarily lessen a person's knowledge or understanding in America's eighteenth-century public sphere. Silas Deane, who helped secure France's assistance for America during the Revolution, observed in his "Memoire" of September 24, 1776, that even "the very poorest" among Americans "are not an ignorant unprincipled rabble, heated and led on to the present Measures by the artful & Ambitious few." Instead, Deane explained, they form their opinions by consulting "Gazettes & political publications, which they read, observe upon and debate in a Circle of their Neighbors."

Finally, the press became the perfect means of manipulating public opinion. John Adams described what happened at the *Boston Gazette* in the post–Stamp Act world as "cooking up paragraphs, articles, occurrences, &c., working the political engine." Naturally all colonials did not believe separation from Britain was the proper or wisest course for America. Even though calls for free speech and a free press continued to sound from America's papers, those who favored independence knew that they somehow had to limit speech by those who did not support the cause. In many ways, the century-long move toward a press unencumbered by sedition charges aided the Patriots. Leonard Levy in *Emergence of a Free Press* concluded that, by the time of the Stamp Act crisis, an atmosphere existed in America that kept printers and essayists from worrying about censure, arrest, or charges of seditious libel. In such an environment, your enemy could be vilified without worry. As Edes and Sam Adams cooked up their paragraphs, wrote the "Journal of Occurrences," and portrayed all things British as the embodiment of evil, they, the Sons of Liberty, and other like-minded colonials began to monopolize the printed word. Their rhetoric was filled with emotion. They worried less about fact and more about arousing negativity toward Britain and positive feelings toward independence. Printers still espoused a free press, but most did so in words only. John Holt said his *New-York Journal* was open to all opinions, but he refused to print what he considered the lies of Tories. He called their polemics on January 5, 1775, "barefaced attempts to deceive and impose upon the ignorant." For Patriot printers, it was very much the old adage that the squeaky wheel gets the grease. The loudest voice wins. That is exactly how the Patriot minister Andrew Eliot of Boston saw it. The newspapers of America must "awaken and rouse" the people, he wrote to another minister in 1765. By the end of the century, when another revolutionary battle of ideology was taking place—that between Federalists and Republicans—a Federalist judge named Alexander Addison accurately described how important the press was to that war and had been decades before: "Give to any set of men the command of the press, and you give them the command of the country," he said in an article in the *Columbian Centinel* on January 1, 1799, "for you give them the command of public opinion, which commands every thing."

Controlling the press is what the propagandists, as Philip Davidson called them, did from about 1765 through the beginning of the Revolution. They gradually silenced the voice of opposition, though never completely. They were able to instill the concept of independence as they vilified British taxes, law, politics, and royalty while painting the American cause as just but oppressed. They could win the war of words because the press in America had achieved a level of freedom by 1765 that allowed people to say just about anything they wanted in the public prints without fear of repercussion by the government. Clever polemists crafted words filled with emotion. Those words were shared in newspapers from New England to Georgia and were then read aloud and debated and discussed in gathering places public and private. By this time, events such as the French and Indian War had created a sense of commonality among colonials on many subjects. It did matter to people in Charleston, South Carolina, what happened to people in Boston, Massachusetts. They were connected, at first economically, then through common causes like fighting off French marauders of the shipping lanes and the Native Americans who terrorized the backcountry. Then, it became British taxes, unjust laws, and a lack of representation. If Boston could be occupied, occupation could just as easily happen in Charleston or Savannah. Revolution did take place in the hearts and minds of the people, as John Adams observed. But for most Americans in the period prior to the Declaration of Independence, their hearts were swayed and their minds made up by what they read in the printed word.

All of the above are reasons that this volume by Carol Sue Humphrey is so important. America's Revolutionary press established an agenda that helped develop the nation and has continued to define it ever since. Within this volume, all the polemics of Revolution play out from the pages of the press, but Humphrey takes the reader further and delves into the pages of the papers that published during the Revolution. Often, that story is lost between our inquiry into the push to revolution and then the development of a new nation and its formation of a radical and new style of government after the war. But in *The American Revolution and the Press,* the reader is immersed in the whole story. Patriots and Tories provide the foundation, and their take on it all comes alive. It is a story that is relived with excitement when one does so through the accounts that the people of the era experienced. *The American Revolution and the Press* helps readers understand the American response to all that was written and shared in a new nation that was about to come into existence against the greatest of odds.

# PREFACE

Americans love stories about the wars their ancestors fought in. Generally leading the way has been the Civil War, primarily because it involved the entire nation fighting itself and had battles scattered across the country from Maryland and Pennsylvania to Oklahoma and New Mexico. In many ways, the Civil War has overshadowed all other military conflicts in American history, including the American Revolution, the war that brought the United States into existence as an independent nation.

That reality has been a part of my entire life in many ways. Growing up in North Carolina, I spent a lot of time in activities related to the history of the Civil War. My family usually went camping for several weeks every summer and we would spend part of the time visiting Civil War battlefields. My mother and one of my brothers were both big Civil War buffs and greatly enjoyed dragging the rest of us around to see everything we could on every battlefield we visited. I can remember walking around Gettysburg, Manassas, the Wilderness, Spotsylvania, Appomattox, Fredericksburg—the list goes on and on. I know that these summer trips helped spark my interest in American history, but the Civil War was never my favorite part of American history. As long as I can remember, I was fascinated with George Washington and the American Revolution and could not understand why my family did not join me in that fascination. When we moved to Wilmington, North Carolina, when I was in the fifth grade, I was ecstatic to learn that there was a Revolutionary War battlefield nearby (Moore's Creek).

Obviously, my fascination with the American Revolution has influenced my career path. In college, I took as many classes related to the eighteenth century and the American Revolution as I could find and I wrote an honors paper and a master's thesis related to the Declaration of Independence. When I started my Ph.D. program at the University of North Carolina, I knew that I wanted to study something to do with the American Revolution, but I had no idea as to what direction that study should take. So, I went to see the History Department's expert on the American Revolution, Dr. Don H. Higginbotham. When I sat down to talk to him about possible directions for my research, he was extremely helpful. He reached in his desk drawer and pulled out a stack of index cards. On these cards he had written various ideas that he had had over the years about good research projects that he was not planning to pursue himself. He figured that these ideas would be good ones to share with students when they came asking for suggestions, and he was right about that. One of the ideas was to pick up the study of the role of the press during the American Revolution at the point that Arthur Schlesinger had stopped in his *Prelude to Independence: The Newspaper War on Britain, 1764–1776.* That possibility fascinated me, and thus my lifelong study of newspapers and their impact during the American Revolution began.

From that day on, Don served as my adviser. I knew that Don was the local expert on the Revolution in the University of North Carolina History Department, but the true depth of his learning on the subject slowly became apparent to me as I worked with him to fine-tune my research directions and to produce my dissertation on the role of the press in New England from 1775 to 1789. Don's own interest in the Revolution helped him ask thoughtful questions that guided my research and my writing. He knew that newspapers had played an important role in the Revolution because the military leaders he had studied had talked about them, so he encouraged me to study how and why that happened. He also served as an amazing editor who took my drafts apart and pushed me to make what I wrote more thoughtful and more focused. As a result, my dissertation was in great shape when I finished it and it was soon published.

Don's encouragement of my research and writing continued as my career progressed. Every so often, he would contact me and ask me how things were going and what my current projects were. The last time I saw him was in March 2007 at the symposium, "A Higginbotham Affair," that the University of North Carolina hosted honoring his retirement and his contributions to the study of history. He asked me then what I was working on and I told him about this book, which was in the very early stages at that point. He encouraged me to keep working on it, and the very last thing he told me as I left to catch my plane was to hang in there and get this book published. I know that he would have been very happy to see it completed.

In this book, I examine the important role played by the press during the Revolutionary era, a period stretching over about twenty years. During this period, newspapers provided the primary mechanism to tie the thirteen colonies together in a way that would mold them into one nation. Whether you are talking about the arguments over taxes in the 1760s that laid the groundwork for the revolt against British rule or the various meetings in the early 1770s that led to declaring independence or the fighting from 1775 to 1781 that produced final victory, newspapers played an essential role in the Revolution's ultimate success. The press gave their readers specific information about these arguments, meetings, and battles in the war as well as how the war was going overall. But the newspapers also worked hard to keep Americans engaged in the war in such a manner that they were willing to fight hard and sacrifice until independence was achieved. Without the press, Americans would not have known much about what was going on.

For modern Americans, living in a world of essentially instantaneous communication in a variety of forms, it is not easy to appreciate how such information was delivered. A "timely" story in the eighteenth century could take six weeks or more to get across the Atlantic from Great Britain or from one end of the colonies to the other. For us, that seems slow. But Americans at that time knew nothing else and so they eagerly waited for the news. Six weeks or less was timely for them because that was the only option they had. What mattered more to the readers of these stories was finding out how the war was going and whether their side was winning or not. Both Americans who favored independence and those who wanted to remain loyal to Great Britain supported the press during the war because it was the major source of information available, no matter which side of the conflict someone was on.

Today, we often talk about television or the Internet serving as the primary means of communication that ties us together and gives us a common outlook. For the eighteenth-century person who lived in what would become the United States, the press filled that role during the Revolution, and it was really the first time that American newspapers served their readers in this fashion. The newspapers that supported the fight for independence came to outnumber those that wanted to stay loyal to Great Britain and this helped produce final victory. People throughout America read the same essays and reports about events, and this common knowledge base helped produce a sense of unity and common purpose that had to occur if the Americans were going to win the war. Thus, newspapers played an essential role in the fight for independence by helping convince people that the war could be won and that the fight was worth the sacrifice.

When Americans think about their nation's victory in the Revolution, many ask how they managed to defeat a major empire that had a great army and the best navy in the world. There are many reasons for the American victory, but the press definitely helped because the newspapers kept people interested and engaged in a way that kept them fighting until the British got tired and quit.

Many people have encouraged me in my research and writing over the years. My parents and my siblings have always been supportive (even if they were more interested in the Civil War than the American Revolution). I am also thankful to my colleagues at Oklahoma Baptist University for their support in granting me a reduced teaching load that gave me time for research and writing on this project. The members of the American Journalism Historians Association have also been encouraging and patient as we have debated the differences that exist between the disciplines of journalism/communications and history. I am particularly thankful to Julie Hedgepeth Williams and David Abrahamson for reading a draft of this manuscript and pushing me to rethink parts of it. It is better as a result of their prodding.

# THE AMERICAN REVOLUTION AND THE PRESS

ONE

# INTRODUCTION

On July 4, 1776, one of the most celebrated events in American history occurred in Philadelphia. On that day, the Second Continental Congress adopted the Declaration of Independence, explaining why the thirteen colonies had chosen to break away from Great Britain. The members of the Congress believed that it was very important to present their reasons for declaring independence in a public, written format. From the very beginning of the disagreements with Britain, published materials had played a central role in presenting the various arguments over taxes and the rights of the colonials, and would continue to be important throughout the American Revolution. Of particular importance were the newspapers published on a regular basis from Maine to Georgia. Americans either sought out copies of the newspapers themselves or went someplace where they could hear them being read aloud. Newspapers were the major source of information about what was happening elsewhere in the colonies.

Historians have long studied and discussed the factors that led to the American Revolution, and they have always given ample credit for the success of the revolt to the press, and particularly the newspapers, for their efforts during the conflict.[1] Even those historians who wrote in the years immediately after the war praised the press for its many contributions to ultimate victory. In discussing the Stamp Act and its impact on New Hampshire, Jeremy Belknap declared that the newspapers were "filled with essays, in which every plea for and against the new duties was amply discussed."[2] Another of the earliest historians of the American Revolution, David Ramsay of Charleston, South Carolina, affirmed that "in establishing American independence, the pen and the press had a merit equal to that of the sword."[3] Yet, although scholars have agreed that the newspapers played an important part in the move toward independence, they have disagreed on the exact nature of that role. Some of these debates have grown out of discussions of how newspapers were produced. Today, the jobs of printer, editor, and publisher are filled by separate individuals, but one person often did most or all of these jobs in the eighteenth century. Thus, over the years, studies have credited eighteenth-century journalists with everything from providing part of the building blocks for American democracy to establishing the beginnings of professional journalism in the United States; from fueling a class conflict between those in and out of power to serving as a reflector of the growing unity that existed in the American colonies long before the first shots were fired at Lexington and Concord.

In general, there are five different views of the role of the mass media during the Revolutionary War. The nationalist/romantic schools dominated prior to the Civil War. The developmental school, which came to prominence after the Civil War, has proved the most pervasive and continues to be the most dominant interpretation. The progressive school appeared in the early twentieth century, but has remained influential since that time. The consensus and cultural schools both appeared following the Second

World War. Obviously, these groups overlap, but each has certain characteristics that differentiate it from the other outlooks. All of these groups have impacted how we think about the influence and impact of newspapers in winning American independence from Great Britain.

During the first half of the nineteenth century, historians emphasized the patriotism of the printers in their efforts to help America establish its republican system of government as a model for the rest of the world to follow. These scholars are often classified as nationalist or romantic in their outlook and conclusions. For these historians, the American colonies had an important role to play in making the world a better place to live through the spread of democracy and freedom, and the newspapers served well in helping to bring about the break with Great Britain that led to these developments.

Much of the history written by these historians discussed the "great men" of journalism who worked during the American Revolution. The emphasis was on the importance of individuals in creating American mass media that kept the people informed on the issues involved in the conflict with Great Britain. The historians of this school knew most of the people they wrote about, and some had experienced the American Revolution personally. They believed strongly in the role of the printers in producing the revolt that led to independence.

The stress on "great men" is most clearly seen in the work of Isaiah Thomas and Joseph Buckingham. Both of these men are very important in the history of American journalism because of their efforts to preserve the records of the work of printers during the American Revolution. Both placed particular importance in their histories on the *Boston Gazette* and its publishers, especially Benjamin Edes. Thomas was himself a printer of note during the

Revolution, but in his *The History of Printing in America,* he cites Edes and the *Gazette* as being extremely important in the move toward independence: "No publisher of a newspaper felt a greater interest in the establishment of the independence of the United States than Benjamin Edes; and no newspaper was more instrumental in bringing forward this important event than *The Boston Gazette.*"[4] Thomas's book was the first major history of American journalism and is worth reading by modern historians because it offers useful insights and many interesting stories about the era of the American Revolution, and is an essential resource for anyone studying the role of newspapers during the Revolutionary era. Thomas is also important in the early history of American journalism because of his efforts to preserve the actual records of the newspaper press from the Revolutionary era. He personally saved many of the newspapers he received through the regular exchange system engaged in by printers during the eighteenth century. He also founded the American Antiquarian Society in Worcester, Massachusetts, in 1812, as an organization that worked to preserve the historical documents that showed the first century of the development of the mass media in America.

Joseph Buckingham sought to preserve the journalistic record of the American Revolution by republishing it in a book that would be easily available to the general American public. His *Specimens of Newspaper Literature* also credited Benjamin Edes and his supporters with an important role in America's fight for freedom and independence. He praised the *Gazette*'s writers as a patriotic group that produced many pieces that urged the colonials to stand up to the British government. According to Buckingham, "One united spirit of hostility to the arbitrary exercise of power and prerogative pervaded their minds, and each seemed strengthened and invigorated by contact with another."[5] This unity of spirit and encouragement of one another enabled the writers in the pages of the *Boston Gazette* to lead others in America to unite in their fight against Great Britain.

As a group, the nationalist/romantic historians had a major impact on our understanding of the role of newspapers during the American Revolution because they preserved so much material that later historians have used for their own research. But these writers also perceived only good in the various efforts of the press of the Revolutionary era. The fact that these historians either experienced the American Revolution directly or knew the people who did made it more difficult for them to see any problems or concerns about the role of the press during the colonies' fight for independence. These historians continually emphasized the importance of the newspapers in bringing on the revolt against British tyranny and praised the printers for their loyalty and patriotism in the fight for liberty and independence.

Following the Civil War, the first generation of professionally trained historians began to produce studies of American history. These writers slowly moved away from the focus on "great men" to produce a more general overview of how the press had grown and developed over time. They thus helped us deepen our understanding of American history beyond a study of individuals to a broader consideration of trends and developments. Influenced by an increasing emphasis on the validity of science and its techniques, these scholars underscored the organic nature of the development of the United States and its institutions. Most historians of American journalism continued to be working journalists (as Thomas and Buckingham had been), but they were influenced by the changes in the newspaper—and how it was produced—that arose in the early nineteenth century. These historians increasingly stressed the professional development of the press, underscoring the origin of the mass media and their progress toward "proper" practices such as an emphasis on news and timeliness. Most of these authors emphasized journalistic "firsts" and, as a result, often still dealt with individual newspapers and publishers rather than the industry as a whole. But their focus pushed their readers to think beyond a handful of individuals to a broader consideration of changes in journalism that affected everyone in the business. This interpretation became the most popular among historians of newspapers and the press and has remained strong for well over a hundred years.

Prominent among the advocates of this interpretation were several authors who produced important surveys of the history of American journalism. This group included such historians as Frederic Hudson, James Melvin Lee, Willard Grosvenor Bleyer, and Robert W. Jones. All of them emphasized the impact of the Revolutionary War in the development of the American press from a trade into a profession, and the influential role the newspapers played in the American Revolution itself. According to Bleyer, the weekly newspapers "played their part in developing a feeling of solidarity among the colonists in the struggle against the mother country" and "the protracted struggle between the colonies and the mother country from 1765 to 1783 demonstrated the value of the press as a means of influencing public opinion." Jones concluded that "the position of the newspaper publisher was now one of greater importance because of the prestige resulting from the success of the Revolutionary War." All of these authors emphasized specific papers and people that they considered to be important, but they also focused on the various changes in all newspapers and their production that occurred during the American Revolution.[6]

The most important member of the developmental school

was Frank Luther Mott, the author of one of the dominant twentieth-century survey histories of American journalism. In many ways, Mott's efforts constituted the height of the dominance of the ideas of the developmental school. In his studies of the American Revolution, he emphasized that deepening public interest in American political affairs as the conflict with Great Britain intensified led to greater influence and prestige for the press. Particularly important in this increase in influence and prestige were the efforts of the mass media during the Stamp Act crisis. Because of the successful fight against the Stamp Act in 1765, colonial leaders "respected this new power" and realized the possibilities for influencing people that the newspapers offered. Mott concluded that "by the end of the war journalism had made a distinct gain in prestige." He also stressed the importance of how news was acquired during the American Revolution. In an important article published in the *Journalism Quarterly* in 1944, Mott traced the spread of the news of the battles of Lexington and Concord through the pages of the colonial newspapers, showing that it took six weeks for the news of the battle to appear in all the newspapers throughout the colonies. But Mott also showed that modern sensibilities of the timeliness of news did not really function in the eighteenth century. The slowness of the mail and other modes of communication meant that three to six weeks for news to spread throughout the colonies represented a timely sharing of information for that period. But even though communication of important events through the newspapers took longer than modern readers would be comfortable with, Mott's work emphasized the growing importance of the mass media as major sources of information as the colonials successfully broke away from Great Britain.[7]

Many other historians have adopted the developmental interpretation of the role of the press in the American Revolution. The result has been a number of studies by authors such as Albert Carlos Bates and Rollo G. Silver that emphasized the growth of American journalism primarily through the study and comparison of the careers of individual people and the records of individual newspapers. C. M. Thomas studied the press of the Revolutionary era by reviewing the careers of three New York printers: John Holt, James Rivington, and Hugh Gaine. He concluded that most American printers in the 1760s and 1770s were good at their jobs, but only those who supported the Patriot cause have been remembered. Capable printers such as Rivington and Gaine "chose the side that lost and were lost with it," though they too played an important part in the growth, development, and improvement of the American press in the eighteenth century.[8]

The developmental outlook has also produced important studies of specific roles that the press generally plays, particularly in the development of the editorial function. Jim A. Hart emphasized the growing use of editorial opinion in the newspapers published during the American Revolution. Before the Revolution, opinions typically took the form of letters and essays from contributors, but Hart concluded that at this time "the first strains of the editorial . . . appeared occasionally." In a similar vein, John M. Harrison concluded that Revolutionary newspaper contributors constituted "the first editorial writers in the American press, establishing one of the primary functions of newspapers as they were to develop in the United States."[9] According to these historians, the printers of the newspapers of the Revolutionary era played an essential role in developing what has become one of the most recognized and widely accepted functions of the mass media, that of expressing opinions about public developments and events through editorials.

Journalism historians who accept the developmental interpretation have often emphasized the growing business acumen and professionalism of the Revolutionary-era printers and the resulting improvements in the mass media that developed during the war. Because of this interest, these historians have appreciated printers' efforts to be good newspapermen and businessmen first and Patriots or Loyalists second. Both Alfred McClung Lee, in a study of printing partners John Dunlap and David C. Claypoole of Philadelphia, and Sidney I. Pomerantz, in a study of the press of New York and New Jersey, concluded that the Revolutionary-era printers were good businessmen who tried to operate their establishments as well as possible. Pomerantz discussed the challenges faced by Loyalist printers Hugh Gaine, James Rivington, and James Robertson, but focused most of his attention on Patriot printers John Holt, Samuel Loudon, Isaac Collins, and Shepard Kollock. Pomerantz praised the men he studied for helping the Revolutionary cause "while observing the canons of journalistic conduct all too often forgotten in wartime." In a study of James Rivington, Robert M. Ours lamented that Rivington has not been remembered for his contributions to American journalism: "Rivington's direct legacy to American journalism was virtually nil—largely because of his reputation as a Tory liar. That was unfortunate, because his newspaper was one of the better ones in the colonies in the early months of its existence. Rivington had an excellent pattern to offer journalists in his policies regarding impartiality and freedom of the press. The evidence is strong that he tried to adhere to his announced policies. That he failed in the long run was largely the result of wartime pressures and polarization."[10] Ours urged his readers to look beyond Rivington's political stance to recognize his major contributions to the development of newspapers in the United States.

As a group, the developmental historians have continued to

emphasize the growth and development of American journalism during the American Revolution, placing particular emphasis on the increasing professionalism of eighteenth-century printers. The American Revolution provided the impetus for colonial printers to become more aware of the potential of their publications, particularly their weekly newspapers. The developmental scholars emphasize this growing awareness among eighteenth-century printers. These historians show the conflict with Great Britain as an essential piece in the press's move from being primarily a source of information to also serving as a medium that influenced public opinion, a move that was necessary if American journalism was to develop into the powerful instrument that it became in the nineteenth century.

After 1900 historians presented a new interpretation of American history that came to be reflected in journalism history. In an era concerned with inequities and the lack of unity in American society in the twentieth century, the progressive historians emphasized the presence of conflict from the initial settlement of the colonies down to the present. Most of the disagreements and arguments occurred between different classes of people or geographic sections in the American colonies, but the Revolutionary era represented a period of both internal and external troubles. Divisions existed both between groups within the colonies and between the colonies and Great Britain. In this environment, the press played an important role in encouraging and carrying out a crusade for change. In pushing for alterations in the relationship between the colonies and Great Britain, the mass media often helped to accentuate the differences and thus helped to make the divisions grow and become worse.

One of the most important historians to present the progressive view of the press was Arthur M. Schlesinger Sr. In research that spanned several decades, he stressed the growing power of the mass media during the 1760s, particularly during the Stamp Act crisis. The press itself changed greatly during the American Revolution, but it also helped produce changes as well. Throughout the crises of the 1760s and 1770s, the Patriot press "fearlessly and loudly championed the American cause, never yielding ground as did some of the politicians." Schlesinger's primary work on the role and influence of the mass media during the American Revolution was *Prelude to Independence: The Newspaper War on Great Britain, 1764–1776.* In this publication, Schlesinger declared that "the patriot journalists sought to activate popular resentment while keeping several paces ahead of it." Thus, the Revolutionary printers worked to use the unhappiness of the colonials to widen the divisions and increase the conflicts that existed with Great Britain. Based on detailed research in the surviving newspapers of the era, Schlesinger provided clear evidence of the influence of the newspapers in forming public opinion in favor of revolting against Britain. Schlesinger showed that the newspapers were the primary mechanisms used to stir up the common people to break away. He also presented an excellent account of how the growing conflict between the colonies and Great Britain affected the publishing business because of changes in editors and other printing problems resulting from censorship and mob violence. The Revolutionary-era newspapers proved essential in creating the colonial discontent that led to revolt and the push for independence because this event changed "routine vehicles of news and miscellany into engines of opinion." Schlesinger concluded that without the press the American Revolution would probably not have occurred at all.[11]

Other progressive historians have gone beyond Schlesinger's conclusions in emphasizing printers' conscious use of propaganda, or pieces designed to influence, mislead, or deceive, to produce changes unsought by the majority of Americans in the late eighteenth century. In *Propaganda in the American Revolution, 1763–1783,* Philip Davidson stated that the use of propaganda by the Patriots indicated clearly that the revolt from Great Britain was not a move supported by the majority of colonials, for "had the Revolution been the work of a majority, united on methods and objects, in sure control of the movement throughout, there would have been little necessity for propaganda." Davidson concluded that colonial leaders who desired to be in control of their own affairs made good use of the American newspaper press to emphasize the differences between the colonies and Great Britain. The result was the independence of the colonies: "Without their work, independence would not have been declared in 1776 nor recognized in 1783."[12] Thus, the newspapers proved to be an essential part in the American fight against Great Britain.

Davidson believed that Patriot leaders were successful in their propaganda efforts, but other progressive historians reached different conclusions. Carl Berger's *Broadsides and Bayonets: The Propaganda War of the American Revolution* said that, while propaganda in the press was important, it did not play a more decisive role in converting neutral Americans into Patriots or Loyalists than did other events. Ultimately, real events had more impact than propaganda efforts and thus military victories and losses as well as issues of politics and economics influenced people's actions the most as they made up their minds which side to support. In several studies of the press, Ralph A. Brown concluded that printers tried to make use of their newspapers to further the cause of the side they supported, but Brown downplayed the impact of these efforts. The Loyalist press in Philadelphia tried, but failed, to convince people that "the rebels were cruel and heartless" and that rebel leaders "were treacherous and self-seeking." In a study of the New Hampshire newspaper press, Brown concluded that the only indication of the effects of Patriot newspaper propaganda was the importance of these printers in the years after the war. Brown's work indicated that Patriot leaders wanted to accentuate the divisions between the colonies and Great Britain while Loyalist leaders sought to emphasize the conflicts between different groups of colonials, but neither group had much success in these efforts.[13]

Another important progressive interpretation appeared in Edwin Emery's *The Press and America: An Interpretive History of the Mass Media.* This survey text, which has gone through multiple editions and been used in numerous journalism history classes, emphasized the internal conflicts of the American Revolution. The war was a "class struggle" in which "printers, publishers, and editors were important influences in preparing the public for revolution and in maintaining the fighting spirit during the War of Independence." Of particular importance in their efforts during the Revolution were Samuel Adams, Isaiah Thomas, and Thomas Paine. But many less well-known printers also played important roles as their productions helped keep their readers informed about issues and events during the years of debate and fighting during the Revolution.[14]

With a growing interest in the role of economics in history, more recent progressive historians have questioned the motives for the actions of Revolutionary printers. Several have concluded that most pressmen supported the Patriot cause for reasons of economic survival rather than any strong ideological commitment. Robert D. Harlan, in his study of David Hall of Philadelphia, stated that, while Hall's support of the colonials proved to be genuine, he began moving in that direction to keep his newspaper alive. Alfred L. Lorenz's biography of Hugh Gaine of New York described the printer as "essentially an apolitical man" who "pursued a course dictated by ambition and expediency." According to Lorenz, Gaine "had no strong political beliefs for which he was willing to risk his life or his fortune." Dwight L. Teeter concluded that the guiding principle of John Dunlap of Philadelphia was a desire to be successful financially, a goal that he accomplished. In a study of Philadelphia printers and their stands on social issues, William F. Steirer stressed that "prudence and caution, not bravery and idealism, dominated the behavior of those newspapermen—indeed, they acted like the small businessmen protecting their investments that they in truth were."[15] Thus, business issues and business decisions, rather than personal ideals and personal beliefs, guided printers' actions.

In recent years, historians have continued to expound the progressive view of the role of the press in the American Revolution, with emphasis on newspapers as propaganda and encouragers of class conflict. In a survey of the impact of journalism in the United States, Robert A. Rutland stressed internal divisions, as well as those from outside, stating that "printers in Boston had to be vigilant, not of the king's attorney but of their own elected representatives." After an uneasy alliance, the printers supported the revolt and helped push public opinion toward independence. Studies of Margaret Draper of Boston, Massachusetts, by Susan Henry and of Clementina Rind of Williamsburg, Virginia, by Norma Schneider found that both of these female printers used their newspapers in the propaganda war against Great Britain after the Boston Tea Party in December 1773. According to Charles Cutler, Connecticut editors "tended to serve one side or the other with a zeal that seemed to blind them to an alternate viewpoint." He stated that "social pressure won willing or unwilling converts to the Patriot cause" and that the press "incited Connecticut citizens against

British rule." William F. Steirer, discussing the Philadelphia press, found that "much of the impetus for the printers' directing the thinking and actions of readers (or at least trying to) initially came from non-journalists." Thomas C. Leonard found that Revolutionary newspapers emphasized "the exposure of injustice" in British-American society.[16]

From the standpoint of these and other progressive historians, the American Revolution produced new conflicts and accentuated the divisions that already existed in colonial society, whether they were internal conflicts between various groups of Americans or growing strains in colonial relations with Great Britain. The result was a war that broke ties with Great Britain and restructured internal relationships in the new nation of the United States. The increasing focus on conflicts by these and other progressive historians has produced major debates among journalism historians about whether the newspapers played a positive or negative role during the American Revolution. Thus, while the progressive historians have added to our detailed knowledge about the mass media during the Revolution, they have also increased the debates and disagreements about the media's overall impact at the time.

Following World War II, American historians began to challenge the progressive interpretation. In the face of growing world conflict, Americans searched for and found much that they had in common, both in the past and in the present. The consensus interpretation of American history downplayed the existence of conflict during the eighteenth century and emphasized the unifying elements that existed during the American Revolution.[17] An important early work reflecting the consensus interpretation was *The Stamp Act Crisis* by Edmund S. and Helen M. Morgan. While not focused exclusively on journalism, the Morgans showed how the Stamp Act controversy produced well-defined constitutional principles that served the colonies well in the years leading up to the Revolution. Their primary sources were the newspapers and other publications of the 1760s that helped spread the ideas that helped unify Americans in their opposition to British policy.[18]

The most important proponent of the consensus outlook was Bernard Bailyn, a historian whose research has had an enormous impact on our perception of the mass media during the American Revolution. All of Bailyn's work stressed the common ideology held by most Americans prior to the American Revolution. In his *The Ideological Origins of the American Revolution,* he focused on the various pamphlets published in the years prior to the war that served to unify Americans in their search for greater political freedom and equality. Bailyn showed how pamphlets provided a printed mechanism for encouraging debate as Americans developed common ideas about government and how it should function. The pamphlets themselves were widely distributed, but many of them were also reprinted in whole or in part in the newspapers published throughout the colonies. Because the colonials agreed on basic issues such as the type of government they wanted, the real revolution was actually over before the fighting started in 1775. In many ways, the revolt from Great Britain was a conservative move because the colonials sought to preserve rights and privileges they had assumed many years before.[19] The Revolution represented the fulfillment of already-accepted ideas rather than growing divisiveness in American society.

In journalism history the consensus interpretation produced an emphasis on the role of the press as a support for the government and a reflection of the ideas and attitudes of the general population. The printers worked hard to maintain both their principles and their business in the face of many obstacles. In doing so they made lasting contributions to the growth of American journalism.

Consensus historians vigorously criticized the progressive interpretation for its emphasis on class struggles and colonial divisions. Maurice Cullen, in "Middle-Class Democracy and the Press in Colonial America" in *Journalism Quarterly* in 1969, concluded that the Revolution, far from being a class struggle, actually constituted a fight to establish democracy in America. In a study of the Stamp Act, Francis G. Walett admitted the importance of the press in bringing on the colonial rebellion, but stressed the unifying efforts of the newspaper press over the divisiveness produced by the revolt. Bill F. Chamberlin's study of postwar Connecticut, "Freedom of Expression in Eighteenth-Century Connecticut: Unanswered Questions," capably summed up the outlook of the consensus historians: "For the most part, the rulers and the ruled shared common interests in order and commercial growth." During the American Revolution, the result was a united effort to throw off the British yoke that controlled the colonies and restricted American growth.[20]

The consensus outlook has not always been strongly supported by historians of the Revolutionary-era press, primarily because of the press's attempts to influence the public's actions during the war. However, the consensus historians emphasized the existence of a unity of ideas prior to the war—that is, that the newspapers of the War of Independence merely reflected opinions already commonly held rather than trying to change the attitudes of the uncommitted. These scholars have successfully argued that these widely held common ideas help explain the strong commitment of many Americans to the fight for independence and their determination to keep fighting until victory over Great Britain was achieved.

Another historical interpretation also appeared after the end of World War II. Represented primarily by the work of Sidney

Kobre, the cultural interpretation stressed the interrelation of the media and the societal/cultural environment. The major concerns were the impact of the media on society, and vice versa. In studying the press of the eighteenth century, Kobre looked at social and economic growth in the colonies as it encouraged the growth of the mass media. He examined the expansion of areas of settlement, the population, and the economy, and how this growth affected newspapers. He concluded that the press "was the only agency of a national character which could act as a channel of news and persuasion." Furthermore, "the press helped develop 'a consciousness of kind,' an emotional, intellectual and economic sympathy for distant colonies. The many newspapers aided in unifying the thirteen separate colonies into one nation and in promoting the solid solidarity required for a war of revolt."[21] Kobre stressed the changes in society that were partially produced by the press and how these changes were necessary for the creation of a new nation.

The debate about exactly what role the press played during the American Revolution has continued. In 1980 the American Antiquarian Society published *The Press and the American Revolution* as its contribution to the bicentennial of the American Revolution. This book contained a collection of essays that reflected the continuing disagreements over the role of the press in the American Revolution. All of the essays in this work emphasized the growth and development of the press during the Revolution, but they did so from several perspectives. The authors clearly did not fully agree on exactly what the role of the press was during the Revolution.

Several essays adopted the progressive interpretation, stressing the conflicts the war produced. Janice Potter and Robert M. Calhoon found that some Loyalist printers thought that "the most substantive threat to their freedom emanated not from Britain but from the patriot congresses, committees, and mobs in their midst." Paul Langford's study of British correspondence in the American press concluded that reports in the colonial newspapers concerning British attitudes toward America only served to worsen misunderstandings and divisions between the colonies and Great Britain. Both Robert M. Weir and Stephen Botein questioned the motives of the printers in supporting the Patriot cause. Weir, in studying the Southern newspaper press, found the printers to be "the voice of the local political establishment" who could not afford to antagonize their major supporters. Botein stressed that printers began to adopt a more partisan stance when it became clear that their traditional neutral position was no longer economically feasible.[22]

All of these essays emphasized the divisiveness and change-producing aspects of the American Revolution, but other essays in the collection represented the consensus view that the press served to reflect the basic unity that existed in the colonies at the time of the Revolution. Willi Paul Adams, in studying the American German-language press, found that it carried out a primarily political function, not the religious role that historians had previously thought. According to Adams, "The German-language press, like its English-language counterpart, made possible rational discussion on questions of statecraft and social betterment beyond the limited circles of the elite, among a population too spread out and too large to assemble in one's city marketplace. Further, it helped create a 'new form' of public opinion essential for the growth of a shared sense of legitimacy. Finally, like the English-language press, the German-language press was an integrating force, essential to the process of nation-building." Thus, the German-language press "helped the German-speaking minority to feel part of and to function in a larger national whole."[23] The newspaper press played a unifying role that helped the American Revolution succeed.

The American Antiquarian Society publication was not the first in which scholars have disagreed about the American Revolutionary press, and it probably will not be the last. Historians have argued about the role of newspapers in the American Revolution ever since the war began in 1775, using much ink and paper in the debate. Much of this debate has also centered on whether the impact of specific individuals mattered more than the overall influence of the entire industry. Isaiah Thomas often zeroed in on individual newspapermen while Frank Luther Mott focused more on the growth of the industry. Another major debate revolved around whether the American society reflected in the newspapers tended to focus on division or agreement and the role the press played in creating that reflection. Arthur Schlesinger declared that newspapers encouraged societal divisions while Bernard Bailyn described the press as reflecting the overall unity that existed among Americans prior to the Revolution. Clearly, historians have not reached agreement about the impact of the press in the eighteenth century. But even with all the many disagreements about the actual function of the press during the American Revolution, all of these studies have pushed us to agree that the newspapers played a very important role in the successful fight for independence.

TWO

# THE COLONIAL PRESS

Newspapers were able to play an important role during the American Revolution because they had already become indispensable to many Americans during the colonial era. Many of the earliest settlers had considered printed materials an essential part of life. This proved particularly true in New England, where the Puritans desired to increase access to the Bible by making it more readily available. As a result of this outlook, the first printing press in the British American colonies was set up in the original Puritan colony in Massachusetts. In 1638, Stephen Daye established this first printing office in Cambridge, across the river from Boston, the colonial capital of Massachusetts. Daye and his successor, Samuel Green, published government materials and religious pamphlets. Other printers opened shops in the area in 1665 and 1675. William Nuthead set up shop in Virginia in 1682, but moved to Maryland in 1685 because the Virginia Royal Council prohibited him from printing. The colony of Pennsylvania also had a print shop open in 1685. Much of the early production revolved around religious materials, primarily because the Puritans in Massachusetts and the Quakers in Pennsylvania used the printing press to spread their ideas and beliefs.

By the time the Revolutionary War broke out in 1775, there were only fifty presses in America. The slow growth in printing in America reflected the slow growth of the colonies in many ways. The difficulties of the printing business itself retarded its expansion, both in Europe and America. By the middle of the eighteenth century, printing as a trade had existed in Europe for over three hundred years, but it had changed very little since Johann Gutenberg had developed the press with movable type. Type was still being cast in the same laborious way, one letter at a time, while paper was still slowly made from rags. Acquiring the necessary materials for printing often proved difficult in the colonies. Paper and ink could be produced locally if supplies were available, but most of these supplies were imported from Great Britain throughout the colonial era. The printing presses and type also had to be imported from Europe. The costs involved proved a challenge that many people simply could not meet.

For printers who attempted to publish a newspaper, there was also the difficulty of getting content and of delivering the publications to readers. With time, the number of newspapers being published increased and thus provided more sources of information. Most printers exchanged newspapers with one another and copied stories and information on a regular basis. But these exchanges were not always easy. The colonies did not have an organized postal system for many years. Several colonies developed their own systems, but efforts to establish an intercolonial postal system did not begin until 1673. These efforts came to nothing until 1692, when the British government finally approved the idea and the first regular delivery was established between the cities of Boston and New York. This postal system provided the primary means for exchanging information and delivering newspapers in the years leading up to the American Revolution.

The printing trade could also be discouraging because it was a very slow and involved process. The two people operating the press had to perform thirteen separate processes to produce one printed page. Type had to be set by hand in the page form and then locked into place in the press. After the form was positioned, one person would ink the type using two large deerskin balls. He would next place a piece of paper on top of the type and ensure that everything was in its proper place. Then the coworker would pull twice on an iron lever that would press the paper onto the inked type, producing one printed page. The sheet would then be hung up to dry, and the process would be repeated with the next page. The hourly output from this procedure averaged two hundred to two hundred fifty sheets, resulting in a total of two thousand to twenty-five hundred pages for a ten-hour day, that is, if nothing interfered with the regular routine.

Despite the difficulties inherent in printing in the colonial era, some entrepreneurs were sufficiently tempted by the prestige and potential income from subscribers and advertisers to establish newspapers. Newspapers had become firmly established in Great Britain by the end of the 1600s, and some American printers sought to emulate this development in the colonies. The first printer to attempt a newspaper in the colonies was Benjamin Harris. He had been a printer and newspaper publisher in London before coming to Boston in 1686. In 1690, Harris decided to produce a newspaper in Boston. On September 25, he produced the first issue of *Publick Occurrences, Both Forreign and Domestick,* declaring that he intended to print an issue at least once a month. This proved to be the only issue of this title, primarily because Harris failed to acquire a government license prior to publication.

This one issue contained several pieces about the Native Americans and Native American warfare. Many government officials believed that Harris had criticized their actions in dealing with the Native Americans and thus they shut him down. The first effort at producing a newspaper in the colonies had failed.

Over ten years passed before someone decided to try publishing another newspaper. John Campbell began publishing the *Boston News-Letter* on April 24, 1704. In his position as the local postmaster, Campbell had access to information from the captains of ships coming into Boston and his post riders, who delivered the mail. He originally produced handwritten newsletters, but decided to start producing a printed version. The newspaper carried the statement "PUBLISHED BY AUTHORITY," showing that Campbell had learned from Harris's troubles and had gotten official permission before printing the first issue. Campbell hesitated to challenge the colonial government in any way. He focused much of his newspaper on foreign news, which he acquired by meeting ships as they docked so he could get copies of London newspapers, letters from correspondents, and gossip from the ship's crew. Thus, most of the material published in the *News-Letter* was borrowed from other sources. Campbell also had no sense of urgency whatsoever when publishing foreign news and stories. Rather, he thought it was important to record all important events in some manner. So, he tried to print as much information from Europe as possible and fell further and further behind in terms of timeliness. By 1718, the European news that appeared in the *Boston News-Letter* was over a year old. Campbell promised his readers that he would catch up, but he never succeeded.

Campbell also published little local news. He knew that news of local events would pass around primarily by word of mouth and that repeating stories about them in his newspaper would be a waste of his limited space. His decision to ignore local news reflected the decisions of most newspaper printers in the colonies in the first half of the eighteenth century. The limitations on local news continued to be true for most colonial newspapers until the outbreak of the French and Indian War in the 1750s increased interest in local events.

Campbell lost his job as postmaster in 1719, but kept the *News-Letter* as the mainstay of his printing business. His successor as postmaster, William Brooker, hired James Franklin (older brother of Benjamin Franklin) to produce a newspaper. The first issue of the *Boston Gazette* appeared on December 21, 1719. Franklin was replaced as the printer of the *Gazette* by Samuel Green when Brooker lost the postmaster position to Philip Musgrave. Franklin soon found other financial supporters in the persons of John Checkley and Dr. William Douglass, who urged him to start a new newspaper. The first issue of the *New England Courant* appeared on August 7, 1721. Franklin's newspaper took the journalism industry in a new direction as it contained editorial comments as well as foreign and local news reports. The supporters of the paper hoped to encourage the growth of the Anglican Church in the colony by weakening the popularity of the Puritan clergy. In the first issue, writers attacked the Puritan Reverend Cotton Mather for his support of smallpox inoculation. A huge debate ensued in the local newspapers in Boston, producing a response from Mather himself in the *Boston News-Letter:* "And for a Lamentation to our amazement (notwithstanding of GOD'S hand against us, in His Visitation of the Small-Pox, in Boston, and the threatening Aspect of the West-Weather) we find a Notorious, Scandalous Paper, called the *Courant,* full freighted with Nonsence, Unmannerliness, Railery, Prophaneness, Immorality, Arrogancy, Calumnies, Lyes, Contradictions, and what not, all tending to Quarrels and Divisions, and to Debauch and Corrupt the Minds and Manners of New-England."[1] The fact that Mather felt he needed to respond to the charges in the *Courant* shows that newspapers were increasingly seen as having an influence on the beliefs and actions of their readers.

As spirited debate over inoculation and other issues continued in the newspapers, the *Courant* increasingly criticized the colonial government. Of particular concern to local authorities was Franklin's apparent criticism of their failure to act quickly in dealing with pirates off the coast of Massachusetts during the summer of 1722. Authorities tried to stop Franklin's criticism by arresting him and jailing him for three weeks. When that did not work, the General Court ordered Franklin to cease publication of the *Courant.* Franklin got around this order by listing his younger brother Benjamin as the printer of the newspaper. Benjamin later left Boston for Philadelphia, in 1723. James Franklin continued to publish the *Courant* for three more years, but moved to Newport, Rhode Island, in 1726, where he founded that colony's first newspaper, the *Rhode Island Gazette,* in 1732. Other newspapers, including the *Boston Evening-Post* published by Thomas Fleet and his sons Thomas and John, appeared in Boston prior to the Revolution, showing that the newspaper business had become firmly established in that city.

Newspapers also began to appear in other cities as merchants and businessmen increasingly saw their usefulness in gaining information and as a means for advertising goods and services. The next colony to gain a newspaper was Pennsylvania. Printer Andrew Bradford founded the *American Weekly Mercury* in Philadelphia on December 22, 1719. Bradford's paper contained similar material to the papers in Boston, with the focus on foreign news rather than local and other domestic reports. Bradford remained the sole newspaper printer in Philadelphia for almost a decade. In 1728, Benjamin Franklin, who had become a successful printer after moving to the city in 1723, decided to establish a newspaper to compete with the *Mercury.* Samuel Keimer, the third printer in Philadelphia, tried to beat Franklin to the punch by establishing the *Pennsylvania Gazette.* A year later, Franklin bought the *Gazette* from Keimer and sought to make it truly successful.

Benjamin Franklin had a better sense of the possibilities of a newspaper than most of his fellow printers at the time. In his first issue, Franklin declared: "We are sensible, that to publish a good News-Paper is not so easy an Undertaking as many People imagine it to be. The Author of a *Gazette* (in the Opinion of the Learned) ought to be qualified with an extensive Acquaintance with Languages, a great Easiness and Command of Writing and Relating Things clearly and intelligibly, and in a few words; he should be able to speak of war both by Land and Sea; be well acquainted with Geography, with the History of the Time, with the several Interests of Princes and States, the Secrets of Courts, and the Manners and Customs of all Nations. Men thus accomplish'd are very rare in this remote Part of the World; and it would be well if the writer of these Papers could make up among his Friends what is wanting in himself."[2] Thus Franklin reached out to the community to participate in the newspaper and boldly stated what was true for most printers at the time—their dependence on volunteer writers to help produce materials for the paper. Franklin himself did not necessarily need the help of such people because he was such a good writer himself, but his attitude reflected the reality that most colonial printers faced in their efforts to gain enough material to produce a local newspaper.

Benjamin Franklin was one of the most successful printers during the colonial era. Besides the *Pennsylvania Gazette,* which constituted 60 percent of his business, Franklin produced many other publications that proved very successful. Of most importance in this group was his very popular annual publication, *Poor Richard's Almanack,* which he began publishing in 1732. Franklin tried a magazine in 1741, but it failed. He also helped establish the first German-language newspaper at Germantown, Pennsylvania. Franklin was so successful financially that he was able to retire from active involvement in his printing business in 1748 at age 42, but he continued to be involved in the printing business in a more indirect way through his support of young printers in a number of other colonies. Franklin's financial success made it possible for him to leave his print shop to serve in a variety of public capacities. He first served Philadelphia as postmaster beginning in 1737 and he later served all of the colonies as deputy postmaster general from 1753 to 1774. He later served as the colonial agent in London for several colonies, such as Pennsylvania and Massachusetts, in the 1760s and 1770s. His most notable service came as the agent of the Continental Congress to France during the Revolution and as a member of the Constitutional Convention that met in Philadelphia in 1787. Much of Franklin's understanding of people came from his experience of dealing with them on a daily basis in his print shop, so his experience as a printer helped him as a public servant. His reputation also helped improve the overall public perception and reputation of printers, which helped set the stage for the growing influence of newspaper printers during the American Revolution and later.

The success of Bradford's *American Weekly Mercury* and Franklin's *Pennsylvania Gazette* persuaded printers in other colonies to try producing a newspaper. Andrew Bradford's father, William, a printer in New York, led the way when he established the first newspaper in that city. The *New-York Gazette* appeared on November 8, 1725. Other colonies followed suit over the next several years. William Parks established the *Maryland Gazette* in Annapolis on September 19, 1727, and he later founded the first *Virginia Gazette* in Williamsburg on August 6, 1736. With the appearance of the *Virginia Gazette,* Maryland, South Carolina, and Virginia each had one newspaper in print, while the colonies of Massachusetts, Pennsylvania, and New York had multiple newspapers. A dozen newspapers were now being published, a number that would stay pretty constant for the next twenty years. All of these publications focused primarily on foreign news, but many also increasingly printed reports of happenings in the other colonies. This growing knowledge base about the other American colonies would prove essential in helping tie the colonies together in the conflicts with Great Britain that led to the American Revolution.

Many of these newspapers appeared with permission of the colonial governments or chose not to challenge the local authorities to more easily remain in business. But other newspapers appeared in various colonies as a mouthpiece for those who opposed the government and its decisions. Such a development resulted in the first major argument over freedom of the press in America. In New York, a group of merchants and businessmen increasingly opposed the actions of the royal governor, Sir William Cosby. In an effort to get their message out to the people, they provided support (both financially and in producing materials for publication) for the founding of the *New-York Weekly Journal.* They hired John Peter Zenger to print the paper, and it began publication on November 5, 1733. For over a year, the pages of the *Journal* contained numerous attacks on the government. Cosby was increasingly upset over the attacks and sought to force the *Journal* to cease publication. He first sought court indictments against Zenger for seditious libel—public criticism of government officials and their actions in a manner intended to demean or challenge the government. These efforts to get an indictment failed. The governor then asked the Colonial Assembly to condemn the *Journal,* but they refused to cooperate. Cosby then had the Royal Council order Zenger's arrest for seditious libel, even though Zenger was only the printer and had not actually written any of the materials considered offensive. Zenger spent nine months in jail, but the paper continued to be published as Zenger's wife, Cathrine, took over the production process. When brought to trial, Zenger was defended by Andrew Hamilton, a lawyer from Philadelphia who argued that the jury should decide the truth of the publications that provided the basis for the trial. The jury found Zenger not guilty. Historians have debated the impact of this verdict on legal issues related to freedom of the press, but it clearly made libel prosecutions in the colonies more difficult. Under English common law, judges decided whether published materials were libelous or not, while the jury only determined whether the accused had been involved in printing the materials in question. The jury in the Zenger case went further and returned a verdict of not guilty on the charge of libel rather than just the issue of whether Zenger printed the materials. This development would prove important as the conflict with Great Britain heated up in the 1760s because it made it increasingly difficult for royal authorities to legally shut down the newspapers that opposed British actions and spoke out in support of American rights and freedoms.

Newspapers in America grew slowly in the first half of the eighteenth century, but people were clearly becoming more interested in what they provided. In January 1750, James Parker, the printer of the *New-York Gazette, or Weekly Post-Boy,* commented on this reality: "This Taste, we Englishmen, have for News, is a very odd one; yet it must be fed; and tho' it seems to be a Jest to

Foreigners, yet it is an Amusement we can't be without."[3] The desire for information produced slow growth prior to 1750, but it took an international event to spark extensive growth and development. The French and Indian War provided a major encouragement for the further growth of newspapers in the American colonies because of the desire for information about the conflict. More printers decided that a newspaper was a good idea, resulting in more sources of information for American colonials. By the end of the French and Indian War in 1763, there was at least one printing establishment in each of the thirteen mainland colonies and the number of newspapers had grown from eleven in 1736 to twenty-three in 1763. Along with an increase in the number of newspapers came an increase in the circulation of the newspapers. In 1750, the average newspaper circulation was about 600 copies per week. By 1765, the average circulation ranged from 600 to 800 but some printers produced as many as 1500 copies per week. These numbers continued to go up throughout the conflict with Great Britain. The population of the cities did not grow that rapidly during the same period, indicating that more people were reading newspapers. Some of the larger cities had several newspapers, another indication that newspaper readership was sizeable enough to sustain the growth in circulation. A steady increase in literacy helped fuel the growth. Newspapers were sold through subscription, but local taverns or coffeehouses often subscribed and customers either read them directly or listened while someone else read them aloud. For example, in 1774, John Adams noted in his diary that he went to the local coffeehouse and read the newspapers while he was there.[4] Hence, the information carried by newspapers was available to many more people than previously.

Great Britain and France had struggled for control of North America almost since the first European settlements in the early sixteenth century. Prior to the French and Indian War, they had fought three wars that each left the issue of control of North America more vexed than before. The fourth war broke out in the Ohio Valley, which both countries claimed, as British and French colonists moved west from the Atlantic seaboard beyond the Appalachian Mountains. The fighting began when French troops and their Native American allies fought Virginia militiamen under the command of a young George Washington. Washington's journal of the Ohio Valley expedition appeared in a number of newspapers throughout the colonies after his return from the fighting.[5] The French victory at Fort Necessity on July 3, 1754, and news of other French activities in the Ohio Valley scared many Americans, who feared that French control of the British colonies would result in severe economic disruption, as trade with Great Britain and within the colonies would change. Probably of even greater concern was the realization that French victory would probably mean a forced conversion to Roman Catholicism, an eventuality that both British and American people had feared since the days of the Restoration of the Stuarts as British monarchs following the end of the Commonwealth in 1660.

Americans increasingly called for the colonies to join together to face this threat. Benjamin Franklin produced one of the first public calls for intercolonial cooperation. He drew up a plan of union and published it in his newspaper, the *Pennsylvania Gazette,* in May 1754, to spark discussion of the issue. He included a woodcut of a divided snake representing the British colonies and calling on Americans to "JOIN, or DIE."[6] This woodcut constituted the first editorial cartoon in American history and would be used again and again during the French and Indian War and also be appropriated to encourage the colonies to join together to fight the British as the fight for independence heated up in the years after the war with France ended.

The calls for cooperation resulted in the meeting of the Albany Congress in June 1754. This meeting produced the Albany Plan of Union, which was published in the newspapers throughout the colonies. Newspaper printers increasingly urged support for the plan because they thought the colonies needed to join together to successfully face the French threat. An anonymous writer in the *Boston Gazette* declared that "an Union of the Colonies was absolutely necessary, in order to defeat the Schemes of the French."[7] The colonial legislatures refused to ratify the Albany Plan of Union, but they did cooperate more in military efforts against the French and their Native American allies.

The war changed from a colonial conflict to an international war in 1756 when Great Britain officially declared war on France. Newspaper printers eagerly sought to publish accounts of fighting from around the globe as well as the growing hostilities in America. As Boston printer Thomas Fleet noted in the *Boston Evening-Post,* the war became "The Main Subject of the Publick Attention."[8] Beyond the basic news content, newspaper printers also sought to rally their readers to the cause by urging everyone to support the war effort. A writer in the *Virginia Gazette,* who called himself the "Virginia Centinel," called on his fellow citizens to join together to face the French and Indian threat: "FRIENDS! COUNTRYMEN! . . . AWAKE! ARISE! . . . When our Country, and all that is included in that important Word, is in most threatening Danger; when our Enemies are busy and unwearied in planning and executing their Schemes of Encroachments and Barbarity . . . when in short our All is at Stake . . . the Patriot Passions must be roused in every Breast capable of such generous Sensations. . . . Countrymen! Fellow-Subjects! Fellow-Protestants! to engage your Attention, I need only repeat, YOUR COUNTRY IS IN DANGER."[9] Such printed efforts in the newspapers aimed at uniting the Americans against the French threat and reflected the growing potential influence of newspapers in the middle of the eighteenth century.

The desire for information produced by the French and Indian War also produced changes in the news business. Printers sought to improve the delivery of newspapers, both to subscribers and to each other. Printers Benjamin Franklin of Pennsylvania and William Hunter of Virginia were appointed deputy postmasters general in 1758. They established a system of postage-free exchange of newspapers, thus encouraging a broader exchange of news and information throughout the colonies. The wider exchange of information also increased the speed by which news was shared. Timeliness in the 1700s was measured in days and weeks, not in seconds as it is today, but news about the war traveled relatively quickly for the time. News of fighting in South Carolina appeared in print in New Hampshire within three weeks in 1760.

Printers also sought to ensure the accuracy of the military reports that they published. They increasingly hesitated to publish stories about the war unless they could confirm them from other sources, and they reported the confirmations in the press. For example, Thomas and John Fleet of the *Boston Evening-Post* did not print the rumors they had heard about the surrender of Canada in 1760 until they could confirm it. When they did print it, they added that "The above account is confirmed by a Gentleman who came to town last Saturday morning from Albany."[10] Printers also began to change how they gathered information. Correspondents of all sorts had always been an important source of news, but printers now began to use more formal correspondents who functioned more like modern reporters. The *Boston Gazette* reprinted a piece from an anonymous correspondent of the *New-York Gazette* to report on the invasion of Canada in 1759. In his reports, this writer stated that "at the rate the British fleets and armies go on, it will be very difficult for a weekly news writer to keep pace."[11] His concern about getting his reports out quickly showed that he recognized the growing interest by all Americans for news stories about the war.

By the end of the French and Indian War in 1763, newspaper printers had managed to improve their business to such an extent that they now had an effective system for gathering and sharing news that would serve them well in the future. Journalism historian Frank Luther Mott referred to the French and Indian War as "the great running story of the period."[12] But it actually was much more than that because it served to give newspaper printers the skills, tools, and experience they needed to cover a major intercolonial event. By the end of the war, the press was ready for the role it would play as tension between the colonies and Great Britain intensified. The printing network that came into existence in the 1750s and 1760s would prove to be essential in the decades of conflict that made up the Revolutionary era.

THREE

# THE CONFLICT EMERGES

The American Revolution began as a result of an argument over taxes. Great Britain began passing additional taxes for the American colonies to pay off the war debt that had resulted from the French and Indian War. The war had been a large-scale one that entailed many sacrifices and the British treasury needed to be replenished. The war had doubled England's national debt, and military and administrative expenses in America had increased several times. Parliament believed that the military victory had benefited all citizens of the British Empire and that all citizens should help pay the costs. Americans, however, rejoiced over the elimination of the French and Indian threat and pondered the possibilities of the victory for expansion and other economic opportunities. Increasingly, the colonials felt less dependent on Great Britain. This feeling was increased because of the difficulties in communication created by 3,000 miles of ocean that separated the colonies from Great Britain. The average sea voyage from Great Britain to America in the 1760s lasted six weeks, which made quick responses to concerns and problems very difficult. The lack of good communication resulted in a growing misunderstanding between Great Britain and its American colonies that would eventually lead to revolution and separation.

In America, the new taxes covered all manner of goods and services. The Sugar Act of 1764, the first in a series of new tax laws, was followed by the Stamp Act of 1765. British officials thought it only fair that colonials should help pay the costs of their protection, but Americans argued that they too had incurred expenses during the war and that they already were taxed by local governments to help pay these debts. As it became clear that Great Britain was determined to raise more money in the colonies in some manner, more and more colonials came to question the ties to Britain and slowly moved toward favoring independence. The primary means of spreading the word about the growing tensions with Britain was through the printed word, particularly newspapers.

As the British government tried to pass new taxes on the colonies, the colonials cried "no taxation without representation," insisting that they were not represented in the British Parliament because they did not vote for its members. The British responded by stating that every member of Parliament represented every citizen of the empire, a view known as "virtual representation." These disagreements produced debates in both British and colonial legislatures. American newspapers printed reports of these debates as well as essays that discussed the issue of representation and what the word really meant. At this time, most newspapers had not become severely partisan and continued to present both sides of any debate. For example, the *Boston Gazette* (though already expressing opposition to the Stamp Act) did present materials supporting both definitions of representation. Reports on debates in Parliament about this issue included speeches by Prime Minister George Grenville, who had proposed the new taxes. As early as 1761, when he was serving as the treasurer of the Royal Navy,

Grenville stated that he could not understand the opposition of Americans to paying for British protection, and called them the "Ungrateful People of *America*!"[1] But most American comments on the issue of taxes and representation in the *Boston Gazette* clearly opposed the idea of virtual representation, such as these by an anonymous writer from 1765, in the weeks before the Stamp Act took effect: "It is a standing Maxim of *English Liberty* 'That no Man shall be taxed but with his own consent,' and you very well know we were not, in any *sober* sense, represented in Parliament, when this Tax was imposed. When the Legislature decree a Tax, as they represent the Community, such Tax ought to be considered as the voluntary Gift of the People to be applied to such Uses, as they, by their Representatives, shall think expedient."[2] Disagreements such as these only hardened with the passage of time and helped produce the split that led to war.

The clamor over the Stamp Act clearly indicated that relations between the British and the Americans likely would worsen. The taxes imposed by the act were, in the colonials' view, excessive. The situation was set for collision. The Stamp Act passed March 22, 1765, and was to become effective on November 1, 1765. Unwisely, the British government selected lawyers, merchants, and printers as the primary targets for the new tax. Those individuals, along with clergymen, were the best educated and most publicly involved citizens in the colonies. The act required that all documents, official papers, books, and newspapers be printed on stamped paper that carried a special tax. It also placed an additional tax on each advertisement in newspapers.

Printers recognized the economic threat to their businesses from the moment word of the legislation reached the colonies. The act levied a tax of a halfpenny per half sheet, a penny for larger page sizes, and two shillings for each advertisement. The income that printers received from subscribers and advertisers generally was only slightly higher than these taxes. The tax on job printing was just as high, and printing in languages other than English was taxed at double the standard rate. Printers who violated the rules could be fined from forty shillings to ten pounds. Anyone found to be publishing anonymously without stamps would be tried in the admiralty court without a jury, which seemed a violation of the traditional practice of trying cases of local offenses in courts before juries of local citizens.

Printers thus had an incentive to use their newspapers to strongly oppose the Stamp Act. But they initially hesitated to come out against the new tax, partially because they had no long history of defying the law and they were also uncertain about how the public would react to the legislation. Instead, they focused their attention on reducing the impact of the taxes by encouraging their readers to pay their debts. In May 1765, the *New Hampshire Gazette* announced the passage of the Stamp Act and stated that it would "oblige the Printers on this Continent to Raise more Money every Year, than was ever raised at the year's end, and perhaps be obliged to pay the Stamp Duty weekly."[3] Other newspapers, such as the *Maryland Gazette* and the *Georgia Gazette,* stated that they would have to raise their subscription rates to make enough money to pay the new taxes and continue in business.[4]

Although hesitant at first in their opposition to the Stamp Act, printers increased their criticisms as the date for the tax to take effect grew closer. They were joined by the merchants and lawyers who would have to pay the tax on essential documents needed to carry out their business as well as many other people who thought the legislation illegal. Merchants had originally organized trade boycotts to protest the Sugar Act in 1764, and they increased these efforts to present a stronger protest against the Stamp Act. All of these criticisms and protests were reported in the newspapers. Clergymen denounced the Stamp Act from the pulpit. Colonial legislatures and town meetings passed strong resolutions against it, and the newspapers published them all. On May 30, 1765, Patrick Henry introduced a series of resolutions opposing the Stamp Act in the Virginia House of Burgesses. They concluded with the following two resolutions: "*Resolved,* That his Majesty's liege People, the Inhabitants of this Colony, are not bound to yield Obedience to any Law or Ordinance whatever, designed to impose any Taxation whatsoever upon them, other than the Laws or Ordinances of the General Assembly aforesaid. . . . *Resolved,* That any Person, who shall, by speaking or writing, assert or maintain, that any Person or Persons, other than the General Assembly of this Colony, have any Right or Power to impose or lay any Taxation on the People here, shall be Deemed, an Enemy to this his Majesty's Colony."[5] The House of Burgesses repealed this part of the resolutions the next day, but some version of what was originally proposed by Henry is what appeared in newspapers throughout the colonies. Because Virginia was the oldest and most populous colony, many people saw this supposed action as a lead for the rest of the colonies to follow. Governor Francis Bernard of Massachusetts feared that this action changed everything: "Two or three months ago, I thought that this people would submit to the Stamp Act without actual opposition. . . . But the publishing of the Virginia Resolves proved an alarm bell to the disaffected."[6] Bernard was clearly concerned that the other colonies would take drastic actions in response to what Virginia had done.

Later events seemed to prove Bernard correct. The Stamp Act Congress, meeting in New York in October 1765, denounced the tax as an unconstitutional invasion of colonial liberties. Besides the trade boycotts organized by merchants, public meetings were called during the summer and fall of 1765 to discuss the Stamp Act. These meetings often led to marches of protest and sometimes turned into brawls, particularly in Boston and the Middle Colonies, and planned protest rallies and other strategies were devised by local leaders to nullify the legislation. In every colony, men came together to form organizations called the Sons of Liberty. They were determined to prevent the enforcement of the Stamp Act as well as to keep British authorities from stirring up trouble. In Charleston, South Carolina, the Sons of Liberty prevented an effort to collect money from the people: "At present every thing is very quiet here; our Liberty Boys being content to keep out the Stamps, do not injure, but protect, the Town; for some Time ago a Parcel of Sailors, having a Mind to make the most of this Suspension of Law, formed a Mob, to collect Money of the People in the Streets; but these Sons of Liberty suppressed them instantly, and committed the Ring-leaders to Goal [*sic*]. While they act thus cooly and determinately we have little Reason to fear they will give up the Point, especially as the Country People are all unanimous in it."[7] Similar actions and protests occurred throughout the colonies.

Probably the most famous public protests occurred in Boston, where the Sons of Liberty regularly organized demonstrations against the Stamp Act. Most of these public protests occurred near the center of town where a tree had been designated the Liberty Tree. On the morning of August 14, 1765, people found an effigy of Andrew Oliver, the stamp master-designate and secretary of the Province of Massachusetts Bay, hanging from the Liberty Tree. With it was a huge boot, symbolic of John Stuart, the third Earl of Bute (generally referred to as Lord Bute), whom everyone blamed for pushing the Stamp Act through Parliament. Out of the boot peeped a stuffed likeness of the devil clutching a copy of the Stamp Act. By the end of the day, the Sons of Liberty had destroyed Oliver's house. A week later, they destroyed the home of

Lieutenant Governor Thomas Hutchinson. After totally destroying the house and all its contents, they went on to cut down every tree on the grounds.

Reports of the events in Boston appeared in newspapers throughout the colonies. For example, an "Extraordinary" issue of the *Providence Gazette* published on August 24 carried a number of reports from Boston as well as some essays reacting to the events. The report described the effigy on the Liberty Tree and quoted the handwritten threat attached to it: "*He that takes this down is an enemy to his Country.*" The report also quoted a poem that had been attached to the effigy: "*What greater Joy can NEW-ENGLAND see, . . . Than STAMPMEN hanging on a Tree!*" In reacting to the events in Boston, "Colonus" worried that "every Privilege which our brave Ancestors, when driven from the Mother country, fought, found, and 'till of late fully enjoyed in America" would be lost. He declared that people throughout the colonies were trying to figure out some way to prevent the Stamp Act from taking effect and that "this laudable Zeal hath burnt into a Flame in BOSTON." He also worried that keeping the "flame" under control might prove difficult.[8]

The growing protests and newspaper discussions related to the Stamp Act reflected growing concerns among Americans about the impact of the legislation on the colonies. More and more people feared that the British government intended for the new tax to muzzle criticism in the colonies. John Adams stated in an essay published in the *Boston Gazette* in August 1765 that authorities sought "to strip us in a great measure of the means of knowledge, by loading the press, the colleges, and even an almanack and a newspaper, with restraints and duties."[9] On the day the new tax took effect, an essay in the *New London Gazette* by "A Freeman of the Colony of Connecticut" called on the people to use the pages of newspapers to discuss and debate the issues related to British taxes. He declared that "the liberty of free inquiry is one of the first and most fundamental of a free people; and where this is denied, there is not so much as the shadow of *Freedom* remaining. . . . The Press is open and *Free,* and how can it be better imployed upon any subject of a civil nature than this, in which the Trade, the Liberties, the Tranquillity and Prosperity of Great Britain and her colonies are so nearly and deeply concerned."[10] Increasingly, newspaper printers throughout the colonies used the pages of their weekly productions to speak out against the Stamp Act and its potential impact on the colonies.

In Massachusetts, the printed opposition to the Stamp Act was led by Benjamin Edes and John Gill of the *Boston Gazette* and Thomas and John Fleet of the *Boston Evening-Post.* Both of these printing partnerships were very important in the development of the newspaper press in Massachusetts in the eighteenth century. Edes and Gill both grew up in Charlestown, Massachusetts, and had entered into a printing partnership in Boston in 1755. This partnership lasted until the outbreak of fighting in 1775 when Edes left with a press and some cases of type to set up a new business in Watertown. Gill remained in Boston during the British occupation. Edes returned in 1776 after the British Army evacuated the city. At that time they dissolved their partnership. Edes continued to publish the *Boston Gazette* while Gill founded a new weekly newspaper, the *Continental Journal.* Edes continued publishing the *Gazette* until his death in 1803 while Gill sold the *Journal* to James D. Griffith shortly before his death in 1785.

Thomas Fleet Jr. and John Fleet were brothers who grew up in Boston and learned the printing trade from their father, Thomas Fleet, who had emigrated from Great Britain to Massachusetts in 1712. Having been apprenticed to the printing trade as a young man, Fleet quickly opened a print shop in Boston. He began publishing *The Weekly Rehearsal* in 1731 and changed the name to *The Boston Evening-Post* in 1735. The printing business and the *Evening-Post* passed to his two sons when he died in 1758. Thomas Jr. and John continued publishing the newspaper until the outbreak of the American Revolution. They remained in Boston during the siege and following the British evacuation, but they never revived the *Evening-Post.* Thomas Jr. died in 1797 and John died in 1806.

These printers published numerous essays opposing the Stamp Act. In the *Boston Gazette* several weeks before the new tax took effect, the essayist "B. W." urged people to step up and oppose the Stamp Act: "AWAKE!—Awake, my Countrymen, and, by a regular & legal Opposition, defeat the Designs of those who enslave us and our Posterity. Nothing is wanting but your own Resolution."[11] Accompanying such essays were also numerous reports of town meetings that discussed the potential impact of the Stamp Act. The town of Marblehead professed loyalty to the king while protesting the new taxes and instructing their representatives to oppose them: "THAT you promote, and readily join in, such dutiful Remonstrances and humble Petitions to the King and Parliament, and other decent Measures, as may have a Tendency to obtain a Repeal of the *Stamp-Act* or Alleviation of the heavy Burdens thereby imposed on the *American British* Colonies."[12] And opposition extended even to editorial comments on regular news stories, as shown by a report of an execution in the *Boston Evening-Post:* "Saturday last was executed Henry Halbert . . . for the murder of the son of Jacob Woolman.—*He will never pay any of the taxes unjustly laid on these once happy lands.*"[13] Printers thus used all means available in their newspapers to criticize the Stamp Act.

In New York, John Holt, printer of the *New-York Gazette, or*

*Weekly Post-Boy,* led the opposition to the Stamp Act. Originally in partnership with James Parker, Holt had become the sole printer in 1762. He used the pages of his newspaper to protest the taxes and to urge people to rally against the Stamp Act. Government authorities in New York debated charging Holt with seditious libel, but chose not to do so. But the possibility led Holt to a more circuitous form of protest. On September 21, 1765, the *Constitutional Courant,* a fake newspaper, appeared in New York. Actually produced in Woodbridge, New Jersey, by William Goddard, an employee of Holt's, the newspaper stated that it was "Printed by ANDREW MARVEL, at the Sign of *the Bribe refused,* on *Constitutional Hill, North-America.*" The first page contained the divided snake cartoon originally developed by Benjamin Franklin at the time of the Albany Congress and it once more urged the colonies to "JOIN or DIE." A number of unsigned articles protested the Stamp Act, fearing "the chains of abject slavery just ready to be riveted about our necks." One writer declared that it might have been better for the colonies if Britain had lost the war with France: "We might as well belong to France, or any other power; none could offer a greater injury to our rights and liberties than is offered by the Stamp Act."[14] Given the huge American fear of French victory in the war, such a statement reflected how upset many Americans were by the Stamp Act.

Other printers throughout the colonies protested the Stamp Act and called for its repeal, but to no avail. As the time for the act to take effect approached, the printers had to decide what to do. Many newspaper printers hesitated to openly violate the law, but they did begin to express concerns about its impact. Some used black borders in their newspapers as a sign of mourning for a free press which they thought would disappear with implementation of the Stamp Act. On October 31, 1765, the *Pennsylvania Journal and Weekly Advertiser* was published with a most garish design, its front page set up to look like a tombstone that was topped with a skull and crossbones. On the left side of the masthead, the printer stated that "THE TIMES ARE DREADFUL DISMAL DOLEFUL DOLOROUS, and DOLLARLESS." At the bottom of the masthead, he declared that the newspaper was "EXPIRING: In Hopes of a Resurrection to LIFE again."[15] Clearly, the printer hoped to grab people's attention to make a point about the impact of the Stamp Act on Americans.

Some printers published their newspapers after the deadline with no stamps on them. John Holt's first edition of the *New-York Gazette, or Weekly Post-Boy* after the Stamp Act took effect appeared with the following motto: "The United Voice of all His Majesty's *free* and *loyal* subjects in America—LIBERTY, PROPERTY and *no* STAMPS."[16] He also included an "anonymous" letter in this edition which threatened both his business and his body if he did not continue to publish the newspaper. Other printers also continued to publish their newspapers without stamps, but hoped to circumvent the penalties for doing so. A number of newspapers appeared with no printer listed or under a new name, assuming that would make it impossible to fine anyone for failing to use stamped paper. Others, such as the *New London Gazette* and the *Connecticut Gazette,* continued to publish without stamps, stating that no stamps were available. (No stamps were available because the stamp distributors in their communities had been forced to resign by mobs threatening physical harm if they tried to do their job.) The end result was that no newspapers appeared on stamped paper in the thirteen colonies that later revolted (newspapers with stamps did appear in other colonies such as Nova Scotia and Barbados).[17]

In one case, the Stamp Act even produced encouragement for

the newspaper business. In Charleston, South Carolina, Charles Crouch actually began publishing a newspaper, the *South Carolina Gazette; and Country Journal,* because some local residents had encouraged him to do so as a way to protest the Stamp Act. In his first issue, published on December 17, 1765, he stated on the first page: "No *STAMPED PAPER* to be had." He also called for "*LIBERTY and PROPERTY, and NO STAMPS.*"[18] He went on over the next several months to print further criticisms of the Stamp Act and to point out the volatility of the situation. He reprinted an essay by "Freeman" from New York that stated, "Let us oppose them with all our might, even though death should be the consequence—we should die gloriously in our duty in the best of causes."[19] Crouch also quoted a London writer who declared that "the bomb has burst in North-America."[20] Crouch used the Stamp Act controversy to spark support for his new printing business while also pointing out the potential volatility that the Stamp Act had produced in the relations between the colonies and Great Britain.

Most of the newspaper printers joined together to protest the Stamp Act and what they believed were unfair economic costs for their businesses. This resulted in what probably constituted one of the first mass-media editorial campaigns in American journalism history. As David Ramsay commented in his book *The History of the American Revolution,* published in 1789: "It was fortunate for the liberties of America, that News-papers were the subject of a heavy stamp duty. Printers, when uninfluenced by government, have generally arranged themselves on the side of liberty, nor are they less remarkable for attention to the profits of their profession. A stamp duty, which openly invaded the first, and threatened a great diminution of the latter, provided their united zealous opposition."[21] The Stamp Act thus produced a strong opposition among printers that helped push them to attempt to unite all Americans to fight the odious British legislation.

Faced with all this opposition, British officials in the colonies reported to their superiors in London that they could not enforce the Stamp Act and asked what they should do. The boycott of British goods began to have an effect as well. Trade with Great Britain dropped precipitously, and colonials refused to pay their British creditors. On June 3, 1765, the *Boston Post-Boy* reported that the number of ships working the West Indies routes had declined by more than 80 percent in the months since the passing of the Stamp Act. Business was suffering tremendously and British merchants implored Parliament to solve the problem. Finally, in March 1766, Parliament repealed the Stamp Act, recognizing that it was unenforceable. Americans rejoiced at their successful opposition to the legislation and hoped that relations with Great Britain would get back to normal. Americans also rejoiced over their successful protests and printers reflected on the role that their newspapers played in the victory. Most newspaper printers in 1766 would have agreed with William Rind's comment in the *Virginia Gazette* in May: "A *well conducted* NEWSPAPER *would, at any Time, be important, but most especially at a Crisis, which makes a quick Circulation of Intelligence particularly interesting to all the* AMERICAN COLONIES."[22] But Great Britain still faced financial difficulties and debt because of the French and Indian War, and British leaders soon sought other ways to raise funds in the colonies.

The situation in the colonies calmed down tremendously following the repeal of the Stamp Act and the political unrest sparked by that piece of legislation might have been the last if the British treasury had not still needed money. To solve the continuing financial problem, Chancellor of the Exchequer Charles Townshend devised a plan in 1767 to place duties on goods imported into the colonies. During the crisis over the Stamp Act, many complaints had centered on the fact that the stamp duty had been an "internal" tax on American production rather than an "external" tax on imports (the type of tax that Great Britain had previously placed on the colonies through the Navigation Acts and other trade duties). Townshend believed that tariff duties would not produce the kind of protests that the Stamp Act had produced, so he proposed duties on American imports of glass, lead, paper, paint, and tea. He also proposed a Board of Customs Commissioners in Boston to administer the new legislation.

Once more, the British government erred by including something in the new legislation that would strike at printers directly. In 1767, very little paper was produced in the colonies, so printers had to import much of what they used. By placing a duty on imported paper, the Townshend duties ensured that printers would strongly oppose the legislation. As one essayist stated in the *Pennsylvania Chronicle* in December 1767, "in *substance* and *right*" no difference existed between paying "the rates mentioned in the *Stamp-Act,* on the *use* of paper" and "these duties, on the *importation* of it. It is nothing but the edition of a former book, with a new title page."[23] Printers sought some relief through the encouragement of domestic papermaking, but they also joined the protests against the Townshend duties in general.

But the differentiation between internal and external taxes that had proved so effective during the Stamp Act crisis produced problems in dealing with the Townshend Acts and printers struggled to find a common platform with which to criticize the new legislation. Royal officials worried that the newspapers would once more lead the people astray because, as Lieutenant Governor Cadwallader Colden of New York stated in a letter to William Petty, the Earl of Shelburne, "The People are familiarised to read Seditious if not treasonable Papers."[24] Governor Bernard also warned Lord Shelburne that "the proceedings in the newspapers are precisely the same as those preceding the former disturbances."[25] But it took some time for those opposed to the new duties to focus their arguments and attentions in a way that would have the biggest impact.

While seeking focus, newspaper printers did not hesitate to criticize the new legislation. Much of the earlier criticism focused on the harmful impact of trade duties and restrictions on an economy already deep in depression. Calls for some sort of retaliation became common. An essayist in the *Boston Gazette* in late 1767 called on "the free-born sons of those truly brave ancestors, who traversed a boisterous ocean, and settled a howling wilderness" to cease, or at least greatly reduce, imports from Great Britain to clearly protest the new duties.[26] Another writer, in the *Pennsylvania Chronicle* in November 1767, implored Americans to "Save your Money, and save our Country!"[27] Such calls for action produced some boycott efforts, but the protests against the Townshend Acts still did not have the focus that had resulted during the Stamp Act crisis.

For newspaper printers to rally their readers as they had done during the Stamp Act crisis, the protests had to move beyond material self-interest to something more philosophical and constitutional in nature. Such an appeal came in December 1767 with the first appearance of the "Letters from a Farmer in Pennsylvania." The *Pennsylvania Chronicle* published these essays in twelve installments between December 2, 1767, and February 15, 1768. The author did such a good job of demonstrating that the Townshend duties were unconstitutional that the entire series was reprinted in most newspapers and also in pamphlet form once all had appeared in the *Chronicle.* Though the pieces were published anonymously, it later transpired that the author was John Dickinson, a prominent lawyer and politician from Pennsylvania. Dickinson went on to represent Pennsylvania in both the First and Second Continental Congresses. Dickinson refused to vote for independence in July 1776 because he thought it was not clear that the colonies could successfully win the fight against Great Britain. He left Congress, but joined the Pennsylvania militia and served in a variety of capacities in Pennsylvania and Delaware during and after the American Revolution. Dickinson's actions in 1776 made some believe that he did not support the move for independence, but his ideas expressed in the "Letters from a Farmer in Pennsylvania" clearly show that he believed that the British government had become tyrannical and that something had to be done if the colonies were going to protect their rights.

In the "Letters," Dickinson clearly stated that the distinction between internal and external taxes was a false one and declared "*that we cannot be* HAPPY, *without being* FREE—that we cannot be free, *without being secure in our property*—that *we* cannot be secure in our property, *if, without our consent, others may, as by right, take it away.*"[28] Dickinson urged Americans to petition the British government for redress of their grievances, to increase their boycott efforts in order to make clear their opposition to the taxes, and to avoid violence at all costs. His advice against violence had little impact, but his constitutional argument against the legitimacy of the Townshend duties provided the focus needed to rally people in opposition.

The primary organized efforts aimed at protesting the Townshend Acts once more revolved around trade boycotts. Following the publication of the "Letters from a Farmer in Pennsylvania," efforts to formalize intercolonial trade boycotts increased. Many colonials joined together in an effort to organize and coordinate the boycotts through the adoption of official nonimportation agreements. These boycotts proved less successful than those entered into to protest the Stamp Act, primarily because the general population did not seem as united against the Townshend Acts as they had been against the Stamp Act. Opponents of the new duties sought ways to once more unify people in opposition to British policy. Opposition leaders in Boston in particular sought support from other communities because Boston was suffering economically from the Townshend Acts and also now had to deal with the presence of British troops, who had arrived in 1768. Fearing that the troops had been sent to Boston to quell colonial opposition to British legislation, opposition leaders turned to the newspapers in hopes of once more unifying Americans against British actions. The result was the first conscious effort to distribute news in an organized manner throughout America: the "Journal of Occurrences."

The original edition of the "Journal of Occurrences" appeared in the *Boston Evening-Post* with the following request to the Fleet brothers who printed the newspaper: "Though you have already published an account of the arrival of the fleet and army at Boston, yet a great number of your customers would be glad to find the following Journal of Occurrences published in your useful and impartial paper, so that they may see in one comprehensive view, the extraordinary transactions of the present day."[29] The "Journal of Occurrences" was the most formal series of reports on the sufferings of the citizens of Boston, but it was not the only such effort. From September 1768 to the summer of 1769, such reports appeared in the Boston newspapers and then spread throughout the colonies and even to Great Britain. The focus was always on the fact that Boston was under military rule, a situation that violated British law and was considered totally unacceptable by many colonials. Numerous reports of brutality and cruelty by the soldiers appeared.[30] The author of the "Journal of Occurrences" stated that the situation was not acceptable:

> In pursuance of this ministerial plan of policy, we now behold a standing army and swarms of crown officers, placemen, pensioners and expectants, co-operating in order to subdue Americans to the yoke. Our hopes are that the people of Britain do now, or will soon fully perceive that they cannot have our monies in the way of a revenue, and trade both; that what the merchants and manufacturers receive, serves to increase the wealth and opulence [*sic*] of the naition [*sic*], while the other only tends to destroy trade and increase ministerial dependence.[31]

Something had to be done to end this intolerable situation.

By the time of the publication of the last issue of the "Journal of Occurrences" on August 1, 1769, readers throughout the colonies had been told over and over again that the British could not be trusted and were not humane. The reports declared that the British government hoped to totally subjugate the Americans by any means necessary: they sought to monopolize trade through illegal taxes, they would not listen to reason, they threatened anyone who interfered with their plans, and they were just plain vulgar. If readers based their opinions of the British solely on the accounts in the "Journal of Occurrences," there seemed to be nothing positive to say about them. The widespread circulation of such news helped many newspaper readers become used to the idea that the British presence was not good for Americans.

Although newspaper printers were increasingly coming out in opposition to British policies, not everyone agreed that Great Britain was in the wrong. The most vocal newspaper supporter of the British government during the argument over the Townshend duties was a relatively recent immigrant from Scotland. John Mein had immigrated to Boston in 1764, where he established himself as a successful bookseller. He originally advertised his business in the *Boston Gazette,* printed by Benjamin Edes and John Gill. He soon decided to enter the newspaper business himself, establishing the *Boston Chronicle* in 1767 in partnership with John Fleeming. Mein and Fleeming originally stated that their newspaper would be impartial, in the tradition long held in the colonies, to "throw some light on the complexion of the times." The *Chronicle*'s motto was: "Be independent—your interest is intimately connected with this noble virtue—if you depart from this—you must sink from the esteem of the public."[32] But the goal of impartiality proved impossible to achieve in the wake of the Stamp Act crisis. Mein found himself irresistibly drawn into the debate over the Stamp Act, and insisted on expressing his opposition to the trade boycotts, which quickly got him in trouble with those American leaders who wanted to use the boycotts to force the British to repeal their taxes.

By nature a stubborn man, Mein did not hesitate to criticize these people. He first reported in June 1769 that 190 Boston importers had violated the nonimportation agreement.[33] The supporters of the boycott accused Mein of padding his list with people who were not merchants and thus not subject to the agreement. Mein supported his claims by printing manifests of ships that had entered Boston Harbor since January 1, 1769. Included in this list were three ships owned by John Hancock.[34] As one of the leaders of the merchants in Boston, Hancock had helped organize the nonimportation agreement. Mein's accusations were intended to embarrass Hancock and other people opposing British policy. Mein also attacked people in Great Britain who supported the colonies. He published an essay from a London newspaper that spoke badly of William Pitt, probably the most popular British statesman in America. Edes and Gill then printed an attack against Mein in the *Boston Gazette.* The next morning, Mein called on Edes and Gill and demanded that they reveal the identity of the author of the attack. They refused, and Mein invited them outside one at a time. Edes and Gill again refused. Mein then promised "to cane the first one of them I meet" and departed. On the next afternoon he spied Gill on the street; and "with force of arms, to wit, with a large club," he laid his adversary low with two blows to the head. Then he "beat, wounded, and evil treated" the downed man.[35] Gill won a court judgment of seventy-five pounds against Mein for the assault. When Mein continued to criticize the opposition leadership in the *Chronicle,* he was hanged in effigy and his home was attacked. On October 28, 1769, a mob assaulted Mein and his partner Fleeming. In defending himself, Mein accidentally shot a bystander. To escape prosecution and in fear of his life, Mein fled to a British man-of-war in Boston Harbor and shortly thereafter left for Britain. Fleeming tried to continue the publication of the *Chronicle,* but shut it down in 1770 and he, too, left Boston. Thus, the primary effort to offer an alternative view in the newspaper press in Boston failed.

Newspapers of the American colonies played an essential role in the debates over the taxes that Great Britain passed following the French and Indian War. Stories about the various protests and resolutions against the taxes appeared again and again from city to city throughout the colonies. Readers of the weekly news sheets perceived that many colonials from New Hampshire to Georgia opposed the parliamentary legislation, and thus they saw that they had something in common. The newspapers thus helped pull the people in the colonies together in the early years of the conflict with Great Britain that would eventually lead to the Revolution.

FOUR

# A TIME OF QUIET

Although the crisis sparked by the Stamp Act was allayed with the act's repeal in 1766, tensions continued and the adoption of the Townshend Acts only added to the disagreements. The situation remained particularly tense in Boston, where the Stamp Act riots were commemorated on an annual basis. Governor Francis Bernard worried that the tensions and arguments would once more degenerate into riots, and he requested that British troops be stationed in Boston to intimidate the citizens of Massachusetts and to serve as a deterrent to such an event. In 1768, several regiments were moved to Boston, partially in response to Bernard's request and also to save money because they could be more easily housed and supplied on the Atlantic coast than in the Ohio River Valley where they had previously been stationed.

Bernard's request ultimately backfired. Rather than intimidating the people, the presence of the troops only increased tensions. Part of the troubles resulted from British troops working at civilian jobs when they were not on duty. The soldiers, desiring to supplement their military pay, would work for less than the going rate. Thus, Boston laborers perceived the troops as stealing their jobs and their livelihood. Boston merchants also continued their boycott of British goods, even though some feared the move of the troops to the city was intended to pressure Bostonians to cease the boycott. As a result of both of these developments, relations between the soldiers and the citizens of Boston grew steadily worse.

Tensions in Boston reached the boiling point in early 1770. On February 22, a crowd gathered to try to force a merchant, Theophilus Lillie, to honor the nonimportation agreement. During the confrontation, one of Lillie's neighbors, Ebenezer Richardson, tried to help him. The crowd followed Richardson home and threw rocks through his windows. Richardson fired a shotgun in response, killing eleven-year-old Christopher Seider.

With Seider's death still fresh in people's memory, rumors circulated through Boston that the soldiers planned to massacre large numbers of Boston citizens. Fights broke out between British troops and the people of Boston. One particularly violent incident took place on March 2, and neither the troops, nor the Bostonians sick of the troops' presence in the city, had gotten over the incident when further trouble broke out three days later.

On March 5, 1770, the defining moment of the crisis arrived. A lone sentry in front of the Customs House was surrounded by a crowd, which began throwing snowballs (possibly rocks covered with snow) at him. He summoned help, and the main guard responded. Seven men under the command of Captain Thomas Preston came to the sentry's aid. Preston tried to reason with the apparent leaders of the mob, but to no avail. A snowball hit Private Hugh Montgomery, who either slipped or fell as a result. When he got up, he fired into the crowd. After a short pause, the rest of the soldiers also fired into the crowd. Eleven men in the crowd were shot; three died instantly and two more died in the next few days. Preston managed to prevent his men from firing again, and the troops withdrew to a place of safety.

For the next day or so, Boston became a place of near anarchy. Crowds marched in the streets demanding justice. The situation calmed somewhat once Preston and the soldiers of the guard were arrested. In November and December 1770, Preston and the enlisted men were tried for murder in separate hearings. John Adams and Josiah Quincy represented the accused. By emphasizing the confusion and the role of the mob, Adams and Quincy were able to convince two juries that the events of March 5, 1770, did not constitute murder. Preston and five of the troops were acquitted, while two soldiers were convicted of manslaughter. They were branded on the hand, a common punishment for such crimes in the eighteenth century.

The Boston Massacre, as the events of March 5 came to be called, produced news reports and reactions in the press and other printed media throughout the American colonies. Probably the most famous "account" of the clash between British troops and the Boston crowd was an engraving of the event produced by Paul Revere. Revere apparently did not witness the Boston Massacre, and he based his engraving on the work of another engraver, Henry Pelham. Color prints of Revere's engraving became available by late March 1770. The engraving shows the British troops firing in an organized manner with Preston standing behind them and issuing the order to fire. Eyewitness accounts of the event indicate that the shooting did not occur in such an organized manner, and most said that Preston was actually standing in front of his troops when the firing began. But Revere's representation came to heavily influence American perceptions of the confrontation in the streets of Boston. Revere used the local newspapers to advertise the availability of prints of his engraving and they became very popular throughout the American colonies, helping to increase the anti-British feelings of many American colonials.

Printed accounts in the newspapers spread the story of the Boston Massacre even further. Leading the way in reporting the events of March 5 and what they meant for Americans were Benjamin Edes and John Gill of the *Boston Gazette.* On March 12, they printed a lengthy account of what had happened. They began their report with an editorial comment about why events had degenerated to such a low point:

> THE Town of Boston affords a recent and melancholy Demonstration of the destructive Consequences of quartering Troops among Citizens in a Time of Peace, under a pretence of supporting Laws and invading Civil Authority; every considerate and unprejudic'd Person among us was deeply imprest with the Apprehension of their Consequences when it was known that a Number of Regiments were ordered to this Town under such a Pretext, but in Reality to enforce oppressive Measures; to awe and controul the legislative as well as executive Power of the Province, and to quell a Spirit of Liberty, which however it may have been basely oppose'd and even ridicul'd by some, would do Honor to any Age and Country. A few Persons amongst us had determin'd to use all their Influence to procure so destructive a Measure with a View to their securely enjoying the Profits of an American Revenue, and unhappily both for Britain and this Country they found a means to effect it.[1]

Edes and Gill clearly believed that actions of greedy British officials had produced the problems in Boston.

Having placed all of the blame on the British authorities, Edes and Gill went on to describe what they believed had happened in some detail. First, they accused the soldiers of causing all the trouble that led to the confrontation: "On the Evening of Monday, being the fifth Current, several Soldiers of the 29th Regiment were seen parading the Streets with their drawn Cutlasses and Bayonets, abusing and wounding Numbers of the Inhabitants . . . they attacked single and unarmed persons until they raised much clamour, and then turned down Cornhill street, insulting all they met in like manner, and pursuing some to their very doors."[2] Edes and Gill then went on to describe the Massacre itself: "Thirty or forty persons, mostly lads being by this means gathered in King-street, Capt. Preston, with a party of men with charged bayonets, came from the main guard to the Commissioners house, the soldiers pushing with their bayonets, crying, Make way! They took place by the custom-house, and continuing to push to drive the people off, pricked some in several places; on which they were clamorous, and, it is said threw snow-balls. On this, the Captain commanded them to fire, and more snow-balls coming, he again said, Damn you. Fire, be the consequence what you will! One soldier then fired, and a townsman with a cudgel struck him over the hands with such a force that he dropt his firelock; and rushing forward aimed a blow at the Captain's head which graz'd his hat and fell pretty heavy upon his arm: However, the soldiers continued the fire, successively, till 7 or 8, or as some say 11 guns were discharged. . . . By this fatal manoeuvre, three men were laid dead on the spot, and two more struggling for life; but what shewed a degree of cruelty unknown to British troops, at least since the house of Hanover has directed their operations, was an attempt to fire upon or push with their bayonets the persons who undertook to remove the slain and wounded!"[3]

Edes and Gill went on to describe the meeting of town leaders and British officials that resulted in the removal of the troops from

Boston to the fortress Castle William in Boston Harbor, a move praised as a good effort to prevent further trouble. Edes and Gill concluded their report with a description of the funerals of the men killed on March 5:

> Last Thursday, agreeable to a general Request of the Inhabitants, and by the consent of Parents and Friends, were carried to their *Grave* in Succession, the bodies of *Samuel Gray, Samuel Maverick, James Caldwell,* and *Crispus Attucks,* the unhappy Victims who fell in the bloody Massacre of the Monday Evening proceeding! . . . On this Occasion most of the shops in Town were shut, all the Bells were ordered to toll a solemn Peal, as were also those in the neighboring towns of Charlestown, Roxbury, &c. The procession began to move between the hours of four and five in the afternoon; two of the unfortunate sufferers, viz. Mess. James Caldwell and Crispus Attucks, who were strangers, borne from Faneuil Hall, attended by a numerous train of persons of all ranks; and the other two, viz. Mr. Samuel Gray, from the house of Mr. Benjamin Gray, his brother, on the North-side the Exchange, and Mr. Maverick, from the house of his distressed mother, Mrs. Mary Maverick, in Union street, each followed by their respective relations and friends. The several hearses forming a Junction in King-Street, the Theatre of that inhuman Tragedy! proceeded from thence thro' the Main-Street, lengthened by an immense Concourse of People, so numerous as to be obliged to follow the Ranks of six, and brought up by a long Train of Carriages belonging to the principal Gentry of the Town. The Bodies were deposited in one Vault in the middle Burying-ground: The aggravated Circumstances of their Death, the Distress and Sorrow visible in every countenance, together with the peculiar Solemnity with which the whole Funeral was conducted, surpass Description.[4]

Edes and Gill thus sought to stir up the passions of their readers through their emotional descriptions of the events related to the Boston Massacre.

Newspaper producers throughout the colonies reprinted the news from Boston because they knew their readers would want to know what happened. Such widespread interest in the actions of the British throughout the colonies indicated the growing frustration with government authorities on the part of many colonials. Americans were increasingly unhappy with the British presence throughout the colonies and thus the Boston Massacre was more than a local story. It constituted a story of interest to all Americans who perceived the British as interfering in American affairs. On March 22, the *Pennsylvania Gazette* carried a summary of several news reports: "The Boston Papers of the 5$^{th}$ Instant, give Accounts of sundry Frays between the People of the Country and Town, and some Soldiers of the 29$^{th}$ Regiment, in which the Soldiers were always the Aggressors, and always worsted. . . . a great Number of People having assembled near the Town-House, where a Sentry is placed, the Regiments in Town appeared also, under Arms, and a Detachment was sent from the Main Guard to the Sentry; 7 Men of this Detachment, it seems, fired among the Crowd—The Post could not certainly tell the Reason,—whether they were assaulted, or too closely pressed, or were ordered to fire. . . . "[5] Printers also promised their readers that they would find out as much as possible once the rumors of the Boston Massacre spread. In late March, Virginia printer William Rind stated that "it is reported that a fray happened lately at Boston, between some of the inhabitants and some of the soldiers, and that the latter fired upon, and killed several of the former, whereupon a large number of the inhabitants rose, and (the report says) drove the soldiers out of the town, and the Commissioners vanished nobody knew where. We hope there is no truth to this report, but if there is, a few days will clear it up."[6] Rind's desire for the report to be false reflected the growing frustration with British officials on the part of many Americans.

Although the bulk of the reports about the Boston Massacre appeared in newspapers opposed to the government, the pro-British press could not ignore the event. On March 8, one of the first reports of the tragedy appeared in John Mein's *Boston Chronicle,* being printed by his partner John Fleeming. Fleeming briefly summarized events, but hesitated to give too much detail because of the fact that the soldiers were going to be put on trial for murder: "For some days bye-past, there have been several affrays between the inhabitants, and the soldiers quartered in this town. . . . Last Monday, about 9 o'clock at night a most unfortunate affair happened in King-street: The centinel posted at the custom-house, being surrounded by a number of people, called to the main-guard, upon which Capt. Preston, who was Captain of the day, with a party went to his assistance: soon after which some of the party fired."[7] The piece then listed the names of those killed and wounded and reported that government leaders had decided to move the troops out of Boston. Fleeming concluded this report by explaining why it was so brief: "*We decline at present, giving a more particular account of this unhappy affair, as we hear the trial of the unfortunate prisoners is to come on next week.*"[8] Fleeming probably wished that he had nothing to report at all.

Other reports from Boston placed the blame for the Boston Massacre squarely on the crowd. A letter from a citizen of Boston appeared in the *New-York Gazette, and Weekly Mercury* about a month after the event and accused the mob of plotting to attack the soldiers: "The 5$^{th}$ and 6$^{th}$ Instant was agreed upon for a general Attack upon the Troops, and great Numbers came in with Arms from the Country, to join their Friends in Town. On the 5$^{th}$ in the Evening, two Soldiers were attack'd and beat, and the Town's People, agreeable to their Plans, broke open two Meeting Houses, and rang the Alarm Bells, which was supposed to be for Fire. Soon after some of the Guard came to Capt. Preston, who was Captain of the Day, and informed him the Inhabitants were assembling to attack the Troops, that the Bells were ringing for that Purpose, and not for Fire." The anonymous writer went on to describe the confrontation, reporting that Captain Preston was standing in front of the troops when the firing began. This report was intended to exonerate the captain from accusations that he ordered the troops to fire into the crowd. This author concluded that he hoped "Truth and Innocence will prevail; that blind Vengeance will not intrude itself into his Tryal."[9] The reports of a plot by the members of the mob continued to appear in print. When the trials ended in not guilty verdicts, a writer to the same New York paper commented that he had been told that "the Jury laid great Stress upon the Evidence, of a Plan having been laid by the Inhabitants to attack the Soldiers, a great Number having met together in the Market Place, breaking the Stalls to furnish them with Clubs, such as were not before provided and amongst the rest, there was one with a white Wig, and a Boston red Cloak, encouraging them to make the Attack."[10] This report showed growing suspicions of plotting on both sides following the Boston Massacre.

The fate of the soldiers arrested in the wake of the Boston Massacre sparked numerous comments in the newspapers. Captain Thomas Preston, the platoon commander of the soldiers who had fired into the crowd, understood the role of the press, and he used the pages of the *Boston Gazette* to communicate to the people of Boston:

> PERMIT me thro' the channel of your paper, to return my thanks in the most publick manner to the inhabitants in general of this

> town—who throwing aside *all* party and prejudice, have with the utmost humanity and freedom stept forth advocates for truth, in defense of my injured innocence, in the late unhappy affair that happened on Monday night last: And to assure them, that I shall ever have the highest sense of the Justice they have done me.[11]

The trials of the soldiers were delayed until the fall of 1770 in hopes that the anger of the citizens of Boston would have cooled by that time. When the verdicts were handed down in November, reports of the results appeared throughout the colonies. The *Boston Gazette* reported Preston's acquittal without much comment, while Isaiah Thomas expressed shock at the outcome in the *Massachusetts Spy:* "Thus ended this long expected and important trial!"[12] Most Americans seemed surprised by the not guilty verdicts because the account they received of the Boston Massacre in the newspapers generally showed an organized attack on the part of the British troops.

Although Isaiah Thomas clearly did not like the results of the trials, their end did mark the beginning of a time of calm as people on both sides of the Atlantic Ocean reacted in horror to the events in Boston. However, Americans opposed to the British used the pages of their newspapers to remind people of the ongoing disagreements with the British government. The Boston Massacre was used to fuel opposition to the government from the point it occurred until fighting broke out in 1775. Commemorations of the conflict replaced the remembrances of the Stamp Act riots as the primary event for rallying opposition to British authorities. And the newspapers helped in these efforts to keep people from forgetting. On the first anniversary of the massacre, Isaiah Thomas called on his readers to never forget the tyranny of the British government:

As a solemn and perpetual Memorial of the Tyranny of the British Administration of Government in 1768, 1769, and 1770: . . . Of the fatal and destructive Consequence of quartering Armies, in Time of Peace in populous Cities: . . . Of the ridiculous Policy, and infamous absurdity, of supporting Civil Government by a Military Force: . . . Of the great Duty and Necessity of Firmly opposing Despotism in its first approaches: . . . Of the detestable Principles and arbitrary Conduct of those Ministers, in Britain who advised, and of their friends in America who desired, the introduction of a Standing Army into this Province in the Year 1768: . . . Of the irrefragable Proof which those Ministers themselves thereby produced, that the Civil Government, as by them administered, was weak, wicked, and tyrannical: . . . Of the vile ingratitude and abominable Wickedness of every American, who abetted and encouraged, either in Thought, Word, or Deed, the Establishment of a Standing Army among his Countrymen: . . . Of the unaccountable Conduct of those Civil Governors, the immediate Representatives of his Majesty, who, while the Ministry were triumphantly insulting the whole Legislative Assembly of the State, and while the Blood of the massacred inhabitants was flowing in the Streets, persisted in repeatedly disclaiming all Authority of relieving the People, by any the least Removal of the Troops: . . . And of the savage Cruelty of the immediate Perpetrators: . . . *Be it forever Remembered*. . . . That this day, the Fifth of March, is the Anniversary of Preston's Massacre, in King-Street, Boston, New-England, 1770: in which Five of his Majesty's Subjects were slain, and Six wounded by the Discharge of a Number of Muskets from a Party of Soldiers under the command of Capt. Thomas Preston. . . . GOD Save the PEOPLE![13]

By reminding his readers of the horror of the Boston Massacre, Thomas implied that British tyranny continued to exist.

In particular, Samuel Adams sought to use the Boston Massacre and its aftermath as a mechanism for continuing to spark further opposition to the British government. Having failed in a number of business ventures, Adams found success as leader of the growing protest movement in Massachusetts against the British government during the 1760s and 1770s. By 1769, he had become the leader of the radicals in Boston. It is unclear whether he supported independence by this time, but he clearly wanted to reduce the control and influence of the British government in colonial affairs. The Boston Massacre provided Adams with useful ammunition in his fight against the British government.

Adams first focused his attention on the results of the trials of the soldiers involved in the Boston Massacre. Beginning on December 10, 1770—the same day that the final official report of the trials appeared—and continuing through January 28, 1771, Adams produced a series of essays that appeared in the *Boston Gazette.* Writing as "Vindex," Adams used the pages of the *Gazette* to retry the cases. In the end he could not change the verdicts, but he did convince many of his readers that the trials had not resulted in a fair judgment for everyone involved.

Over the course of two months, Adams deftly used the press to shape public opinion about the Boston Massacre and to turn it into a major crime by the British government. Through Adams's skillful writing, Captain Preston, the eight soldiers, and the entire British government were portrayed as the murderers of five patriots killed in front of the Boston Customs House that bitter March evening.

At first, Adams praised all of the participants in the trials for their conscientious efforts in carrying out their respective assignments. However, he quickly moved to the issue of whether the soldiers were justified in firing into the crowd. Adams questioned why the soldiers did not just retreat to the barracks. Adams also wrote that there existed ample proof that the soldiers had stirred up the crowd and caused the trouble in front of the Customs House. "The behavior of the party as they went from the main guard discover'd an haughty air—they push'd their bayonets and damn'd the people as they went along."[14] According to Adams's analysis, the troops brought the trouble on themselves by stirring up the crowd with their own belligerent attitudes.

Throughout the series of essays, "Vindex" continually returned to the issue of who was at fault on the night of March 5, 1770. In a piece published on December 31, he concluded that during the trials, "not a single instance was prov'd, of abuse offer'd to Soldiers that Evening, previous to the insolent behavior of those who rush'd out of Murray's Barracks, with cutlasses, Clubs and other Weapons, and fell upon all whom they met." Rather, there had been many instances of the troops "insulting and even assaulting the Inhabitants in every part of the Town."[15]

Adams left the final judgment to the people of Boston, but his language left no room for doubt as to who he believed was responsible for the Boston Massacre. He concluded that the soldiers pushed the crowd too far and that the people responded to the threats in self-defense. "Vindex" wrote that after the initial shots into the crowd the soldiers continued to fire because their commanding officer did not control them: "Capt. Preston, at so alarming a juncture, took no method to prevent the rest from firing, if what was testified in court is to be credited; or, if his own account must be rely'd upon, he exerted no authority over his men, but used expostulations only."[16] Thus, the British only had themselves to blame for what happened on that evening.

Adams also emphasized the barbarity of the event. In doing this, he presented to the public questionable evidence never aired at the trial. Of particular importance was the issue of Private Kilroy's bayonet, which "was prov'd to be the next morning bloody five inches from the point." Adams stated that many believed the bayonet had fallen into human blood "which ran plentifully in the street," which accounted for its condition the next morning. But, it was "much more likely that this very bayonet was stab'd into the head of poor Gray [one of the dead] after he was shot." Adams reported that "such an instance of Savage barbarity there undoubtedly was.—It was sworn before the Magistrate who first examined into this cruel tragedy." However, when the case came to trial, the witness who made this statement was out of the province and could not attend to testify. Adams believed that government collusion lay behind this.[17]

Besides asking why certain witnesses did not appear for the prosecution, Adams questioned the validity of witnesses who testified for the defense. In particular, he challenged the evidence given by Andrew, a slave, which supported the story that the crowd threw coal at the sentry. The great propagandist declared that Andrew was "remarkable for telling romantick stories in the circles of his acquaintance." People believed Andrew's testimony, Adams wrote, primarily because "his master, who is in truth an honest man, came into court and swore to his character." Adams hinted that the master might be mistaken because "no man knows so little of the real character of his servant, as the master himself does: It is well known, that the Negroes of this town have been familiar with the soldiers; and that some of them have been tamper'd with to cut their master's throats: I hope Andrew is not one of these."[18] Such comments weakened the strength of defense testimony, at least in the minds of many who already believed the soldiers were guilty.

Adams also attempted to put events in historical perspective:

"The trial of the soldiers concern'd in the carnage on the memorable 5th of March, was the most solemn trial that ever was had in this country, was pronounc'd from the bench. To see eight prisoners bro't to the bar together, charg'd with the murder of five persons at one time, was certainly, as was then observ'd, affecting."[19]

Finally, Adams slyly reversed himself on the issue of how good a job those involved in the trial had done. He declared: "I am not about to arraign the late jurors before the bar of the public." But, he concluded, "They are accountable to God and their own consciences, and in *their* day of trial, may God send them good deliverance."[20]

Newspapers throughout the colonies reprinted all or part of the "Vindex" essays and thus helped facilitate Adams's desire to convince many Americans that the trials had not produced fair and objective verdicts. Adams then focused his attention on an effort to convince Americans that they could no longer trust Great Britain and that the Boston Massacre and its aftermath provided clear proof of this fact. Again, Adams used his efforts in the pages of the *Boston Gazette* to keep the discussion about British tyranny alive. In 1771, writing as "Candidus," Adams called on Americans to recognize that British law amounted to slavery:

> Is it impossible to form an idea of *slavery* more complete, more miserable, more *disgraceful,* than that of a people where justice is administer'd, government exercis'd, and a standing army maintain'd at the expense of the people, and yet without the least dependence upon them? If we can find no relief from this infamous situation,—I repeat it, *if we can find no relief from this infamous situation,*—let the ministry, who have stripped us of our property and liberty, deprive us of our understanding too; that, unconscious of what we have been or are, and ungoaded by tormenting re-

> flections, we may tamely bow down our necks with all the stupid serenity of servitude to any drudgery which our lords and masters may please to command.

Adams went on:

> I appeal to the common sense of mankind to what a state of infamy and misery must a people be reduced! To have a Governor by the sole appointment of the crown; under the absolute control of a weak and arbitrary minister, to whose dictates he is to yield unlimited obedience or forfeit his political existence; while he is to be supported at the expense of the people by virtue of an authority claimed by *strangers* to oblige them to contribute for him such an annual stipend, however unbounded, as the Crown shall be advised to order? If this is not a state of despotism, what is? Could *such* a governor, by all the *arts of persuasion,* prevail upon a people to be quiet and contented under *such* a mode of government, his noble patron might spare himself the trouble of getting a Charter vacated by a formal decision of parliament or in the tedious process of law.—Whenever the relentless enemies of America shall have completed their system, which they are still, though more silently pursuing, by subtle arts, deep dissimulation, and manners calculated to deceive, our condition will then be more humiliating and miserable, and perhaps more *inextricable too,* than that of the people of England in the infamous reigns of the Stuarts, which blacken the pages of history.[21]

Adams thus urged Americans to remember their situation in order to be better prepared to defend themselves in the future.

Adams's lack of editorial neutrality was increasingly typical of newspapers of this period. Prior to the conflict with Great Britain, newspapers had declared themselves open to all outlooks and had published a range of different views and opinions. The Stamp Act controversy had changed that, and newspapers increasingly served as organs for the promotion of a specific ideology. Although British officials had the desire and, in theory, the power to prosecute printers for speaking out against British authorities, they hesitated to do so because of popular support for the printers and their stand. Grand juries, made up of colonials, would not indict offending printers; and authorities feared that more high-handed or extralegal measures would invite violent opposition. Despite complaints such as one by Lord Frederick North, first lord of the treasury, that no one could "recollect a period when the press groan'd with such a variety of desperate libels,"[22] the government grew increasingly lax in restricting printers. As the arguments between the colonies and Great Britain continued into the 1770s, authorities discovered they had more and more difficulty reining in outspoken printers. They faced the dilemma of wanting to punish offenders while fearing the result if they attempted to do so.

Increasingly, printers chose to take advantage of this lack of control, assuming that government officials would not try to shut them down. But some government officials did try to encourage newspaper printers to be less critical. In Massachusetts, Isaiah Thomas, printer of the *Massachusetts Spy,* faced such an effort. Summoned before the governor's council for essays critical of Governor Thomas Hutchinson, Thomas snubbed the council's messenger and ignored the order to appear.[23] The council then voted to prosecute him for seditious libel, to which Thomas, joined by a chorus of writers in other papers, responded with strong attacks on those officials who would regard freedom of the press so lightly and attempt to punish someone for printing the truth. The council persisted in pursuing the case, presenting its charges to a grand jury three months later. The jury refused to indict Thomas. The council believed that the jury had been packed but decided to drop the case. An essayist in the *Massachusetts Spy* declared to Governor Hutchinson that "no writer needs now to stand in fear of you."[24] This realization gave printers encouragement to continue their attacks against British officials when government actions once more stirred up trouble.

The efforts of Samuel Adams and others to keep the debate going paid off because they were ready when word of new legislation reached the colonies. In 1773, the British Parliament passed the Tea Act. The goal was to save the East India Company from bankruptcy by eliminating most of the taxes on tea and by allowing the East India Company to ship tea directly to the colonies without going through Great Britain first. This increased tensions between Britain and the colonies because the colonials perceived the act as an attempt to establish an illegal trading monopoly for the East India Company. Merchants engaged in smuggling tea into the colonies opposed the legislation because it would make East India tea even cheaper than smuggled tea. More important in increasing tensions, however, was the fact that for many the Tea Act represented a further attempt to establish the right of Parliament to tax the colonies. Samuel Adams and others opposed to British legislation feared that the East India Company tea would be so inexpensive that people would not think about the fact that they were still paying some parliamentary taxes when they bought the tea. Colonial leaders looked for a way to avoid this possibility.

Newspapers throughout the colonies carried numerous essays criticizing the British efforts at monopoly. In December 1773, a writer in the *Pennsylvania Gazette,* signing himself "A Mechanic," clearly expressed the concerns of many related to the Tea Act. He declared that Great Britain practiced "TYRANNY, PLUNDER,

OPPRESSION and BLOODSHED" and hoped to "become your Masters" through legislation such as the Tea Act.[25] Other writers had earlier reflected this fear of slavery as a result of British legislation. In October, an essay by Scaevola printed in the *Boston Gazette* declared that "if the East India company can establish warehouses in America for the sale of TEA, *on which a duty is imposed for the purpose of raising a revenue in America,* they may vend, in like manner any other articles of their trade. Thus the imposition may be increased at pleasure, and America be subjugated without the possibility of redemption."[26] Another essayist in the *Pennsylvania Chronicle* in November worried that, if all British companies gained similar special privileges, "have we a single chance of being any Thing but *Hewers of Wood and Drawers of Waters* to them?"[27] On November 11, Isaiah Thomas used the pages of his *Massachusetts Spy* to call on Americans to stand up to British tyranny: "Shall the island BRITAIN enslave this great continent of AMERICA which is more than ninety-nine times bigger, and is capable of supporting hundreds of millions of people? Be astonished all mankind, at their superlative folly!"[28] Only by standing united could Americans defeat British attempts to enslave the colonials.

By sometime in November or December 1773, East India Company tea shipments were scheduled to arrive in Boston, New York, Philadelphia, and Charleston. In New York and Philadelphia, American leaders successfully persuaded British authorities to allow the ships to leave without unloading their cargoes. In Charleston, the tea was seized by a group of citizens following a town meeting and stored until the conflict over the Tea Act could be settled. (The Revolutionary government of South Carolina later sold the tea and used the proceeds to fight the war against Great Britain.) Only in Boston did the argument over the East India Company tea degenerate into a major conflict.

As news of the imminent approach of the tea ships reached Boston, discussions occurred over what to do once the tea arrived. Edes and Gill reported on town meetings that protested the Tea Act and these reports were reprinted throughout the colonies. For example, the *Pennsylvania Gazette* printed a lengthy article on December 9, 1773, that summarized a series of town meetings in Boston that had discussed the tea and what to do with it. As a result of these meetings, local leaders also approached Governor Thomas Hutchinson to request that the tea ships be allowed to leave without paying the required duties. Hutchinson refused because he believed that it was essential to enforce British law to maintain the proper relationship between Great Britain and its colonies. With both sides digging in their heels, the stage was set for a major confrontation. Time ran out on December 16, 1773. According to British law, the governor could order the tea ships seized on December 17 for failure either to unload their cargoes or leave port. The governor would not let the ships leave, and local leaders refused to allow the tea to be unloaded. The Sons of Liberty knew that Hutchinson would seize the tea if given the chance, so they determined to prevent that from happening.

On the night of December 16, about sixty men thinly disguised as Mohawk Indians boarded the three East India Company ships and dumped all the tea into the harbor. The 342 chests of tea that were destroyed were worth more than 10,000 pounds. The Americans were careful to destroy only the tea. A door lock broken during the raid was quietly replaced the next day. News reports of this event quickly appeared and spread throughout the colonies and, once more, Edes and Gill used the *Boston Gazette* to lead the way. Their account of the event first reported on the failed efforts to get the tea shipped back to London. The report concluded with a description of what followed these failed efforts:

> The people finding all their efforts to preserve the property of the East India company and return it safely to London, frustrated by the tea consignees, the collector of the customs and the governor of the province, DISSOLVED their meeting.—But, BEHOLD what followed! A number of brave & resolute men, determined to do all in their power to save their country from the ruin which their enemies had plotted, in less than four hours, emptied every chest of tea on board the three ships commanded by the captains Hall, Bruce, and Coffin, amounting to 342 chests, into the sea!! without the least damage done to the ships or any other property. The masters and owners are well pleas'd that their ships are thus clear'd; and the people are almost universally congratulating each other on this happy event.[29]

Edes and Gill thus stated that a majority of the people in Boston supported what happened to the tea because there was no other option.

This first report of the Boston Tea Party was fairly straightforward and to the point in comparison to later reports, which added to the drama of the event. For example, a report in the *Boston News-Letter* a week after the event focused attention on the "disguises" that the participants had worn:

> Just before the dissolution of the meeting, a number of brave and resolute men, dressed in the Indian manner, approached near the door of the assembly, and gave the war whoop, which rang through the house and was answered by some in the galleries, but silence being commanded, and a peaceable deportment was again enjoined till the dissolution. The Indians, as they were then called, repaired to the wharf, where the ships lay that had the tea on board, and were followed by hundreds of people, to see the event of the

> transactions of those who made so grotesque an appearance.... They, the Indians, immediately repaired on board Captain Hall's ship, where they hoisted the chests of tea and when upon deck stove the chests and emptied the tea overboard. Having cleared this ship, they proceeded to Captain Bruce's and then to Captain Coffin's brig. They applied themselves so dexterously to the destruction of this commodity that in the space of three hours they broke up 342 chests, which was the whole number in those vessels, and discharged their contents into the dock. When the tide rose it floated the broken chests and the tea insomuch that the surface of the water was filled therewith a considerable way from the south part of the town to Dorchester Neck, and lodged on the shores.... There was the greatest care taken to prevent the tea from being purloined by the populace. One or two being detected in endeavoring to pocket a small quantity were stripped of their acquisitions and very roughly handled. It is worthy of remark that although a considerable quantity of goods were still remaining on board the vessels, no injury was sustained. Such attention to private property was observed that a small padlock belonging to the captain of one of the ships being broke, another was procured and sent to him.... The town was very quiet during the whole evening and the night following. These persons who were from the country returned with a merry heart; and the next day joy appeared in almost every countenance, some on occasion of the destruction of the tea, others on account of the quietness with which it was effected. One of the Monday's papers says that the masters and owners were well pleased that their ships were thus cleared.[30]

The "Indians" thus had carried out a successful attack against the unjust British tea tax by destroying just the tea and nothing else.

The Boston Tea Party produced an immediate reaction in Great

Britain. British authorities were furious and responded with legislation designed to punish Boston and the colony of Massachusetts for their actions. They hoped that such action would sever the unity of the colonies, but that proved a false hope. The press had helped tie the colonies closer together during the quiet years between the Boston Massacre and the Boston Tea Party and printers all over the colonies rallied to the support of their friends and neighbors in the face of British tyranny. It was now only a matter of time until the arguments degenerated into something more.

FIVE

# NO HOPE OF A SOLUTION

The Boston Tea Party and its aftermath probably marked the point of no return in the conflict between Great Britain and the American colonies. The British Parliament passed the Coercive Acts to punish the colony of Massachusetts, and particularly the city of Boston, which saw its port closed by the legislation. The acts also gave the colonial government of Massachusetts more power by restricting the number of town meetings to one a year and allowing the governor to quarter troops more easily in private facilities. Leaders throughout the American colonies perceived the Coercive Acts as further proof of British plans to deny the rights of the colonials. Americans called the Coercive Acts the Intolerable Acts because they believed they were a totally unacceptable reaction on the part of the British government. Furthermore, Americans responded to the legislation by supporting Boston in particular and Massachusetts in general by passing numerous resolutions of support and providing needed supplies for the people in Boston, who faced starvation because of the closing of the port.

Newspapers throughout the colonies joined in the protests against the Coercive Acts. On June 13, 1774, Peter Timothy, printer of the *South Carolina Gazette,* printed his paper with a black border, "in mourning," as some printers had during the Stamp Act controversy.[1] In July, an anonymous writer from Georgia complained in the pages of the *Georgia Gazette* that the British could tax anything if the tea tax was allowed to stand: "Why not on my breath, why not on my daylight and smoak, why not on everything."[2] In August, an anonymous writer in the *Virginia Gazette* published by Alexander Purdie and John Dixon described the Coercive Acts as "pregnant with great Evils."[3] And, in September, James Davis, the printer of the *North Carolina Gazette* in the colonial capital of New Bern, adopted a new motto for the newspaper to reflect public reaction to the British legislation: "SEMPER PRO LIBERTATE, ET BONO PUBLICO" ("always for liberty, and the public good").[4] Other anonymous newspaper writers throughout America worried that the British government would spread the restrictions to the rest of the colonies if Boston and Massachusetts submitted without a fight. They thus urged all Americans to support the people of Massachusetts in their efforts to stand up to the British government so that British authorities, both in the colonies and across the Atlantic in London, would realize that they could not force the colonies into submission.

Although most newspapers supported Boston and Massachusetts in the face of the tough British legislation, some writers called on the people in the colonies to calm down and obey the law. An anonymous essayist in the *New-York Gazette, and Weekly Mercury* in May suggested that paying for the destroyed tea could have solved the problem:

> A British American, who is a Lover of Peace, as well as a Hater of every Species of Tyranny, whether Monarchial or Parliamentary, proposes to the Consideration of the Publick of Boston, whether

> it would not be their wisest Course in the present critical Situation of Affairs, to raise immediately, by Subscription, a Sum equal to the estimated Value of the drowned Teas, and deposit it in some publick Office, ready to be tendered to his Excellency General Gage, immediately on his first Requisition for Restitution of the India Company's Loss, with a solemn Declaration . . . that they make the Reimbursement with sincere Pleasure, as they thereby have at once an Opportunity of testifying their Readiness to repair every private Loss that Individuals may sustain in the present unhappy Struggle for the Maintenance of their just Rights. . . . The Querist presumes that by adopting some such Mode of Management as this, "Good may be brought out of Evil," and that hasty Act of Violence which moderate Men now look on with high Disapprobation, be thereby rendered a Circumstance honourable to the Bostonians in particular, and advantageous to the Colonies in general, who doubtless would chearfully bear their Proportions in the Sum to be raised.[5]

A piece originally published in London and reprinted in the *Boston News-Letter* in November declared that breaking the law was no solution to a disagreement: "Whenever a factious set of People rise to such a Pitch of Insolence, as to prevent the Execution of the Laws, or destroy the Property of Individuals, just as their Caprice or Humour leads them, there is an end of all Order and Government, Riot, and Confusion must be the natural Consequence of such Measures. It is impossible for Trade to flourish where Property is insecure."[6] Thus, breaking the law only led to more troubles.

But the majority of newspapers throughout the colonies called on their readers to stand with the people of Boston and Massachusetts against what they described as British tyranny. Some writers called for a meeting of representatives from all of the colonies to discuss ways and methods of expressing colonial grievances against Great Britain. Leading the way in these calls for some sort of action was Samuel Adams. Even before the Boston Tea Party occurred, Adams had declared in the *Boston Gazette* that an intercolonial meeting was needed to properly address the issues of British tyranny and how the colonies should respond to it: "This very important dispute between Britain and America has, for a long time, employed the pens of statesmen in both countries, but no plan of union is yet agreed on between them; the dispute still continues and everything floats in uncertainty. As I have long contemplated the subject with fixed attention, I beg leave to offer a proposal to my countrymen, namely, that a CONGRESS OF AMERICAN STATES shall be assembled as soon as possible, draw up a Bill of Rights, and publish it to the world; choose an ambassador to reside at the British court to act for the United colonies; appoint where the congress shall annually meet, and how it may be summoned upon any extraordinary occasion, what further steps are necessary to be taken, &c."[7] The colonies would only be able to adequately address British tyranny if they joined together.

Not long after the Boston Tea Party had taken place, an anonymous writer signing himself "Union" declared in the *Boston Gazette* that an intercolonial meeting was the only way to ensure that the colonials got what they desired from Great Britain: "There is no time to be lost, a Congress or meeting of American states is indispensable. Let the Gordian knot be tied, and whatsoever the people do shall prosper.... If we have not a free fair equitable government, we will have; and what the people wills shall be effected.... The politician and general act from the simple principles, though in different departments; and neither has much to fear from action, when there is a probability of defeating the designs of their enemy. And when the consequence resulting from a failure, cannot be worse than what would have happened in the course of the enemy's operations without the attempt."[8] The military reference by "Union" probably was not a real call for war at this time, but it clearly reflected the desire by some for the proposed intercolonial meeting to figure out a way to punish the British for what they considered unlawful actions. Some of those calling for such an intercolonial meeting also called for a search for ways to hurt the British financially through trade embargoes in hopes that the British merchants would suffer like the people of Boston and maybe call for repeal of the punishing legislation.

In an effort to rally the colonies to the cause, several printers revived Benjamin Franklin's "JOIN, or DIE" cartoon of the divided snake that had first appeared during the French and Indian War. John Holt included the divided snake in the masthead of his *New York Journal* from June 23 to December 8, 1774. The snake was divided into ten pieces and each was labeled as a section of America. Holt revised the snake in the December 15, 1774, issue. The masthead now featured a united and coiled snake which declared that "UNITED NOW ALIVE AND FREE FIRM ON THIS BASIS LIBERTY SHALL STAND AND THUS SUPPORTED EVER BLESS OUR LAND TILL TIME BECOMES ETERNITY!"[9] Isaiah Thomas included a version of the snake fighting the dragon of Great Britain in his *Massachusetts Spy* beginning on July 7, 1774, while William and Thomas Bradford, printers of the *Pennsylvania Journal,* included a copy of Holt's original snake cartoon beginning on July 27, 1774.

The issues reflected by the snake cartoon produced debates of all kinds. It even appeared in poetry published in the newspapers. One poet in the *New-York Gazetteer* criticized the effort to unite the colonies in a poem titled "On the SNAKE, depicted at the Head of some American NEWSPAPERS":

YE Sons of Sedition, how comes it to pass,
That America's typ'd by a SNAKE—in the grass?
Don't you think 'tis a scandalous, saucy reflection,
That merits the soundest, severest Correction,
NEW-ENGLAND's the Head too;—NEW ENGLAND's abused;
For the Head of the serpent we know should be Bruised.[10]

But most people supported the efforts to oppose the British punishment of Massachusetts, as reflected in this poem published in the *Pennsylvania Journal* in August in response to the poem in the *New-York Gazetteer:*

THAT New England's abus'd, and by the sons of sedition,
Is granted without either prayer or petition.
And that "'tis a scandalous, saucy reflection,
That merits the soundest, severest correction,"
Is as readily granted, "How comes it to pass?"
Because she is pester'd with snakes in the grass,
Who by lying and cringing, and such like pretensions.
And you, Mr. Pensioner, instead of repentance,
(If I don't mistake you) have wrote your own sentence;
For by such Snakes as this, New-England's abused,
And the head of these serpents, "you know, should be bruised."[11]

For this poet, the colonies needed to do something to address British tyranny and uniting in a joint effort was the best answer.

Many colonial leaders agreed with this idea. The town meeting of Providence, Rhode Island, adopted a formal call for an intercolonial meeting on May 17, 1774. City leaders were instructed "*to use their Influence, at the approaching session of the General Assembly of this Colony, for promoting a CONGRESS, as soon as may be, of the Representatives of the General Assemblies of the several Colonies and Provinces of North-America.*"[12] Within a month, practically every colony adopted a similar call. During this process, the newspapers throughout the colonies carried a variety of letters and essays that debated both whether an intercolonial meeting was needed and what it should deal with if such a meeting took place. In June, John Holt reported in his *New York Journal* that all Americans wanted a congress to meet:

> The News-Papers from all Quarters, in every British American Colony, so far as we have yet received Intelligence, are chiefly filled with Accounts of Meetings and Resolutions of Towns and Counties, all to the same Purpose—complaining of Oppression, proposing a general Congress, and Cessation of Intercourse with Great-Britain, and a Contribution for Relief of the Poor of Boston, so that it now evidently appears, that all the Colonies are unanimous in Sentiment and will be so in Conduct. . . . These Accounts of Facts are so lengthy, that we have not had Room to insert the Reflections upon them—which must be the Subject of future Papers.[13]

But an anonymous writer in the *New-York Gazetteer* in July disagreed, fearing the outcome of such a meeting:

> NEVER did AMERICA behold so alarming a time as the *present*. The *parent state* is big with resentment against us for our late proceedings; and seems determined, at all events, either to make us obedient to the laws of the *British Parliament,* or to cast us off. . . . How shall the dispute between us be adjusted? How shall FIRM FOUNDATION be laid for the *future* PERMANENT UNION? Surely not by opposing a *military force,* which, in the event, must infallibly overpower us;—and *then* we shall have no *claim of right,*—as being a *conquered country.* Surely not by making resolves in *town,* and *country,* and *parish* meetings;—for they can do nothing. . . . Surely not by a GENERAL CONVENTION; for *that* is a mea-

> sure which *never* should be adopted, unless we have *resolved* on the *last extremes.* Whatever may be the proceedings of such a body, it is too much to be apprehended that they will have no salutary influence on the British policy; because the *convention itself* will be deemed unconstitutional; and having no existence in *law,* it may also be judged to be *illegal. . . . Let* every COLONY *instruct its* REPRESENTATIVES *in* GENERAL ASSEMBLY, *to present an* humble address *to* the KING, *requesting the liberty of sending a certain number of their body to England, at a fixed time, for the* express purpose *of settling, with the national Council, a* CONSTITUTION FOR AMERICA; *which hitherto we have not enjoyed, but in idea; and let that settlement be* FINAL.[14]

But an anonymous writer in the *New Hampshire Gazette* later that same month declared that an intercolonial meeting would be a good idea:

> IT must revive the drooping Spirits of every desponding AMERICAN, to see all the Provinces *uniting* to withstand Oppression: And as a GENERAL CONGRESS of DELEGATES is proposed, and will shortly meet, whatever is by them concluded upon, for the Benefit of the whole, let every Man, who values Life, Liberty and Property, sacredly abide by their Determination. And whoever shall dare to act counter, let them be stigmatized by the Sons of true Americans, and their Names handed down with Infamy to the latest Posterity; and may every Female detest a Connection with them.[15]

An intercolonial meeting was essential to maintain American freedom.

Along with the calls for an intercolonial meeting appeared discussions of what such a meeting should do and how it should oppose British authority. In August, a correspondent of the *New York Journal* stated that "The Delegates must certainly desire to know the mind of the country in general. No rational man will think himself so well acquainted with our affairs as that he cannot have a more full and better view of them."[16] Writers insisted that whatever actions were taken must be stronger than what had been done during the Stamp Act crisis, but they disagreed about what those actions should be. Another writer in the *New York Journal* summarized the major issues:

> Shall we stop importation only, or shall we cease exportation also? Shall this extend only to Great Britain and Ireland, or shall it comprehend the West India Islands? At what time shall this cessation begin? Shall we stop trade till we obtain what we think reasonable, and which shall secure us for time to come; or shall it be only till we obtain relief in those particulars which now oppress us? Shall we first apply for relief and wait for an answer before we stop trade, or shall we stop trade while we are making application?[17]

While many writers believed that an intercolonial meeting was essential, they were not sure exactly what action should be taken at the meeting.

The result of such calls was the meeting of the First Continental Congress in Philadelphia from September 25 to October 26 in 1774. Fifty-six delegates eventually attended the meeting. In many ways, this meeting constituted one of the most illustrious gatherings in American history. Among the very talented men who attended were Patrick Henry and George Washington of Virginia, John and Samuel Adams of Massachusetts, John Jay of New York, and John Dickinson of Pennsylvania. But each colony had capable representatives and they sought to find a way to get the attention of British officials concerning colonial opposition to government actions. On October 26, 1774, the Congress adopted a petition to King George III asking him to intervene on behalf of the colonies to force Parliament to honor the rights of the colonials. Reports of this petition and other actions by the First Continental Congress appeared in newspapers throughout the colonies.

The Congress also declared British actions against Boston and Massachusetts to be unconstitutional and called on Americans to cease all trade with Great Britain. The Congress warned Americans that the situation could worsen and urged them to "acquaint themselves with the Art of War as soon as possible."[18] The actions of the Congress gave many people hope concerning the future, as reflected in a statement in an essay by VOX POPULI in the *South Carolina Gazette:* "THE AMERICANS ARE INVINCIBLE. The untutored savages of the new world and the polished sons of freedom in the old, when they know our manly opposition, with admiration will exclain [*sic*], *Brave Americans, worthy of liberty!* And join in their united supplications to the known and unknown God to smile upon our glorious struggle."[19] The Congress seemed to reflect a unity among Americans that would force British officials to cease their tyrannical actions.

The First Continental Congress adopted the Continental Association, which established a comprehensive trade boycott with Great Britain and her other colonies. Nonimportation and nonconsumption were to begin on December 1, 1774, while nonexportation of all goods would begin on September 10, 1775. Local committees were to be appointed in each town to ensure that the boycott was enforced and that the names of violators would be published in the local newspapers. Most writers praised the members of the Congress for their actions. One author in the *Pennsyl-*

*vania Packet,* whose comments were widely reprinted throughout the colonies, declared that "The Congress, like other legislative bodies, have annexed penalties to their laws.... They have held out no punishments but INFAMY, a species of infamy which sounds more dreadful to a freeman than the gallows, the rack or the stake. It is this, he shall be declared in the public papers to be an ENEMY TO HIS COUNTRY."[20] Congress had bravely stood up to British authorities.

Most newspapers supported the actions of the First Continental Congress because it seemed the best way to get Great Britain to listen to the frustrations of the colonials. An anonymous writer in the *South Carolina Gazette* rejoiced in November 1774 that "We now know our Duty, happy for us, if we reduce our Knowledge into Practice.... The Wit of Man could not have devised any Thing more likely to obtain a Redress of our Grievances than the Plan concerted."[21] But not everyone agreed. Some writers worried that they were trading one tyrant for another. In January 1775, "A Freeholder of Essex, and *real* Lover of Liberty" declared in the *New-York Gazetteer* that he "had rather submit to acts of Parliament implicitly, nay to the *will* of a King, than to the *caprice* of Committee-men."[22]

But by the time the First Continental Congress adjourned, most newspaper printers had come out clearly supporting the stands that had been adopted by that meeting. And this development reflected changes that had occurred in how the press was being operated. Most printers prior to the 1760s had declared that they would present all sides of any argument and they had earnestly tried to do that. But the growing disagreements and arguments with Great Britain increasingly made this more difficult and even dangerous to do. Andrew Steuart, printer of the *North Carolina Gazette* in the mid-1760s, had worried then about what direction he should take: "What Part is [a printer] now to act? . . . Continue to keep his Press open and free and be in Danger of Corporal Punishment, or block it up, and run the risque of having his Brains knocked out? Sad Alternative."[23] By the mid-1770s, many printers questioned whether maintaining a fully open press as had been done in the past should even be attempted. John Holt declared in his paper, the *New York Journal,* that "My paper is sacred to the cause of truth and justice, and I have preferred the pieces, that in my opinion, are the most necessary to the support of that cause" rather than those that were "barefaced attempts to deceive and impose upon the ignorant."[24]

But some writers and printers disagreed with this outlook. One anonymous writer in the *New-York Gazetteer* in September 1774 urged the First Continental Congress to protect press freedom so that adequate debate could take place: "That whoever, as an instrument of tyranny, or abetter of a mob, shall go about, either by threats, or any other methods to violate the liberty of the press, is an enemy to everything for which a man of sense would think it worth his while to live, or would dare to die."[25] Another anonymous writer in the *Gazetteer* in December 1774 complained that the approach of the majority of American printers shut down debate which could lead to the truth: "The ears of a genuine son of liberty are ever open to all doctrines; it is his glory to hear them, examine them, to adopt them if they are true, to confute them if they are false."[26] But such complaints became fewer and fewer as time passed and newspaper printers increasingly had to take one side or the other in the arguments between Great Britain and the colonies because of pressure from local citizens and government officials.

The First Continental Congress constituted the final effort to peacefully settle the differences between the colonies and Great

Britain. This effort failed, primarily because the Americans were slowly growing apart from Great Britain and increasingly thinking that separation might be the only answer. Before adjourning, the Congress agreed that a second meeting should take place in May 1775 unless Great Britain repealed the Intolerable Acts. Before the delegates could return for that meeting, however, shots were fired at Lexington and Concord in Massachusetts.

Tensions in Massachusetts had increased throughout 1774 and early 1775. People in Boston and elsewhere in Massachusetts began to gather arms and to organize in preparation for the confrontation they expected to come. By mid-April, General Thomas Gage had determined that some sort of demonstration by the Royal Army was needed to maintain control. On the evening of April 18, 1775, Gage organized his forces to march from Boston to Concord to seize military supplies stored there by the Americans.

Even though the British troops left Boston by ferry instead of marching out, their movement was observed and messengers rode toward Lexington and Concord to warn people of the approaching troops. The first shots of April 19 were fired before sunrise, and their importance was quickly recognized. Just who fired first, the Americans or the British, was never determined, and it became fodder for speculation in the newspapers. The "battles" of Lexington and Concord mark the beginning of the American Revolution. The Americans suffered 49 killed, 41 wounded, and 5 missing, while the British had 73 killed, 174 wounded, and 26 missing. These were not extensive casualties, but the British losses indicated that the Americans could not be ignored. News reports of what happened at Lexington and Concord "flew" across the colonies, and almost everyone knew that war had begun between Great Britain and her colonies.

Printers produced newspapers on a weekly basis, and none

were scheduled to be printed in Boston during the latter part of the week following the fighting at Lexington and Concord except the *Boston News-Letter,* which carried the first published account the day after the battles occurred. After summarizing the movement of the troops from Boston, the printed report stated:

> A general Battle ensued, which from what we can learn, was supported with great Spirit on both Sides, and continued until the King's Troops retreated to Charlestown, which was after Sunset. Numbers are kill'd and wounded on both Sides. The Reports concerning this unhappy Affair, and the Causes that concurred to bring on an Engagement, are so various, that we are not able to collect any Thing consistent or regular, and cannot therefore with certainty give our Readers any further Account of this shocking Introduction to all the Miseries of a Civil War.[27]

The paper gave no specific facts about the confrontations in Lexington and Concord, but it did accurately predict the questions that would surround the skirmishes and their repercussions.

One question that arose quickly related to whether both sides obeyed the conventions of war in dealing with each other. Samuel and Ebenezer Hall, printers of the *Essex Gazette* in Salem, Massachusetts, quickly praised the members of the American militia for their actions: "We have the Pleasure to say, that, notwithstanding the highest Provocations given by the Enemy, not one Instance of Cruelty, that we have heard of, was committed by our victorious Militia; but, listening to the merciful Dictates of the Christian Religion, they 'breathed higher Sentiments of Humanity.' "[28] The printers of the *Essex Journal,* Ezra Lunt and Henry Walter Tinges, reprinted an account of the action at Lexington from the *Salem Gazette* that accused the British forces of savagery:

> Last Wednesday the 19th of April, the troops of his Britannic Majesty commenced hostilities upon the people of this province, attended with circumstances of cruelty not less brutal than what our venerable ancestors received from the vilest savages of the wilderness. The particulars relative to this interesting event, by which we are involved in all the horrors of a civil war, we have endeavoured to collect as well as the present confused state of affairs will admit.[29]

Several days later, John Carter, former apprentice of Benjamin Franklin in Philadelphia, jumped into the discussion. Following his departure from Philadelphia, Carter had joined in a partnership with Sarah Goddard to produce the *Providence Gazette* in Rhode Island. He had been the sole proprietor since 1768 and often commented on the conflicts with Great Britain in the pages of his newspaper. In discussing the fighting in Massachusetts, Carter concluded that Americans were witnessing history in the making:

> Thus, through the sanguinary measures of a wicked Ministry, and the Readiness of a standing Army to execute their Mandates, has commenced the American Civil War, which will hereafter fill an important Page in History. That it may speedily terminate in a full Restoration of our Liberties, and the Confusion of all who have aimed at an Abridgement of them, should be the earnest Desire of every real Friend to Great-Britain and America.[30]

Americans needed to unite to win the war.

Accounts in the newspapers presented descriptions of what people thought had happened at Lexington and Concord and speculations as to the results. A letter from Boston reprinted in Philadelphia in the *Pennsylvania Gazette* a week after the skirmishes in Massachusetts reflected the fears of the residents of Boston:

> I have yet an opportunity of writing from my own house, but how long that privilege is to continue God only knows. Yesterday morning, or rather late in the night of the 18th, a brigade, or four regiments, were carried from the west part of the town, in boats of the men of war, to Cambridge, from whence they marched on toward Concord; which is about 20 miles from hence; on their way, in passing through Lexington, the troops came unexpectedly on a company of our country people (who are called Minute Men) that were early in the morning exercising with guns, without ammunition. The Officer of the troops is said to have ordered them to lay down their arms;—the Captain replied, he was on his own ground, that his company were without ammunition, and had no intent but that of improving in the military art: After some altercation, report says the Captain and his men turned to go off, and that the Light Infantry fired on them, killed six, and wounded mortally two others. The troops continuing their rout to Concord, the country by the time of their getting there were alarmed, and our people, taking to a hill, began firing upon the troops with about 200 men, which number receiving continual additions, the troops were all the remainder of the day on their retreat to Charlestown, and many of the Officers who have returned, say they never were in a hotter engagement. Many are killed on both sides, and were left on the roads, neither side having time to collect their dead. Our people came to no regular battle, but annoyed their whole passage back. We could see the flashes, and hear the reports of the guns for hours, the warmest fire being about two miles from the town, where only water parted us. . . . The marching of the troops to the water side was so sudden and silent, that few of the inhabitants knew of it till next morning.[31]

The people in Boston were unsure about what the British would do now that fighting had begun.

Some printers also sought to provide proof of what happened at Lexington and Concord by printing the sworn statements of the men who were present at the battles. For example, the *New-York Gazette, and Weekly Mercury* ran a series of such statements over the course of several issues:

> AFFIDAVITS AND DEPOSITIONS relative to the commencement of the late hostilities in the province of Massachusetts Bay; continued from our last: . . . LEXINGTON, April 25, 1775 . . . JOHN PARKER, OF LAWFUL AGE, and commander of the colonial militia in Lexington, do testify and declare, that on the 19th instant, in the morning, about one of the clock, being informed that there was a number of regular officers riding up and down the road, stopping and insulting people as they passed the road; and also was informed that a number of regular troops were on their march from Boston, in order to take Concord; ordered our militia to meet on the common in said Lexington, to consult what to do, and conclude not to be discovered, nor meddle or make with said regular troops (if they should approach) unless they should insult or molest us, and upon their sudden approach I immediately ordered our militia to disperse and not to fire; immediately said troops made their appearance and rushed furiously, fired upon and killed eight of our party, without receiving any provocation therefore from us. John Parker. . . . We, Nathaniel Parkhurst, Jonas Parker, John Munroe, junior, John Winship, Solomon Pierce, John Murray, Abner Meeds, John Bridge, junior, Ebenezer Bowman, William Munroe, the 3d, Micah Hager, Samuel Sanderson, Samuel Hastings, and John Brown, of Lexington, in the county of Middlesex, and colony of Massachusetts Bay, in New England; and all of lawful age, do testify and say, that on the morning of the nineteenth of April inst. about one or two o'clock, being informed that a number of

> regular officers had been riding up and down the road the evening and night preceding, and that forms of the inhabitants as they were passing had been insulted by the officers, and stopped by them; and being also informed that the regular troops were on their march from Boston, in order (as it was said) to take the colony stores there deposited at Concord! We met on the parade of our company in this town; after the company had collected, we were ordered by Captain John Parker (who commanded us) to disperse for the present, and be ready to attend the beat of the drum; and accordingly the company went into houses near the place of parade. We further testify and say, that about five o'clock in the morning we attended the beat of our drum and were formed on the parade—we were faced towards the regulars then marching up to us, and some of our company were coming to the parade with their backs towards the troops, and others on the parade began to disperse when the regulars fired on the company, before a gun was fired by any of our company on them; they killed eight of our company, and wounded several, and continued the fire until we had all made our escape.[32]

With such reports, printers were attempting to prove that the British were at fault in starting the fighting.

Those who supported Great Britain in the arguments over taxes regretted the fighting and also worried about what it meant. James Rivington, printer of the *New-York Gazetteer,* quickly urged his readers to remain calm: "The late melancholy accounts from Boston have filled the minds of the good people of this city with the most anxious concern. It was the wish of every generous mind that the unhappy contest with Great Britain would have been compromised without the shedding of blood; and the time when it would become necessary to enter into an unnatural civil war with those, with whom we are connected by the tenderest ties, has ever been depreciated as the most horrid calamity. May the Almighty interpose his gracious providence and avert the impending miseries, and may the blessings of peace be restored to this great continent upon the principles of liberty and the constitution."[33] Rivington and others hoped that a real war could be avoided.

Some British officials also tried to encourage a settlement of the arguments to avoid further conflict and bloodshed. Governor William Franklin of New Jersey, son of Benjamin Franklin, summoned the General Assembly and urged them to take action:

> THE sole occasion of my calling you together at this time is to lay before you a resolution of the House of Commons wisely and humanely calculated to open a door to the resolution of that harmony between Great-Britain and her American colonies on which their mutual welfare and happiness so greatly depend. . . . His Majesty, ardently wishing to see a reconciliation of the unhappy difference by every means through which it may be obtained without prejudice to the just authority of Parliament, which his Majesty will never suffer to be violated, has approved the resolution of his faithful Commons, and has commanded it to be transmitted to the governors of his colonies, not doubting that this happy disposition to comply with every just and reasonable wish of the King's subjects in America will meet with such a return of duty and affection on their part as will lead to a happy issue of the present dispute, and to re-establishment of the public tranquility on those grounds of equity, justice and moderation which this resolution holds forth.[34]

Franklin clearly thought a peaceful resolution was still possible.

But most American printers believed that the events at Lexington and Concord marked a turning point in relations between Great Britain and her American colonies. Isaiah Thomas, printer of the *Massachusetts Spy,* was forced to flee Boston and move his print shop and newspaper westward to Worcester because of the fighting. Once he had established his shop in early May, Thomas printed what became the most famous and most reprinted account of the battles. Besides describing the events as reported to him, he also called on Americans to take action:

> Americans! Forever bear in mind the BATTLE OF LEXINGTON!—where British troops, unmolested and unprovoked, wantonly, and in a most inhuman manner fired upon and killed a number of our countrymen, then robbed them of their possessions, ransacked, plundered and burnt their houses! nor could the tears of defenseless women, some of whom were in the pains of childbirth, the cries of helpless babes, nor the prayers of old age, confined to beds of sickness, appease their thirst for blood!—or divert them from the DESIGN of MURDER and ROBBERY!

Thomas went on to give a detailed account of the events that occurred on April 19 and concluded with praise for the Americans and their actions on that memorable day:

> We have the pleasure to say that notwithstanding the highest provocations given by the enemy, not one instance of cruelty that we have heard of was committed by our militia; but listening to the merciful dictates of the Christian religion, they "breathed higher sentiments of humanity." . . . The public most sincerely sympathize with the friends and relations of our deceased brethren, who sacrificed their lives in fighting for the liberties of their country. By their noble intrepid conduct, in helping to defeat the force of an ungrateful tyrant, they have endeared their memories to the present generation, who will transmit their names to posterity with the highest honor.[35]

Thomas also reflected the debate among Americans about the impact of the fighting at Lexington and Concord on public attitudes toward Great Britain as he discussed where the guilt for starting the fighting lay by accusing the British soldiers of treachery and deceit:

> Some officers in the King's army, it is said, have sworn that the Americans fired first. Their method of cheating the Devil, we are told, has been by some means brought out. They procured three or four traitors to their God and country, born among us, and took with them, and they first fired upon their countrymen, which was immediately followed by the regulars. It is also said these wretches were dressed in soldiers cloathing.[36]

But no matter who was to blame, Thomas and most Americans believed the event would be remembered for years to come because of the events that would follow. As one anonymous writer stated in the *Newport Mercury* on May 8, "Some future historian will relate, with pleasure, and the latest posterity will read with wonder and admiration, how three hundred intrepid, rural sons of freedom drove before them more than five times their number, of regular, well appointed troops, and forced them to take shelter behind their bulwarks!"[37] American printers reflected the concerns of most people on both sides of the Atlantic that the outbreak of fighting would result in major changes in the relationship between Great Britain and the American colonies. It was now impossible to go back to the way things had been before the arguments over British taxes and colonial rights had begun back in the 1760s.

SIX

# THE SPLIT BECOMES PERMANENT

Although the Boston Tea Party and its aftermath was probably the real point of no return in the conflict between Great Britain and her colonies, many people did not see this clearly. But they did see the apparently irreparable division when fighting broke out in Massachusetts on April 19, 1775. When news of the fighting at Lexington and Concord reached Philadelphia, men from throughout the colonies were gathering for the meeting of the Second Continental Congress. As the meeting began on May 10, 1775, the delegates realized that the conflict with Great Britain had changed. Part of the debates centered on the question of what should be done about the collection of New England militiamen that surrounded Boston. They soon organized these men into a permanent army and sought to unify the colonies by appointing a commander in chief for the army who came from outside New England. John Adams began to push for the appointment of George Washington of Virginia because Adams thought it was essential for Virginia, the oldest colony, to support the fight against Great Britain. On June 15, 1775, the Second Continental Congress voted unanimously to appoint Washington as the commander in chief of the newly created Continental Army, reflecting their desire to pull the colonies closer together by appointing a Virginian to command the troops in Massachusetts, who would provide leadership over the military actions to be carried out by the colonies in the future.

In many ways, George Washington was a good choice for this position. Hailing from an upper-crust Virginia family, Washington represented a more conservative element of American colonial society than the radical Sons of Liberty such as Samuel Adams in Boston. He also looked the part of a leader. Standing six feet two-and-a-half inches tall, Washington was a capable rider and looked impressive on horseback in his uniform. He had earned a national reputation for bravery during the French and Indian War. During the terrible defeat of the British army under General Edward Braddock near Fort Duquesne in July 1755, Washington had had two horses shot out from under him. The members of Congress knew that Washington's reputation for bravery would precede him to New England and help him gain the respect and loyalty of the troops under his command.

Newspapers throughout the colonies praised the decision because of Washington's reputation and the desire and need to pull the colonies closer together. The printers throughout the colonies quickly spread the word that the fight in Massachusetts was everyone's war. Shortly after his appointment, Washington was honored with a military parade that was reported in the *Pennsylvania Packet* on June 26:

> Yesterday morning the three battalions of this City and Liberties, together with the artillery company, a troop of light horse, several companies of light infantry, rangers and riflemen, in the whole about 2000, marched out to the Commons, and, having joined in

> brigade, were reviewed by General WASHINGTON, who is appointed Commander in Chief of all the North-American forces by the Honourable CONTINENTAL CONGRESS, when they went through the manual exercises, firings and manoeuvres, with great dexterity and exactness.[1]

The *Packet* later printed a letter to a member of the Continental Congress from the army camp outside Boston. Besides providing details of the military actions in the area, the letter writer also praised the appointment of Washington as commander in chief and stated that everyone in the army was excited about the decision: "We greatly rejoice to hear of the coming of the good, the brave, and great General Washington, we shall receive him with open arms."[2] Such a statement provided an endorsement for Congress's action.

Washington soon left to join the army outside of Boston and newspapers reported his trip northward. The *Pennsylvania Gazette* reported his departure for Massachusetts: "On Friday morning the Generals WASHINGTON and LEE set off from this city to take the command of the American Army at Massachusetts-Bay. They were accompanied from town by the troop of light horse, and by all the officers of the city militia on horseback, who attended them about five miles, when they returned, but the former continued with them."[3] In each major city, Washington was greeted in some formal manner by the local inhabitants. John Dixon and William Hunter, printers of one of the newspapers titled *Virginia Gazette* in Williamsburg, reported Washington's passage through New York City:

> Yesterday arrived here from Philadelphia, on their way for the camp at Boston, General Washington, appointed by the Hon. Continental Congress commander in chief of all the provincial troops

> in North America, attended by the Generals Lee and Schuyler: They were escorted by a party of light horse: The Generals landed at the seat of Col. Lispenard about 4 o'clock yesterday afternoon, from whence they were conducted by nine companies of foot, in their uniforms, and a greater number of the principal inhabitants of this city, than ever appeared here on any occasion before.[4]

The *Pennsylvania Gazette* reported Washington's reception in Watertown, Massachusetts: "The Hon. GEORGE WASHINGTON, Esq; appointed by the Continental Congress General and Commander in Chief of all the New-England forces, passed through this town yesterday, on his way to Cambridge, attended by a Committee from the Provincial Congress, and a train of other gentlemen, escorted by a company of horse from Marlborough."[5] Newspaper printers included such reports because they knew their readers would be interested in Washington's trip to Boston to take command of the army.

News of his taking command of the army appeared throughout the colonies. On July 10, the *Connecticut Courant* reported Washington's arrival in Boston:

> Last Sabbath came to Town from Philadelphia, his Excellency George Washington, Esq; appointed, by the Continental Congress, General and Commander in Chief of the American Forces, and was received with every Testimony of Respect due to a Gentleman of his real Worth and elevated Dignity. His Excellency was accompanied by the Hon. Charles Lee, Esq; and a Number of other Gentlemen.[6]

And Dixon and Hunter printed a letter from the camp of the Continental Army at Cambridge in their *Virginia Gazette.* This letter reported that Washington and the officers with him quickly got to work: "The Generals have spent this whole day in reviewing the troops, lines, fortifications, &c. They find the troops to be 15000 strong, and the works to be in as good order as could be expected." The letter concluded that an attack might be imminent, but that the American troops were ready: "The regulars have been sounding the shore this afternoon, and we are in some expectation of a visit at the next high water. Our men are all in good spirits, and wish they may come out."[7]

The newspapers also reported on the fighting that continued to occur between British troops and the Americans. Initial reports usually contained a brief account of the fighting while later accounts praised American bravery. For example, the initial report of the Battle of Bunker Hill appeared in Benjamin Edes's *Boston Gazette,* which he had moved to Watertown after Lexington and Concord:

> Friday Night last a Number of the Provincials Intrenched on Bunker-Hill in Charlestown; and on Saturday about Noon a large Number of Regulars from Boston came across Charles's River, and landed a little below the Battery near the point, when a bloody Battle commenced (many being killed and wounded on both sides). The very heavy Fire from the Shipping, the Battery on Cop's Hill, Boston, together with the Train of the Enemy, obliged the Provincials to retreat a little this Side Charlestown Neck about Sunset, when the Enemy took Possession of our Entrenchment; after which they set the Town of Charlestown on Fire, beginning with the Meeting-House, and we hear they have not left one Building unconsumed. The Engagement continues at this Publication, 9 o'Clock, with Intermissions. The Confusion of the Times render it impracticable to give a particular Account of what has

> already occur'd, but hope to give a good one in our next. The Provincials are in high spirits.[8]

A month later, the *Virginia Gazette* published by Dixon and Hunter carried a more detailed report, which praised the efforts of the Americans:

> On the evening of the 16th, Col. Putnam took possession of Bunker's Hill, with about 2000 men, and began an entrenchment, which they had made some progress in. At 8 in the morning, a party of regulars landed at Charlestown, and fired the town in divers places. Under cover of the smoke, a body of 5000 men marched up to our entrenchments, and made a furious and sudden attack; they were drove back three times; and when they were making the third attack, one of our people imprudently spoke aloud that their powder was all gone; which being heard by some of the regular officers, they encouraged their men to march up to the trenches with fixed bayonets, and entered them; on which our people were ordered to retreat, which they did with all speed, till they got out of musket shot; they then formed, but were not pursued: In the mean time six men of war, and four floating batteries were brought up, and kept up a continual fire on the causeway that leads on to Charlestown; our people retreated through the fire, but not without the loss of many men. Our loss is 60 men killed and missing, and about 140 wounded. The brave Dr. Warren is among the former, and Col. Gardiner among the latter. We left 6 field pieces on the hill; our people are now entrenched on Pleasant Hill, within cannon shot of Bunker's Hill. The loss of the King's troops must be very considerable; the exact number we cannot tell. If our people had been supplied with ammunition they would have held possession most certainly. They have begun firing on Roxbury, with

> carcases [hollow shells] to set it on fire, but have not yet succeeded. Our people are in high spirits, and are very earnest to put this matter on another trial.[9]

Printers hoped that such high spirits among the troops would offset the impact of heavy battlefield losses by restoring and even increasing support for the war among their readers.

One of the foci of the newspaper reports about the fighting around Boston was the fact that the troops in the Continental Army continued to be in good spirits even after losing a battle. The *Connecticut Courant* printed an account of the battle of Bunker Hill that declared: "Our Troops continue in high Spirits. They are fortifying a very high Hill, about a Mile and a half from this Town, and within Cannon Shot of the Enemy on Bunker-Hill."[10]

Other accounts of the fighting around Boston attacked the British for lying about what actually occurred:

> The miserable Tools of Tyranny in Boston appear now to be somewhat conscious of their Infamy in burning Charlestown, and are, with the Assistance of the Father of Liars, devising Methods for Clearing up their Characters. One of them, in Mrs. Draper's Paper, asserts, that the Provincials, on the 17th of June, after firing out of the Houses upon the King's Troops, set the Buildings on Fire: This, doubtless, is as true as that the Provincials fired first upon the King's Troops at Lexington. Both of them are equally false, and well known to be as palpable Lies as ever were uttered. The Propagation of them are, however, perfectly consistent with the Perfidy, Cowardice and Barbarity of Gage and his Detestable Understrappers.[11]

Such reports served to increase American distrust of the British.

Besides news about the fighting and other events of the Revolution, most newspapers continued to publish letters and essays discussing the growing conflict with Great Britain. Some authors tried to convince Americans that a peaceful solution could still be found. Prior to the fighting at Lexington and Concord, the essayist "Rusticus" declared in the *Pennsylvania Packet* that being subjects of Great Britain was the best possible situation for the colonies:

> I cannot nor will imagine that any of my countrymen entertain even a secret wish, that America shall be freed from all political connections with Great-Britain. The peace and security we have already enjoyed under her protection, before the mistaken system of taxation took place, must make us look back with regret to those happy days whose loss we mourn, and which every rational man must consider as the golden age of America. . . . Let us then, my friends and countrymen, patiently attend this expected important period, in the mean time avoiding all inflammatory publications, and such as are disrespectful to our most gracious Sovereign, still looking forward with an anxious hope to an happy termination of our present disputes, and a cordial reconciliation with our mother country, on constitutional principles, as a consummation most devoutly to be wished for by every true and sincere lover of his country.[12]

An essay signed "Cato" in the *New-York Gazette, and Weekly Mercury,* published in April 1776, declared that war could be avoided:

> It will be *asserted*—indeed it has been already *asserted*—that the animosities between Great-Britain and the Colonies are now advanced to such a height, that RECONCILIATION is impossible. But *assertions* are nothing, when opposed to the nature of things. . . . There never was a war so implacable, even among states naturally

> rivals and enemies, or among savages themselves, as not to have *peace* for its object as well as end! And, among people naturally friends, and connected by every dearest tie, who knows not that their quarrels (as those of *lovers*) are often but a stronger renewal of *love*?[13]

These writers clearly believed the colonies and Great Britain could settle their disagreements short of a major fight.

But most of the letters and essays published were designed to convince more Americans of the reality of British tyranny. By the fall of 1775, some essays even started to call for Americans to break away from Great Britain by declaring independence. In September, a Patriot poet in the *New Hampshire Gazette* declared that people had come to America seeking freedom and that Great Britain could not change that fact:

> What! Can those British Tyrants think
> Our Fathers cross'd the main;
> And savage Foes and Dangers met,
> To be enslav'd by them?
> If so, they are mistaken,
> For we will rather die;
> And since they have become our Foes,
> Their Forces we defy.
> And all the world shall know,
> Americans are free;
> Nor slaves nor cowards we will prove—
> Great Britain soon shall see.[14]

In December of that same year, an anonymous writer in John Pinkney's *Virginia Gazette* declared:

> Our cruel enemies have forced us to pass the rubicon; we have begun the noble work, and there is no retreating; the king of Britain

> has proclaimed us rebels. The sword is drawn, the scabbard must be thrown away; there is no medium between a glorious defence and the most abject slavery. If we fail in our endeavours to repel the assaults of tyranny, we are to expect no mercy.

This author concluded that victory could be won in a fight with Great Britain and that the results would be wonderful:

> A few more noble exertions, my brave fellow soldiers, a few more spirited struggles, and we secure our liberties; a few more successful battles, and we are a free and happy people. We will then retire to our families, and, whilst we are regaling ourselves with social festivity, entertain our listening children with the fatigues and dangers to which they owe their freedom, and shew the scars of the honourable wounds we received in the field of battle. Happy the man who can boast that he was one of those heroes that put the finishing stroke to this arduous work . . .[15]

A successful fight for independence would result in peace and prosperity.

The most famous of the calls for independence came from the pen of Thomas Paine, a recent emigrant to Pennsylvania from London. Having left England in October 1774 because of financial troubles, Paine arrived in Philadelphia with a letter of introduction from Benjamin Franklin. Paine had originally become involved in British politics by writing an article supporting increased pay and better working conditions for excise officers. His interest in improving the situation of people at the bottom of society would continue for the rest of his life, no matter where he was living. After arriving in Pennsylvania, Paine quickly became convinced that breaking away from Great Britain was the only real option for the colonies. Writing in the *Pennsylvania Journal* under the pseudonym Humanus in late 1775, Paine declared that "I hesitate not for a moment to believe that the Almighty will finally separate America from Britain. Call it independence or what you will, if it is the cause of God and humanity it will go on."[16]

On January 10, 1776, Paine went even further with the publication of *Common Sense.* It first appeared as a pamphlet. It quickly went through several printings, but it was also reprinted in whole or in part by newspapers throughout the colonies. Paine placed the blame for the troubles of the colonies at the feet of King George III and called on Americans to kick off their chains and declare independence. Many printers endorsed this call as they sought to spread Paine's ideas by reprinting all or parts of *Common Sense* in their newspapers. For example, the printer John Pinkney of Williamsburg, Virginia, published the pieces of *Common Sense* that he considered to be the most important in February 1776:

> I challenge the warmest advocate for reconciliation to shew a single advantage that this continent can reap by being connected with Great Britain. I repeat this challenge; not a single advantage is derived. Our corn will fetch its price in any market in Europe, and our imported goods must be paid for, buy them where we will. . . . But the injuries and disadvantages we sustain by that connection are without number, and our duty to mankind at large, as well as to ourselves, instruct us to renounce the alliance, because any submission to, or dependence on Great Britain, tends directly to involve this continent in European wars and quarrels. As Europe is our market for trade, we ought to form no political connection with any part of it. It is the true interest of America to steer clear of European contentions, which she can never do while, by her dependence on Britain, she is made the makeweight in the scale

> of British politics. . . . Every thing that is right or reasonable pleads for separation. The blood of the slain, the weeping voice of nature, cries *'tis time to part.*[17]

Pinkney agreed with Paine that independence was the goal the colonies should strive for.

Thomas Paine had declared that the colonies had no real option but to declare independence. And in many ways he was right. Some Americans had foreseen this development back during the time of arguments over taxes in the late 1760s and early 1770s. In 1768, William Livingston, writing for the *New-York Gazette, or Weekly Post-Boy* as "The American Whig," almost prophetically urged Americans to stand up to Great Britain:

> Courage, then Americans! liberty, religion, and sciences are on the wing to these shores: The finger of God points out a mighty empire to your sons. . . . The day dawns in which the foundation of this mighty empire is to be laid, by the establishment of a *regular American Constitution.* All that has hitherto been done, seems to be little beside the collection of materials, for the construction of this glorious fabrick. 'Tis time to put them together . . . before seven years roll over our heads, the first stone must be laid.—Peace or war; famine or plenty; poverty or affluence; in a word no circumstance, whether prosperous or adverse, can happen to our parent . . . no conduct of hers . . . no possible temper on her part . . . will put a stop to this building. There is no contending with Omnipotence, and the *predispositions* are so numerous, and so well adapted to the rise of America, that our success is indubitable.[18]

Americans had to take control and be responsible for their future.

In 1773, an anonymous writer in the *Boston Gazette* took the situation a step further and called for the colonies to be independent:

> How shall the Colonies force their oppressors to proper terms? This question has often been answered, already by our politicians: "Form an independent state," "AN AMERICAN COMMONWEALTH." This plan has been proposed, and I can't find that any other is likely to answer the great purpose of preserving our liberties. I hope, therefore, it will be well digested and forwarded, to be in due time put into execution, unless our political fathers can secure American liberties in some other way. As the population, wealth, and power of this continent are swiftly increasing, we certainly have no cause to doubt our success in maintaining liberty by forming a commonwealth, or whatever measure wisdom may point out for the preservation of the rights of America.[19]

Declaring independence would ensure America's future success.

By the time Paine published *Common Sense,* anyone strongly opposed to the conflict with Great Britain no longer had much of a voice in the press because most of the newspapers that would have previously published opposing viewpoints had gone out of business. A few writers tried to respond to Paine's call for a revolution in the few remaining pro-British newspapers, but with little impact. Using the pseudonym of "Candidus," Marylander James Chalmers wrote a pamphlet titled "Plain Truth" that vigorously attacked Paine's conclusions in *Common Sense.* The newspaper advertisement for this pamphlet summarized the author's argument: "the Scheme of INDEPENDENCE is Ruinous, Delusive, and impracticable: That were the Author's Asseverations, respecting the Power of AMERICA, as Real as Nugatory, Reconciliation, on liberal Principles with GREAT-BRITAIN would be exalted Policy: And that, circumstanced as we are, permanent Liberty, and true Happiness can only be obtained by Reconciliation with that Kingdom."[20] Chalmers hoped Americans would face reality and not do something dangerous by declaring independence.

The most famous opposing response to *Common Sense* came in a series of essays signed "Cato" which appeared in newspapers in the spring of 1776. Written by the Reverend William Smith, the provost of the College of Pennsylvania, "Cato" first accused Paine of taking advantage of the situation surrounding the growing conflict with Great Britain:

> The authors—or (if I must say) author of what is called *Common Sense,* has certainly had fair play. Full time has been allowed him by the sale of his pamphlet to reap the fruit of his labours, and gratify that avidity with which many are apt to devour doctrines that are out of the common way—bold, marvellous, and flattering. What was intended as a compliment to the publick—to give them time to gaze with their own eyes, and reason with their own faculties, upon this extraordinary appearance—the author's vanity has construed wholly in his own favour.

"Cato" went on to declare that Paine's ideas were not common sense: "If what is called *Common Sense* be really *common sense,* it is invulnerable, and every attack upon it will but add to the author's triumph. If it should be proved, in any instances to be *nonsense,* millions will be interested in the discovery; and to them I appeal." Instead, "Cato" concluded that Paine's ideas could be very dangerous:

> In short, I am not able, with all the pains I have taken, to understand what is meant by a Declaration of Independence; un-

> less it is to be drawn up in the form of a solemn abjuration of *Great Britain,* as a nation with which we can never more be connected. And this seems the doctrine of the author of *Common Sense.* But I believe he has made but few converts to this part of his scheme; for who knows to what vicissitudes of fortune we may yet be subjected? . . . We have long flourished under our Charter Government. What may be the consequences of another form we cannot pronounce with certainty; but this we know, that it is a road we have not travelled, and may be worse than it is described.[21]

Smith feared that declaring independence would lead to disaster.

Some real debates in the newspapers did ensue following the publication of *Common Sense,* but they primarily centered on how far to go. As "A Friend to Posterity and Mankind" declared in the *Pennsylvania Packet,* "We all agree in this, that Great Britain is unjust and arbitrary"—the debate was over "the mode of opposition."[22] Several people in New Jersey wrote a letter to their delegates in the Continental Congress urging them not to vote for independence and to work for a peaceful settlement of the arguments with Great Britain. This letter was published in several newspapers throughout the colonies:

> We trust that you will be too deeply impress'd with the Recollection of the peculiar Happiness and Prosperity heretofore enjoyed by the Inhabitants of this Continent, connected with and subject to the government of Great-Britain, not to dread the Consequences of a declar'd Separation from that Country . . . a change of government will prevent a safe, honourable, and lasting Reconciliation with Great-Britain on constitutional Principles.[23]

For these people, splitting from Great Britain was unthinkable. Some people also worried that the conflict with Great Britain would result in the destruction of the colonies because they would end up fighting against one another. An anonymous essayist in Dixon and Hunter's *Virginia Gazette* stated that "our fertile fields will be deluged with blood, our wives & children be involved in the horrid scene; foreign powers will step in and share in the plunder that remains, and those who are left to tell the story will be reduced to a more abject slavery than that which you now dread."[24] Trying to become independent would produce more problems than it would solve.

But other writers disagreed with this outlook. A contributor to the *Pennsylvania Journal* declared that "To see a society of farmers, tradesmen and merchants, quit their peaceful employments, and make war upon one another, would be a phenomenon which the world has not yet beheld, and I will venture to say never will."[25] And others, like an essayist in the *Pennsylvania Evening Post,* declared that a final break would benefit the colonies greatly because it would result in:

> A free and unlimited trade; a great accession of wealth, and a proportionate rise in the value of land; the establishment, gradual improvement and perfection of manufactures and science; a vast influx of foreigners, encouraged by the mildness of a free, equal, and tolerating government to leave their native countries, and settle in these colonies; an astonishing encrease of people from the present stock. Where encouragement is given to industry, where liberty and property are well secured, where the poor may easily find subsistence, and the middling rank comfortably support their families by labour, there the inhabitants must encrease rapidly; to some of these causes we owe the doubling of our numbers in somewhat

> more than twenty-five years. If such hath been the progress of population under the former restraints on our trade and manufactures, a population still more rapid may be reasonably expected when these restraints come to be taken off.[26]

Independence would result in amazing growth and prosperity in America.

The press increasingly urged the Continental Congress to take action. In May 1776, a writer in the *Constitutional Gazette* declared that "Many honest persons two years ago, would have trembled at the thought of such a thing, who are now fully convinced of the expediency, the safety and necessity of this measure, as our only security."[27] Another essayist in the *Boston Gazette* stated that "independence is now become the universal cry; all ranks and conditions of men seem to be waiting in silent and anxious expectation of a formal declaration." This writer concluded that such a step would "give vigor to our military operations."[28] Another writer in the *New York Packet* stated that the people "wait with impatience for our Honourable Continental Congress to cut the Gordian Knot."[29] These essayists believed the time for declaring independence had arrived.

In an essay published in the *Connecticut Courant* on April 22, "Juvenis" asserted that declaring independence was the only real option open to the colonies:

> These political sages, by a long chain of reasoning, and the help of the most cogent arguments, have fully demonstrated the necessity of an entire separation from the mother country; and one would think that the arguments they have adduced, were sufficient to convince every honest mind; but, as it is difficult to eradicate an opinion, imbibed in youth, and corroborated by long habit, I

> would subjoin one, which . . . will, I doubt not, have some weight with the more sensible and unprejudiced part of the people. This argument in favour of independence is derived from the natural situation of this country. . . . The vast oceans that wash two sides of this continent, the numerous large and navigable rivers that penetrate into the very heart of it, and not only fertilize the land, but render the carrying on of trade and commerce so convenient, are strong and almost convincing proofs that North America was designed for the seat of a great empire.[30]

Declaring independence would enable America to achieve the glorious future it was destined for.

Even though the colonies had not declared independence, most of them had slowly transformed themselves into states through the establishment of new governments. They then authorized their delegates to the Continental Congress meeting in Philadelphia to vote for independence. In May, the Virginia Convention adopted a series of resolutions calling for independence, which were quickly published in the local newspapers:

> FORASMUCH as all the endeavours of the UNITED COLONIES, by the most decent representations and petitions to the king and parliament of Great Britain, to restore peace and security to America under the British government, and a re-union with that people upon just and liberal terms, instead of a redress of grievances, have produced, from an imperious and vindictive administration, increased insult, oppression, and a vigorous attempt to effect our total destruction. . . . *RESOLVED, unanimously,* that the delegates appointed to represent this colony in General Congress be instructed to propose to that respectable body TO DECLARE THE UNITED COLONIES FREE AND INDEPENDENT

> STATES, absolved from all allegiance to, or dependence upon, the crown or parliament of Great Britain; and that they give the assent of this colony to such declaration, and to whatever measures may be thought proper and necessary by the Congress for forming foreign alliances, and A CONFEDERATION OF THE COLONIES, at such time, and in the manner, as to them shall seem best.[31]

On June 7, 1776, Virginia delegate Richard Henry Lee followed these instructions and introduced a resolution calling for independence and the establishment of an American confederation. Although a number of colonies followed the lead of Virginia and favored independence, others such as New York hesitated. Because of this hesitation, Congress voted to postpone action for at least three weeks.

In the interim, Congress appointed a committee to draw up an official statement to explain the break from Great Britain. Members of the committee included John Adams of Massachusetts, Benjamin Franklin of Pennsylvania, Roger Sherman of Connecticut, Robert R. Livingston of New York, and Thomas Jefferson of Virginia. Jefferson did most of the writing of the Declaration of Independence, which was adopted by Congress on July 4 (following the vote for independence on July 2). The bulk of the declaration consisted of twenty-seven charges against George III because the document's primary goal was to explain the reasons for the revolt against Great Britain.

American newspapers quickly spread the word about the break from Great Britain. Benjamin Towne, printer of the *Pennsylvania Evening Post,* published three times a week, included the following statement in his July 2 edition: "This day the CONTINENTAL CONGRESS declared the UNITED COLONIES FREE and INDEPENDENT STATES."[32] Newspapers printed the Declaration of

Independence when it became available so that all Americans could see what the Continental Congress had done. They also reported the reactions to the news as it slowly spread throughout the colonies. Isaiah Thomas rejoiced over the news when it arrived in Worcester, Massachusetts: "It is reported that the Honorable Continental Congress have declared the American colonies INDEPENDENT of that Monster of imperious domination and cruelty—Great Britain! Which we hope is true."[33] In the *New Hampshire Gazette,* an anonymous poet rejoiced over the possibilities of freedom:

Freedom's Charms alike engage
Blooming Youth and hoary Age;
Time itself can ne'er destroy
Freedom's pure and lasting Joy:
Love nor Friendship ever gave
Half their Blessings to the Slave;
None are happy but the Free;
Bliss is born of Liberty;
Which from fair America
Tyrants strive to take away.[34]

Dixon and Hunter of Williamsburg, Virginia, described the public celebration in Richmond in early August:

> On Monday last, being court day, the Declaration of Independence was publicly proclaimed in the town of Richmond, before a large concourse of respectable freeholders of Henrico county, and upwards of 100 of the militia, who assembled on that grand occasion. It was received with universal shouts of joy, and re-echoed by three vollies of small arms. The same evening the town was illuminated, and the members of the committee held a club, when many patriotic toasts were drank. Although there were near 1000 people present, the whole was conducted with the utmost decorum, and

> the satisfaction visible in every countenance sufficiently evinces their determination to support it with their lives and fortunes.

In the same issue, they also carried a report from New York that indicated that the celebration there had not been as calm: "Thursday the Declaration of the Independency of the United States of America was published at the courthouse, where a number of people, true friends to the rights and liberties of this country, attended, and signified their approbation to it by loud acclamations. After which the coat of arms of his Majesty George III was torn to pieces and burnt in the presence of the spectators."[35] Such celebrations took place throughout the colonies.

The newspaper printers clearly understood the potential impact of the Declaration of Independence and reflected that in their published reports. An account of the public celebration in Trenton, New Jersey, carried in Dixon and Hunter's *Virginia Gazette,* stated: "The people are now convinced, of what we ought long since to have known, that our enemies have left us no middle way between perfect freedom and abject slavery." This writer went on to say, "In the field, we hope, as well as in council, the inhabitants of New Jersey will be found ever ready to support the freedom and independence of America."[36] The printers also took particular notice of the impact of the decision to declare independence on the soldiers. George Washington had the declaration read to the troops assembled in New York City on July 9, 1776. They responded with three cheers, and reports of this event appeared throughout the press. A report from Ticonderoga in the *Pennsylvania Evening Post* rejoiced over the reaction of the troops there to the news:

> We hear from Ticonderoga, that on the 28th of July, immediately after divine worship, the Declaration of Independence was read

> by Col. St. Clair, and having said, "God save the Free Independent States of America!" the army manifested their joy with three cheers. It was remarkably pleasing to see the spirits of the soldiers so raised after all their calamities; the language of every man's countenance was, Now we are a people! we have a name among the states of this world.[37]

Printers hoped such reports would encourage people to believe that independence could be won.

The adoption of the Declaration of Independence provided a focus for the Americans in their conflict with Great Britain. After July 4, 1776, the air in America seemed to clear. The Continental Congress had the declaration proclaimed to the public from the steps of the State House in Philadelphia on July 8. The American colonies had severed their ties with Great Britain, and Americans began to focus their attention and effort on gaining their freedom by winning the war. Newspaper printers joined in that process by encouraging their readers to do all they could to aid in that effort in order to achieve victory.

The TIMES are Dreadful, Dismal, Doleful, Dolorous, and DOLLAR-LESS.

An Emblem of the Effects of the STAMP

O! the fatal Stamp

Thursday, October 31, 1765. THE NUMB. 1195.

PENNSYLVANIA JOURNAL; AND WEEKLY ADVERTISER.

EXPIRING: In Hopes of a Resurrection to LIFE again.

I AM sorry to be obliged to acquaint my Readers, that as The STAMP-ACT, is fear'd to be obligatory upon us after the First of November ensuing, (the fatal To-morrow) the Publisher of this Paper unable to bear the Burthen, has thought it expedient to STOP awhile, in order to deliberate, whether any Methods can be found to elude the Chains forged for us, and escape the insupportable Slavery, which it is hoped, from the last Representations now made against that Act, may be effected. Mean while, I must earnestly Request every Individual of my Subscribers, many of whom have been long behind Hand, that they would immediately Discharge their respective Arrears, that I may be able, not only to support myself during the Interval, but be better prepared to proceed again with this Paper, whenever an opening for that Purpose appears, which I hope will be soon.

WILLIAM BRADFORD

**Figure 1.** *Pennsylvania Journal and Weekly Advertiser,* October 31, 1765. Printer William Bradford configured the first page of his newspaper to look like a tombstone to protest the Stamp Act.

Hours to the Gates of this City many Thouſands of our brave Brethren in the Country, deeply affected with our Diſtreſſes, and to whom we are greatly obliged on this Occaſion—No one knows where this would have ended, and what important Conſequences even to the whole Britiſh Empire might have followed, which our Moderation & Loyalty upon ſo trying anOccaſion, and ourFaith in the Commander'sAſſurances have happily prevented.

Laſt Thurſday, agreeable to a general Requeſt of the Inhabitants, and by the Conſent of Parents and Friends, were carried to their *Grave* in Succeſſion, the Bodies of *Samuel Gray, Samuel Maverick, James Caldwell,* and *Criſpus Attucks,* the unhappy Victims who fell in the bloody Maſſacre of theMonday Evening preceeding!

On this Occaſion moſt of the Shops in Town were ſhut, all the Bells were ordered to toll a ſolemn Peal, as were alſo thoſe in the neighboring Towns of Charleſtown Roxbury, &c. The Proceſſion began to move between the Hours of 4 and 5 in the Afternoon; two of the unfortunate Sufferers, viz. Meſſ. *JamesCaldwell* and *Criſpus Attucks,* who were Strangers, borne from Faneuil-Hall,

**Figure 2.** *Boston Gazette,* March 12, 1770. Printers Benjamin Edes and John Gill included woodcuts of coffins in their account of the Boston Massacre to represent the men killed in the conflict between the British soldiers and the crowd. COURTESY OF THE LIBRARY OF CONGRESS.

**Figure 3.** Paul Revere's engraving of the Boston Massacre, which shows the troops following orders to fire into the crowd in an organized manner. Although not totally accurate, this account of the events of March 5, 1770, became widely accepted. COURTESY OF THE LIBRARY OF CONGRESS.

**Figure 4.** Benjamin Franklin's original version of the divided snake, which encouraged the colonies to "JOIN, or DIE." Franklin created the cartoon image in 1754 to urge the colonies to work together to oppose French efforts to extend their power in America. COURTESY OF THE LIBRARY OF CONGRESS.

**Figure 5.** *Massachusetts Spy,* July 7, 1774. Isaiah Thomas used a variation of the divided-snake cartoon as part of the masthead for his newspaper, thus urging the colonies to unite in opposition to British actions. COURTESY OF THE LIBRARY OF CONGRESS.

RIVINGTON'S

NEW-YORK GAZETTEER;

OR, THE

Connecticut, Hudson's River, New-Jersey, and Quebec

WEEKLY ADVERTISER.

PRINTED at his OPEN and UNINFLUENCED PRESS, fronting HANOVER-SQUARE.

**Figure 6.** Rivington's *New-York Gazetteer,* February 15, 1775. James Rivington, a printer in New York, supported the British and became the most infamous Tory newspaper producer during the Revolution.

**Figure 7.** Isaiah Thomas, printer of the *Massachusetts Spy*.

WORCESTER, May 3.

AMERICANS! forever bear in mind the BATTLE of LEXINGTON!—where British Troops, unmolested and unprovoked, wantonly, and in a most inhuman manner fired upon and killed a number of our countrymen, then robbed them of their provisions, ransacked, plundered and burnt their houses! nor could the tears of defenceless women, some of whom were in the pains of childbirth, the cries of helpless babes, nor the prayers of old age, confined to beds of sickness, appease their thirst for blood!—or divert them from their DESIGN of MURDER and ROBBERY!

The particulars of this alarming event will, we are credibly informed be soon published by authority, as a Committee of the Provincial Congress have been appointed to make special enquiry, and to take the depositions, on oath, of such as are knowing to the matter. In the mean time, to satisfy the expectation of our readers, we have collected from those whose veracity is unquestioned the following account, viz.

**Figure 8.** *Massachusetts Spy,* May 3, 1775. Isaiah Thomas's famous account of the Battle of Lexington on April 19. It did not appear for several weeks because Thomas decided to move his printshop from Boston to Worcester before the fighting began.

**Figure 9.** Thomas Paine is best known for his 1776 pamphlet *Common Sense,* which encouraged the colonials to rebel against Great Britain. But his *Crisis* essays, published from 1776 to 1783, also proved important because they encouraged Americans to keep fighting until victory was achieved. COURTESY OF THE LIBRARY OF CONGRESS.

VOL. VI.
DUNLAP'S
Pennsylvania Packet
OR THE
GENERAL ADVERTISER
FRIDAY, DECEMBER 27, 1776.

**Figure 10.** *Pennsylvania Packet,* December 27, 1776. The front page held Thomas Paine's first *Crisis* essay. It is probably the most famous of the series because of its first lines: "These are the times that try men's souls: The summer soldier and the sunshine patriot will, in this crisis, shrink from the service of their country; but he that stands it NOW, deserves the love and thanks of man and woman."

( 335 )

# The PENNSYLVANIA EVENING POST.

*Price only Two Coppers.* Published every *Tuesday, Thursday,* and *Saturday* Evenings.

Vol. II.] SATURDAY, JULY 6, 1776. [Num. 228.

## In CONGRESS, July 4, 1776.

## A Declaration by the Representatives of the United States of America, in General Congress assembled.

WHEN, in the course of human events, it becomes necessary for one people to dissolve the political bands which have connected them with another, and to assume, among the powers of the earth, the separate and equal station to which the laws of nature and of nature's God intitle them, a decent respect to the opinions of mankind requires that they should declare the causes which impel them to the separation.

We hold these truths to be self-evident, That all men are created equal; that they are endowed, by their Creator, with certain unalienable rights; that among these are life, liberty, and the pursuit of happiness. That to secure these rights, governments are instituted among men, deriving their just powers from the consent of the governed; that whenever any form of government becomes destructive of these ends, it is the right of the people to alter or to abolish it, and to institute new government, laying its foundation on such principles, and organizing its powers in such form, as to them shall seem most likely to effect their safety and happiness. Prudence, indeed, will dictate that governments long established should not be changed for light and transient causes; and accordingly all experience hath shewn, that mankind are more disposed to suffer, while evils are sufferable, than to right themselves by abolishing the forms to which they are accustomed. But when a long train of abuses and usurpations, pursuing invariably the same object, evinces a design to reduce them under absolute despotism, it is their right, it is their duty, to throw off such government, and to provide new guards for their future security. Such has been the patient sufferance of these colonies, and such is now the necessity which constrains them to alter their former systems of government. The history of the present King of Great-Britain is a history of repeated injuries and usurpations, all having in direct object the establishment of an absolute tyranny over these states. To prove this, let facts be submitted to a candid world.

He has refused his assent to laws, the most wholesome and necessary for the public good.

He has forbidden his Governors to pass laws of immediate and pressing importance, unless suspended in their operation till his assent should be obtained; and, when so suspended, he has utterly neglected to attend to them.

He has refused to pass other laws for the accommodation of large districts of people, unless those people would relinquish the right of representation in the legislature, a right inestimable to them, and formidable to tyrants only.

He has called together legislative bodies at places unusual, uncomfortable, and distant from the depository of their public records, for the sole purpose of fatiguing them into compliance with his measures.

He has dissolved Representative Houses repeatedly, for opposing with manly firmness his invasions on the rights of the people.

He has refused for a long time, after such dissolutions, to cause others to be elected; whereby the legislative powers, incapable of annihilation, have returned to the people at large for their exercise; the state remaining in the mean time exposed to all the dangers of invasion from without, and convulsions within.

He has endeavoured to prevent the population of these states; for that purpose obstructing the laws for naturalization of foreigners; refusing to pass others to encourage their migrations hither, and raising the conditions of new appropriations of lands.

He has obstructed the administration of justice, by refusing his assent to laws for establishing judiciary powers.

He has made judges dependent on his will alone, for the tenure of their offices, and the amount and payment of their salaries.

He has erected a multitude of new offices, and sent hither swarms of officers to harrass our people, and eat out their substance.

He has kept among us, in times of peace, standing armies, without the consent of our legislatures.

He has affected to render the military independent of and superior to the civil power.

He has combined with others to subject us to a jurisdiction foreign to our constitution, and unacknowledged by our laws; giving his assent to their acts of pretended legislation:

*For* quartering large bodies of armed troops among us:

*For* protecting them, by a mock trial, from punishment for any murders which they should commit on the inhabitants of these states:

*For* cutting off our trade with all parts of the world:

*For* imposing taxes on us without our consent:

*For* depriving us, in many cases, of the benefits of trial by jury:

*For* transporting us beyond seas to be tried for pretended offences:

*For* abolishing the free system of English laws in a neighbouring province, establishing therein an arbitrary government, and enlarging its boundaries, so as to render it at once an example and fit instrument for introducing the same absolute rule into these colonies:

*For* taking away our charters, abolishing our most valuable laws, and altering fundamentally the forms of our governments:

*For* suspending our own legislatures, and declaring themselves invested with power to legislate for us in all cases whatsoever.

He has abdicated government here, by declaring us out of his protection and waging war against us.

He has plundered our seas, ravaged our coasts, burnt our towns, and destroyed the lives of our people.

He is, at this time, transporting large armies of foreign mercenaries to complete the works of death, desolation, and tyranny, already begun with circumstances of cruelty and

**Figure 11.** *Pennsylvania Evening Post,* July 6, 1776. Printer Benjamin Towne published the Declaration of Independence on the front page of his newspaper two days after its adoption. This was the first publication of the declaration in a newspaper following its adoption.

COURTESY OF THE LIBRARY OF CONGRESS.

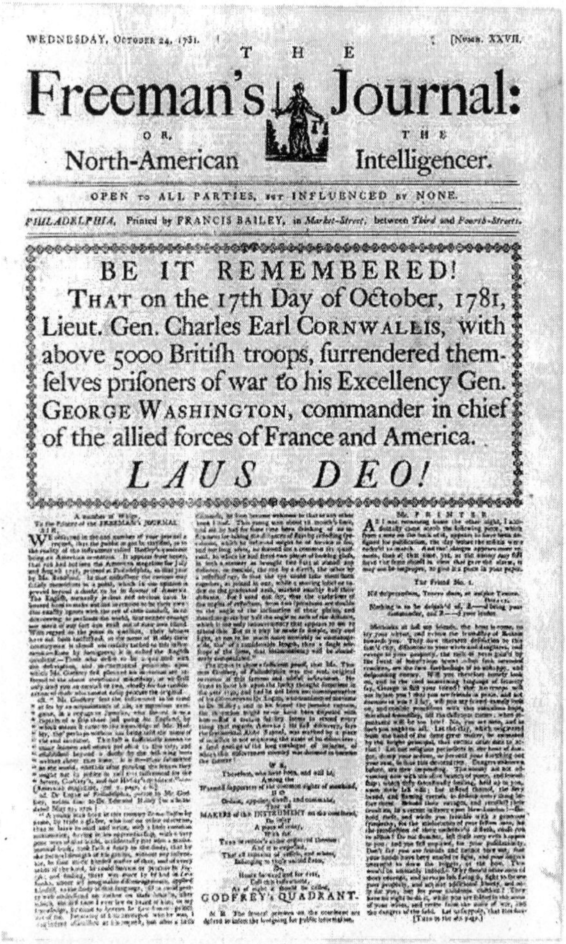

WEDNESDAY, October 24, 1781. [Numb. XXVII.

THE

# Freeman's Journal:

OR, THE

North-American Intelligencer.

OPEN to ALL PARTIES, but INFLUENCED by NONE.

PHILADELPHIA, Printed by FRANCIS BAILEY, in Market-Street, between Third and Fourth-Streets.

BE IT REMEMBERED!

THAT on the 17th Day of October, 1781, Lieut. Gen. Charles Earl CORNWALLIS, with above 5000 Britiſh troops, ſurrendered themſelves priſoners of war to his Excellency Gen. GEORGE WASHINGTON, commander in chief of the allied forces of France and America.

*LAUS DEO!*

GODFREY'S QUADRANT.

**Figure 12.** *Freeman's Journal,* October 24, 1781. This account of the surrender of Lord Cornwallis at Yorktown uses a headline to catch the attention of readers, an unusual technique at the time. COURTESY OF THE LIBRARY OF CONGRESS.

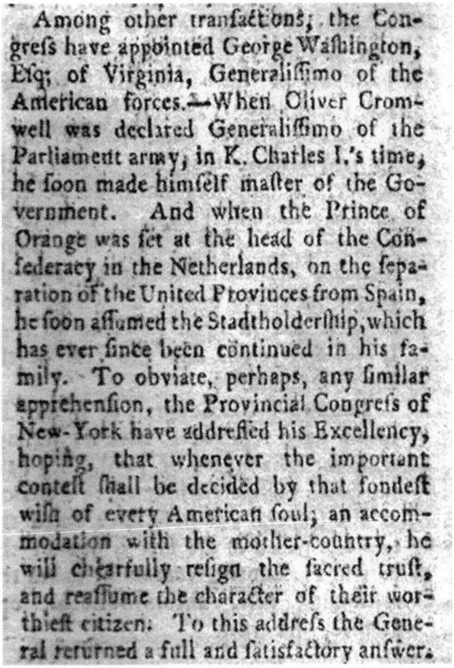

Among other tranſactions, the Congreſs have appointed George Waſhington, Eſq; of Virginia, Generaliſſimo of the American forces.—When Oliver Cromwell was declared Generaliſſimo of the Parliament army, in K. Charles I.'s time, he ſoon made himſelf maſter of the Government. And when the Prince of Orange was ſet at the head of the Confederacy in the Netherlands, on the ſeparation of the United Provinces from Spain, he ſoon aſſumed the Stadtholderſhip, which has ever ſince been continued in his family. To obviate, perhaps, any ſimilar apprehenſion, the Provincial Congreſs of New-York have addreſſed his Excellency, hoping, that whenever the important conteſt ſhall be decided by that fondeſt wiſh of every American ſoul, an accommodation with the mother-country, he will chearfully reſign the ſacred truſt, and reaſſume the character of their worthieſt citizen. To this addreſs the General returned a full and ſatisfactory anſwer.

**Figure 13.** *Gentleman's Magazine,* August 1775. This issue reported that George Washington had been appointed commander in chief of the Continental Army.

1043.

THE Boston-Gazette, AND COUNTRY JOURNAL.

*Containing the freshest Advices, Foreign and Domestic.*

*MONDAY*, *April* 10, 1775.

*To the Inhabitants of the Colony of* MASSACHUSETTS-BAY.

MY FRIENDS,

THE cases of Wales and Ireland are not yet exhausted.—They afford such irrefragable proofs, that there is a distinction between the crown and realm, and that a country may be annexed and subject to the former, and not the latter, that they ought to be thoroughly studied and understood.

The more these cases, as well as those of Chester, Durham, Jersey, Guernsey, Calais, Gascoine, Guienne, &c. are examined, the more clearly it will appear, that there is no precedent in English records, no rule of common law, no provision in the English constitution, no policy in the English or British government, for the case of the colonies; and therefore that we derive our laws and government solely from our own compacts with Britain and her kings, and from the great legislature of the universe.

We ought to be cautious of the inaccuracies of the greatest men, for these are apt to lead us astray.—Lord Coke, in 7 rep. 21. 6 says "Wales was sometimes a kingdom, as it appeareth by 19 H. 6. fol. 6, and by the act of parliament of 2 H. 5. cap. 6. but whiles it was a kingdom, the same was holden, and *within the fee of the king of England*: and this appeareth by our books, Fleta, lib. 1. E. 3. 14. 8. E. 3. 59. 13. E. 3. Tit. Jurisdict. 10. H. 4. 6. Plow. com. 368.—And in this respect, in diverse ancient charters, kings of old time stiled themselves in several manners, as king Edgar, Britanniæ. Basileus, Etheldros, Totius Albionis Dei providentia Imperator, Edredus magnæ Britanniæ Monarcha, which among many *glorum imperii omnia regna insularum oceani, &c. Cum suis ferocissimus regibus usque Norvegiam, maximamque partem Hiberniæ, cum sua nobilissima civitate de Dublina, Anglorum regno subjugare, quapropter et ego Christi gloriam et laudem in regno meo exaltare, et ejus servitium amplificare devotus disposui, &c.*—Yet for that it was wholly conquered in the reign of H. 2. The honour of the conquest of Ireland is attributed to him. That Ireland is a dominion separate and divided from England it is evident by our books, 20 H. 6. 8. Sir John Pilkington's case, 32. H. 6. 26. 20 Eliz. Dyer 360 Plow. com 360, and 2 r. 3. 12. *Hibernia habet parliamentum, et faciunt leges, et statuta nostra, non ligant eos, quia non mittunt milites ad parliamentum* (*which is to be understood unless they be specially named*) *sed personæ eorum sunt subjecti regis, sicut inhabitantes in Calesia, Gasconia et Guigan.* Wherein it is to be observed, that the Irishman (as to his subjection) is compared to men born in Calice, Gascoin and Guien. Concerning their laws, *Ex rotulis patentium de anno* 11. Regis H 3, there is a charter which that king made beginning in these words: *Rex Baronibus, Militibus et omnibus libere tenentibus L. salutem, satis, ut credimus vestra audivit discretio, quod quando bonæ memoriæ Johannes quondam Rex Angliæ, pater noster venit in Hiberniam, ipse duxit secum viros discretos et legis peritos, quorum communi consilio et ad instantiam Hibernensium statuit et præcepit leges Anglicanas in Hibernia, ita quod leges easdem in scripturas redactas reliquit sub sigillo suo ad scaccarium Dublin.* So as now the laws of England became the proper laws of Ireland; and therefore because they have parliaments holden there, whereat they have made diverse particular laws, concerning that do- edict: or unless it goes upon the supposition of Blackstone, that there had been an express agreement and consent of the Irish-nation to be bound by acts of the English parliament; and in either case it is not applicable even by analogy to America, because that is not a conquered country, and most certainly never consented to be bound by all acts of parliament, in which it should be named.—3. That the *instance, request & consent* of the Irish is stated, as a ground upon which king John and his discreet law-sages, first established the laws of England in Ireland.—4. The resolution of the judges in the cases of Orurke and Perrot, is express that Ireland was *without the realm of England*, and the late resolutions of both houses of parliament and the late opinion of the judges, that Americans may be sent to England upon the same statute to be tried for treason, is also express that America is *out of the realm of England*. So that we see what is to become of us, my friends. When they want to get our money by taxing us, our privileges by annihilating our charters, and to screen those from punishment who shall murder us at their command, then we are told that we are within the realm; but when they want to draw, hang and quarter us, for honestly defending those liberties which God and compact have given and secured to us, oh, then we are clearly *out of the realm!* 5. In Stowell's case it is resolved that Ireland is out of *this land*, that is, the land of England.—The consequence is, that it was out of the reach and extent of the *law of the land*, that is the common law.—America surely is still further removed from that *land*, and therefore is without the jurisdiction of that law which is called the law of the land in England.—I think it must appear by this time, that America is not parcel of

**Figure 14.** *Boston Gazette,* April 10, 1775. This issue contained the eleventh essay by John Adams writing as "Novanglus." In these essays, Adams argued that British authority was not absolute in the colonies.

**Figure 15.** Samuel Adams was an important Patriot in the early years of the Revolution. Adams understood the possibilities of using the press to unite Americans in their fight against Great Britain.

SEVEN

# THE WAR FOR INDEPENDENCE

Once independence had been declared, Americans focused on winning the war against Great Britain. The newspapers fulfilled an important function, primarily as a fount of information and inspiration. The role of the press as a source of news proved so essential that Congress provided for a printer for the army so the troops could maintain access to a newspaper. George Washington also arranged to keep abreast of events throughout the colonies and Britain by exchanging, through enemy lines, local news sheets for the papers of New York. By the beginning of the war, the weekly newspapers constituted the only truly national medium for news. Although pamphlets, letters, and broadsides continued to be useful methods of communication, the newspapers had become the public's major source of information.

In attempting to keep their readers informed about the progress of the war, Patriot printers included accounts of the actions of the Continental Army. The first battle of great interest occurred at Trenton, New Jersey. Loyalist printers downplayed the victory as unimportant, as shown by Hugh Gaine's brief report: "Wednesday Morning last one of the Hessian Brigades stationed at Trenton, was surprised by a large Body of Rebels, and after an Engagement hich lasted for a little Time, between 3 and 400 made good ieir Retreat, and the whole Loss is about 900 Men."[1] The Patriot rinters emphasized the importance of the victory in numerous ublished accounts. Of particular interest were the official reports f the engagement, as shown by Dixon and Hunter's publication i their *Virginia Gazette* of George Washington's official report to ongress about this first important victory for the Continental rmy: "Sir, I have the pleasure of congratulating you upon the iccess of an enterprise, which I had formed against a detachment f the enemy lying in Trenton, and which was executed yesterday iorning." Washington concluded by praising his men:

> In justice to the officers and men I must add, that their behavior upon this occasion reflects the highest honour upon them. The difficulty of passing the river, in a very severe night, and their march through a violent storm of snow and hail, did not in the least abate their ardour; but when they came to the charge, each seemed to vie with the other in pressing forward, and were I to give a preference to any particular corps, I should do great Injustice to the others.[2]

uch comments by George Washington and other Continental rmy officers helped convince many Americans that the war gainst Great Britain could be won.

Patriot newspaper printers also rejoiced over other military vicories and described the celebrations that followed the receipt of the ews of such victories. People in Williamsburg, Virginia, rejoiced hen they received the news of the victory at Saratoga as shown by iis report published in Alexander Purdie's *Virginia Gazette:*

> By the Northern post yesterday are received a solid confirmation of the success of arms to the North, in the surrender of General

> Burgoyne, with his whole army, to the victorious and immortal GATES. Upon receiving this great and glorious news a general joy diffused itself amongst all ranks, the regular troops and militia of the city were instantly paraded, and both from artillery and small arms resounded the glad tidings, the inhabitants illuminated their houses, and, with the gentlemen of the General Assembly, spent a cheerful and agreeable evening, wherein the names of WASHINGTON, GATES, ARNOLD, LINCOLN &c. &c. &c. were often bumpered, with huzzas to the independence of America.[3]

A young Continental Army officer wrote in a letter published in the *Boston Gazette* that the army planned to formally celebrate the victory at Saratoga:

> I most heartily congratulate you on the very happy, extraordinary, and unexpected news from the Northern Army, which we received this morning. I think the most sanguine heart could not have form'd an expectation equal to the success—We are to celebrate it this afternoon with 13 pieces of cannon, and a feu de joy from the whole army. We are now about 20 miles from Philadelphia, the ground we march'd from to the last action, and I suppose in a day or two we shall march to another. I think I would not but be in it for a world of happiness. The great almighty Governor of the universe, of his mercy grant that we may be able to give our countrymen as good an account of ourselves as our Northern Brethren have done, or at least gain a share of the glory of setting our country free from tyranny, and independent of the world.[4]

Such reports showed the hopes of many Patriot printers throughout America that the victory at Saratoga marked a turning point in the war.

While the Patriot newspapers rejoiced over the outcome of e Battle of Saratoga, the Loyalist printers downplayed the loss d even accused the Americans of exaggerating the results. James ivington reported in the *Royal Gazette* that "various reports have een propagated in this city since our last, relative to the situation f General Burgoyne's army; some of them too ridiculous to jus-fy a repetition. . . . It seems this news originated with, and came om the rebels, who fabricated the story with a view to inlist men; d, to give an air of truth to it, at Elizabeth Town they caused uns to be fired, bonfires to be made, and every other demonstra-on of joy and triumph, at the same time dealing out rum to the bble, without measure."[5] Such comments from Rivington and is fellow Loyalist printers reflected their hope the American vic-ory at Saratoga would not result in the British losing the war.

Patriot printers also reported on military losses and debated hat they would mean for America's future. Following the loss Germantown in late 1777, Dixon and Hunter's *Virginia Gazette* rinted a letter in which a Continental Army officer expressed oncern over the potential impact of the loss: "I sit down to give ou an account of one of the most important actions that ever hap-ened in America. I call it important, for it was, I think, very near utting an end to the campaign, and perhaps the war."[6] But even ough he worried about the results, this officer also concluded at victory was still possible: "Our army never were in better spir-s; the officers and soldiers desire another opportunity of drubbing ur enemies, and I believe will improve from the late unhappy rcumstance, and not imagine they are surrounded, when they in-nded to be supported."[7] Needless to say, Loyalist printers rejoiced ver the British victory at Germantown, as shown by Hugh Gaine's port in his *New-York Gazette, and Weekly Mercury:* "Glorious news om the southward: Washington knock'd up,—the bloodiest battle in America,—6000 of his men gone,—100 wagons to carry the wounded. General Howe is present at Germantown,—Washington 30 miles back, in a shattered condition,—their stoutest frigate taken, and one deserted. They are tired, and talk of finishing this campaign."[8] According to the Loyalist printers, such victories showed that the British would ultimately win the war.

Because many battle reports often proved unreliable, in June 1777 John Adams urged Major General Nathanael Greene, commander of a force near Philadelphia, to arrange for publication of accurate descriptions of the actions in which he fought to prevent the spreading of false information:

> I wish our N. England Men would practice a little honest Policy for their own Interest and Honour, by transmitting to Congress and publishing in the Newspapers, true States of the actions in which they are concerned. The Truth alone would be sufficient for them, and surely they may be allowed to avail themselves of this Shield of Defence when so many Arts of dishonest Policy are practiced against them.[9]

Along with battle tales, printers also published troop movements, a practice that concerned American leaders because they feared what the British would do if they acquired the information. For example, the *Connecticut Gazette* reported in 1781 that "the main army, under the command of his Excellency, General Washington, removed to White Plains on Monday last."[10] George Washington once worried that "it is much to be wished, that our Printers were more discreet in many of their Publications. We see almost in every Paper, Proclamations or Accounts transmitted by the Enemy, of an injurious nature. If some hint or caution could be given them on the Subject, it might be of material service."[11] Pleas for men and supplies became common in the newspapers. Important public ɔcuments, such as the Declaration of Independence and the Ar-cles of Confederation, were published in full, while important ;says such as *Common Sense* appeared everywhere. By publishing l of these different types of materials, Patriot printers hoped to ılly Americans to keep fighting until independence was achieved.

While not always accurate in their reports, printers did the best ith what they had. No reporters traveled with the army at this me, so much of the material printed consisted of rumor and earsay. The primary sources of information used by newspaper rinters consisted of official and unofficial letters as well as per-ɔnal reports from individuals, but most of these materials were mited in what they reported. These materials were reprinted all ver the country as printers sought whatever information they ɔuld find about the conflict with Great Britain. Printer John ;arter of Providence, Rhode Island, urged Colonel Joseph Trum-ull, the first commissary general of the Continental Army, to help ith the problem of acquiring information by sending accurate ports whenever possible: "As Matters seem coming to a Crisis at ıe Camp, I would thank you much for a Line occasionally—our ccounts here are generally very imperfect."[12] Delays in receiv-ıg existing information often made stories several weeks out of ate. Most newspapermen, however, felt that any information was etter than none at all. As Robert Luist Fowle said in the Exeter *Iew Hampshire Gazette* in July 1776, "At such a Day as this, where the Man that is not anxious for himself, and all his Connections, ıd from Week to Week is uneasy till he receives his News-Paper, hich these shocking Distresses had induced a much greater Iumber to take then was ever known before."[13] People turned ɔ the public prints for news of the war from other parts of the ɔuntry. Inclusion of such items made readers more aware of a na-onal war effort. In case Americans doubted that there really was a war in progress, the press made clear that Americans from other colonies were, indeed, fighting. Items from colonies all over the seaboard illustrated clearly that this was a widespread rebellion, not a disturbance isolated to the reader's own colony. By that means, the rebellion gained strength in numbers. Through the newspapers, rebellious colonists were cast as part of a large movement and their cause as important, helping persuade and convince doubters.

More importantly, the local printers used their newspapers to maintain morale and public support for the war. Using both essays and regular news columns, publishers continually painted the best picture possible of the rebellion. They strove diligently to convince their readers that the colonies had ample justification for their revolt and that Great Britain was, as described by Isaiah Thomas in the *Massachusetts Spy* in 1776, a "Monster of imperious domination and cruelty."[14] Americans' rights had been violated time and again by the British Parliament, threatening the freedom so deeply cherished by the colonials. Independence was the only possible solution: "It is the opinion of many wise and sagacious men, that a connexion with Great Britain is an indissoluble bar to the prosperity of these American colonies; and that independence is the only means by which we can preserve that freedom of which we are now possessed, and which is the foundation of all national happiness."[15] War constituted the final recourse, turned to only after all other avenues had failed. The press pounded home the themes that war was needed, war was necessary, war was right, and war was thus unavoidable if Americans were to remain free.

Probably the most famous essay in support of the war effort came from the pen of Thomas Paine, the author of *Common Sense*. During the tough winter of 1776, after the losses around New York City and prior to the victory at Trenton, Paine wrote the first of the "Crisis" essays to boost morale and keep the soldiers fighting:

> These are the times that try men's souls. The summer soldier and the sunshine Patriot will, in this crisis, shrink from the service of his country; but he that stands it NOW deserves the love and thanks of man and woman. Tyranny, like hell, is not easily conquered; yet we have this consolation with us, that the harder the conflict, the more glorious the triumph. What we obtain too cheap, we esteem too lightly:—'Tis dearness only that gives every thing its value. Heaven knows how to set a proper price upon its goods; and it would be strange indeed, if so celestial an article as FREEDOM should not be highly rated.[16]

)riginally published as a pamphlet in December 1776, this essay ıd the succeeding twelve "Crisis" essays published between Janu- ·y 1777 and April 1783 got reprinted in newspapers throughout ıe country and served to encourage the American Patriots to eep fighting for independence from Great Britain.

Some newspapers reminded their readers that the cause they ·ere fighting for was worth the effort. For example, Benjamin des continually used the pages of his *Boston Gazette* to remind his ·aders that the American cause was just and they would win the ·ar. In June 1777, he declared that the Americans would succeed: Our prospect brightens every day. A manly enduring for a little ·hile some difficulties ever to be expected in such a struggle, and few more spirited exertions, may sooner than many are ready to nagine, place our country in the most happy security, and render the praise of the whole earth."[17] Later that summer, Edes de- ·ared the glory of the American cause:

> The greatness of the American spirit appears to more advantage from the difficulties and disappointments we have met with in this struggle. It rises unappall'd above them all, and must soon, by the

> favour of Heaven, be superior to the arts and menaces, to the pride, injustice, and unparalled cruelty of Britain. This blow [the American victory at Bennington on August 16, 1777] must greatly weaken and dispirit Burgoyne's army. Howe never recovered the stroke at Trenton & Princeton: Our militia are gone in great number & with uncommon ardor: The present Leaders of our Northern Army, we are persuaded, know how to improve so great an opportunity. If the advantage is early and well taken, it may soon finish the War.[18]

And following the loss at Brandywine, Pennsylvania, in the fall of 1777, Edes summarized a letter in the *Boston Gazette* that reported the loss but emphasized that morale remained high. The battle was a big loss in many ways because it set the stage for the British to occupy Philadelphia following another loss at Germantown, Pennsylvania, several weeks later. But Edes affirmed that the fight would continue:

> By a letter from an officer of distinction dated Head-Quarters, Sept. 14, we learn . . . That on the 11th instant, our army had an obstinate engagement with the enemy, with the loss of some men and artillery; but from every account there was reason to believe the enemy suffer'd much more than we did, in the number of kill'd and wounded. That our troops were in high spirits, and in hopes of soon compensating for the loss they had received.[19]

Edes's focus on the morale of the soldiers sought to convince Americans that ultimate victory over Great Britain was still possible.

Patriot printers also emphasized that the Continental Army was capable of winning and that the American people should continue to support its efforts. A soldier at Valley Forge declared in a 1778 report in the *Boston Gazette:* "I have the satisfaction to inform you, ıat the greatest harmony subsists in our army, all in high spirits ıd earnestly wishing for the opening of the campaign, when 'e expect to make the haughty tyrant of Briton tremble on his ırone, and the astonish'd would gaze with wonder on the rising .ory of America. Our army is strong, healthy and daily encreas- ıg."[20] Clearly, Edes hoped this affirmation of the high spirits of ıe army would serve to increase the expectations of his readers ıd keep them engaged and interested in the war with Britain. 'his was particularly true for Massachusetts because there had not een any serious fighting there since 1776.

Furthermore, printers declared that George III, the "whining King f Great Britain,"[21] no longer deserved American loyalty because he ad failed to defend American interests against the encroachments of arliament. In a response to a Loyalist defense of the British monarch ı 1782, a Boston writer averred that "Tories may perhaps think the yrant is ill-used, but his crimes are so black and numerous, that it perhaps impossible to represent him worse, on the whole, than he :ally is, or even so bad:—and the Tories may as well undertake to indicate the conduct of the Devil, as that of the Tyrant."[22] According ) Patriot newspapers, Great Britain and her monarch had under- ıined any claims they had ever had to American support and loyalty.

In addition to attempts to undermine loyalty to the British gov- :rnment, the Patriot newspapers tried to show that the majority of ıe British people did not support the war. Most of these efforts ıme in the form of letters from Great Britain that attacked the ıinistry and the Crown for fighting the colonies. Several pieces, ıcluding one that summarized a Parliamentary speech by General urgoyne after the loss at Saratoga, insisted that Britain could not af- ›rd to lose America's commerce. For example, an essay by "Juvenis" 'hich appeared in the *Boston Gazette* in early 1776 supported the ›lonies in their protests and stated that Great Britain would lose if a settlement was not reached: "The absurd notion of their being reduced to obedience by force of arms is vain and groundless . . . what distresses the one, must injure the other . . . they have proved very useful and valuable brethren; and should this nation lose their lucrative commerce with America, it will be a very essential injury."[23] Others insisted that the government planned to enslave America first and then subdue its own people at home—"the present plan of royal despotism is a plan of general ruin."[24] One British response to the outbreak of fighting at Lexington and Concord bemoaned that "the sword of civil war is drawn, and if there is truth in Heaven, The King's Troops Unsheathed It. Will the English nation much longer suffer their fellow subjects to be slaughtered? It is a shameful fallacy to talk about the Supremacy of Parliament; it is the Despotism of the Crown and the Slavery of the people which the ministry aim at; for refusing these attempts, and for that only the Americans have been inhumanly murdered by the king's troops."[25] In 1779, the *Boston Gazette* summarized accounts from London newspapers that reflected the surprise of some in Europe that Great Britain continued to fight the war: "It puzzles all the politicians in Europe to account for Britain's continuing the war, when all the prospects on which she so unjustly commenced it, are vanquished; and every campaign, for which she pays immense sums, only increases her humiliation, and adds to her embarrassment."[26] By printing such statements, Patriot printers sought to show that, for many people throughout Europe, British victory over the colonies seemed out of reach.

From the moment fighting broke out at Lexington and Concord, the Patriot printers blamed British leaders for the war. They insisted that future generations would agree with them "that Britain is guilty of waging the present war against America, not only without provocation, but in defiance of entreaties the most tender, and submission the most humiliating, faithful history will in time vince."[27] According to the Patriot printers, the British only had hemselves to blame for the war.

Newspaper printers accused British officials of failing to be ccurate in their reports of the fighting with the colonials. For xample, in January 1777, Isaiah Thomas published a variety of xtracts about the fighting in New Jersey from New York papers ) show how the British downplayed their losses. He concluded hese reports with the following comment:

> Our Readers will here see, that the Account of the loss on the part of the Americans is painted and represented in the highest and most formidable colors, and exhibited in a most pompous manner, to attract the Eye and fright the Timid,—while the loss on the part of the British troops is contracted and shewn in a view as little conspicuous as possible:—Their refuge of prevarication will not always secret the true state of this affair:—The loss of our men is much exaggerated![28]

Thomas and other Patriot printers declared that the British thus ied to mislead people in Great Britain and America about how he war was actually going.

Patriot printers also filled their newspapers with accusations f cowardice and cruelty on the part of their enemy. Upon the vacuation of Boston in 1776, the *Newport Mercury* declared that he redcoats left in such a panic that they were unable to carry all heir military stores with them:

> We are assured that General Howe fled from Boston in such a terrible panick, that he left behind cannon and other military stores to the amount of sixty thousand pounds sterling; and that the whole gang of mandamus counsellors and commissioners, with a number of other infamous Tory Traitors to their country, pushed off so

> horribly affrighted, that some left their wives and some their children, to the mercy of that people, the Yankies, whose destruction they had for many years been seeking.[29]

Some believed that the British feared to fight the Americans and intended to hire others to do their fighting for them. Stories of plots to emancipate the slaves for use against the colonials became common, as well as discussions of plans to hire European mercenaries, stories that later proved to be true.

Accounts of British cruelty proved even more popular than stories of British cowardice. Tales of the redcoats plundering and pillaging the countryside appeared frequently. For example, the *Providence Gazette* in January 1778 accused the troops in Newport of grave robbing:

> Our Neighbours, the British savages on Rhode Island, we learn by several Persons from thence, have given fresh proof that they are more savage than their Brethren of the Wilderness. It is an undoubted Fact, that the Body of Mr. John Magee, late a reputable Inhabitant of Newport, was about a Fortnight since taken from the Grave, stripped of the funeral Vestments, and left above Ground. The Body had been interred two Months. It is also said that other Instances of a like Nature have lately happened there.[30]

This story was clearly designed to make the British appear to be uncivilized and less than human and it increased American fears and concerns about their former countrymen. A story in the *American Journal* reported about British raids in the summer of 1779:

> In both these excursions the enemy, "with their usual activity," plundered and abused the inhabitants, sparing neither age nor sex.—One Mr. Beers, about 80 years of age, we are informed was inhumanly

murdered by a British soldier, in his own house, and 'tis said, two children were burnt in the conflagration of Fairfield. ['Tis hoped those lukewarm patriots who oppose RETALIATION will speedily point out some more eligible method to put a stop to such barbarities.][31]

atriot printers hoped such reports would further distance Americans from their former mother country.

British military officers also came under attack for their ques-onable actions. Most criticized were their supposed attempts to read disease, particularly smallpox, among the general popula-on. In December 1781, the *Salem Gazette* reprinted an essay by An American Soldier" which originally appeared in the *Mary-nd Gazette.* This writer declared, "Lord Cornwallis's attempt spread the small-pox among the inhabitants in the vicinity of ork, has been reduced to a certainty, and must render him con-mptible in the eyes of every civilized nation, it being a practice inconsistent with the law of nations and, as repugnant to hu-anity." He went on to accuse Cornwallis of mistreating the slaves ho had run away to fight with the British forces:

Your inhuman treatment to the wretched slaves who fled to you for freedom and protection, is more than sufficient to entitle you to the heaviest calamity. . . . It must inspire every feeling bosom with horror and resentment, when they are told, that out of upwards of 2000 slaves who joined Lord Cornwallis's army, upwards of 1500 have perished from disease and famine. It is a fact, which can be proved by innumerable evidences, that provisions were given to those men only who were able to work, whilst the women, children, and men debilitated by sickness, were left to linger out a miserable existence embittered by the rage of hunger. Many were turned out in such a situation, that they expired before they could reach our army.[32]

Such reports emphasized that the British were not truly civilized and did not deserve American loyalty.

Rumors of various plots and conspiracies on the part of British officials also appeared frequently in the newspapers. For example, in the summer of 1775, Benjamin Edes printed a story that reported that the British regretted not sending 20,000 Swiss troops "to cut the throats of the Americans in conjunction with the Negroes, who were to be emancipated to slaughter their masters."[33] Such accusations, particularly those that focused on threatened slave revolts, emphasized that the British lacked civility and would use any means necessary to defeat the colonials.

Perhaps the most damaging accounts, however, concerned how the British treated American prisoners of war. Accusations of cruelty and lack of concern for the well-being of the captives abounded. The Rhode Island printer John Carter declared in January 1777 that many American soldiers died after their exchange: "A number of Americans have lately arrived here from Newport in a flag of truce, having been exchanged there; one of them is since dead, and some others cannot long survive, owing to the inhuman treatment they received from the enemy."[34] When the war finally ended, an essayist in the *Continental Journal* signing himself "An American" urged all of his fellow printers to publish the following charge against the British concerning American prisoners of war:

> Tell it to the world, and let it be published in every newspaper throughout America, Europe, Asia and Africa, to the everlasting disgrace and infamy of the British King's commanders at New York. That during the late war, it is said, ELEVEN THOUSAND SIX HUNDRED and FORTY-FOUR American prisoners, have suffered death by their inhuman, cruel, savage and barbarous usage on board the filthy and malignant British Prison Ship called the *Jersey*,

> lying at New-York. Britons tremble lest the vengeance of Heaven fall on your isle, for the blood of these unfortunate victims![35]

More popular than castigations of the British, however, were at-cks on those Americans who remained loyal to Great Britain. Tales f Loyalist troubles proved very popular. One humorous piece in the *Jewport Mercury* in the summer of 1775 concerned a house where large number of martins usually spent the spring. The house was ought by a Loyalist, but the martins continued to nest there, "hoping at he might reform; but upon their return this spring, finding that e was incorrigible, determined no longer to build under the roof of Despot, and entertain him with their music, so, with one voice, quit-d his house, and flew away to the dwellings of the Sons of Liberty."[36]

Although useful in spreading information concerning Loyalist ctivities, the newspapers proved most helpful as a means to la-el publicly those who did not support the American cause. Lists f such people appeared regularly, along with the recantations of ose who had seen the error of their ways. In 1776 the *Connecticut Courant* declared that everyone labeled "inimical to the Coun-y" by the Committees of Inspection would have their names ublished in the paper weekly "till a deep Sense of their Guilt, nd Promise of Amendment, shall restore them to the Favour of eir insulted Country." Although desirous of aiding the cause, the rinters of the *Courant* did not forget finances. They also requested at the Committees of Inspection charge a dollar for every con-ssion that had to be published to pay the printing costs.[37]

Public attacks against some of these people also became normal ewspaper fare. Particularly hated by Americans was the former gov-rnor of Massachusetts, Thomas Hutchinson, who became a favorite rget for writers—some even placed total blame for the war on his oulders. Upon Hutchinson's death in 1783, John Gill insisted in the *Continental Journal* that Hutchinson had cut his own throat for "the probability was so great, that he could never have died a natural death (having contracted at least as much guilt of any traitor since the apostacy of Adam) that without any direct information, it might reasonably have been thought that this, or something equally shocking, was the manner of his exit.—May it prove to the end of time, a solemn warning to all hypocrites and traitors."[38] Many of the accusations against the British proved groundless, but these statements still helped the war effort because many colonials believed them.

Loyalist printers tried to show that the American rebels acted as badly as the Patriots accused the British of behaving. In May 1777, the *Newport Gazette* carried a number of comments about this concern. One stated that "the Sufferings of his Majesty's liege Subjects, who are in the power of those imperious Demagogues, are beyond Description."[39] Another comment had originally appeared in a Boston newspaper: "Can there be any propriety in a people fasting and praying, making solemn addresses to Heaven, for deliverance from the oppression of their enemies, while at the same time, they are wantonly practicing the vilest oppression upon one another?"[40] In July, the printer declared that "The Rebels, with the greatest Rigour, continue their Persecution of those whom they barely suspect of being inimical to their mad Undertaking."[41] But such accusations and comments did not get reprinted in very many newspapers.

While condemning the British for their plots and their inhuman treatment of the populace, most newspapers had only praise for the Continentals. Throughout the war, Patriot printers expressed no doubts that the American forces would ultimately prevail. By 1779, Bennett Wheeler, the printer of the *American Journal,* concluded:

> It is allowed on all hands that the American army is now equal at least to any in the world for discipline, activity, and bravery.

> There are no soldiers in Europe more exemplary for subordination, regularity of conduct, patience in fatigues and hardships, perseverance in service, and intrepidity in danger. To whatever quarter of the Continent they belong, they are all animated with one spirit to honour and defend their country; are all equally and invincibly attached to their General, ready to follow him through every hazard and toil, and determined not to relinquish the glorious service in which he is engaged till it shall be happily compleated.[42]

ccording to Patriot printers, the Americans would ultimately in their independence.

Most newspapers attributed the success of America's armed rces to the leadership of George Washington. They even praised im when a battle was lost. Following the retreat from Long Island late August 1776, a writer in Dixon and Hunter's *Virginia Gaette* gave credit to Washington:

> Saturday's post brings us to the agreeable intelligence of General Washington having effected a safe retreat for our army out of Long Island, in spite of the great numbers in that commanded by Howe. They have brought every thing off with them, except some very large cannon, which they spiked up, and a few out sentries. In the skirmishes, which have been for these several days past, the enemy have lost upwards of 1000 men, and we not much more than 500. They have sent a flag of truce offering to exchange General Sullivan and Lord Stirling for two Generals they have missing; but as we have them not, it is supposed they are killed. The manner in which our retreat was performed reflects the highest credit upon our Commander in Chief, and the officers in general.[43]

By 1777, following the victory at Trenton, the public prints had made Washington into a national hero. He could do no wrong and was constantly praised in the newspapers. Even in 1779, when the military conflict did not always favor the Americans, the *American Journal* declared that "this great man was born to give a consistency and cement to the military efforts of these States, in one of the most important and honorable causes that any nation was engaged in."[44]

Praise for this apparently almost perfect man filled the columns of the local newspapers. Numerous poems were written in his honor. In July 1777 the *Independent Chronicle* printed one of the best of these efforts, an acrostic of Washington's name:

**G**enuine production of the God's above,
**E**merg'd from Heav'n on Wings of sovereign love,
**O**ver Columbia's host to take command,
**R**egain her freedom, and defend her land;
**G**reatness of language can't his praise express,
**E**clipses but his fame and makes it shine the less.
**W**isdom and knowledge all his deeds inspire,
**A**nd his vast soul warm'd with angelic fire;
**S**tatesman accomplished, hero Brave and Bold,
**H**is matchless virtue like the Stars untold;
**I**n utmost perils calm and most serene,
**N**or over flush'd when he's victorious been;
**G**odlike his mind's from common changes free,
**T**urns o'er the fate of nations and their end does see,
**O**f all the heroes, history doth record,
**N**one ever were so great, so free from vice,
and so well serv'd the Lord.[45]

Just over a year later, a poet in the *Independent Ledger* produced another acrostic of Washington's name that praised his service to the nation:

**G**enius of Praise, assist my Lays,
while I recount his Virtues o'er;
**E**cho resound to Worlds around,
and waft his fame from shore to shore;
**O**rdain'd by Fate to save the State,
when Foes invade to Arms he flies,
**R**esolv'd to fight, maintain our Right,
or fall a noble sacrifice.
**G**low every Heart, your Joy impart,
exalt the worth of Freedom's Friend;
**E**mploy your Tongues in grateful songs,
'till time itself shall have no end.
**W**orthy to sit at Helm of State,
he Danger courts and Ease declines;
**A**rous'd to arms by War's Alarms,
where brutal Foes terrific join;
**S**trait to the Field (Virtue his Shield)
his vengeful Arm their host o'erthrown;
**H**esse's proud slaves, with Britain's knaves,
submit, nor dare his Powers oppose.
**I**nspire'd by Thee, fair Liberty,
his Bosom glows with martial Flame:
**N**ations shall rise and to the Skies
in Rapture bear the Hero's name.
**G**enerous and Free beyond Degree,
his out-stretch'd Arm compassion bears,
**T**o mitigate the Rod of Fate,
and free the Slaves in captive Wars,
**O**! may each Soul, without controul,
from his example take the Fire,
**N**or sheath their swords, till Britain's Lords,
humbled, shall grant what we require.[46]

or Patriot printers, George Washington was the ultimate example f a noble American engaged in the fight for freedom and inde- endence.

Printers also reported British efforts to bribe George Washington. In July 1781, the *New Hampshire Gazette* reported that the British had offered the following bribe to Washington: "To be given rank in the British service; a landed estate in England, purchased for him, of 7000 l. a year, and great promotions for such 12 persons as he should name."[47] Reports of such bribery efforts provoked ridicule and laughter among the Patriots. So great was the aura that surrounded Washington that his name alone was invoked in the *Providence Gazette* as a reason for joining the army:

> Such, my countrymen, is the General who directs the military operations of America; such the glorious leaders of her armies; such the Hero whose bright example should fire every generous heart to enlist in the service of his country. Let it not be said, you are callous to the impressions of such noble considerations, but, by following his glorious example, shew yourselves worthy of possessing that inescapable jewel Liberty, and reflect that you have nothing to dread whilst you are engaged in so glorious a cause, and blessed with a Washington for a leader.[48]

Many printers believed that no true American could refuse to fight with George Washington.

If George Washington was America's national hero, then Benedict Arnold became its archfiend. Arnold had originally been a hero for Americans because of his efforts to defeat the British, but he never felt that he received proper credit or compensation for his military successes. He first gained fame for his participation in the expedition that took Fort Ticonderoga and seized the cannons later used to force the British Army out of Boston. Arnold so led the expedition to take Quebec in late 1775. This attack iled, but Arnold's fame grew in the next several years as he first irected the construction of a fleet to defend Lake Champlain. he fleet lost the Battle of Valcour Island in October 1776, but ie action slowed the advance of the British Army from Canada ito New England. Hailing from Connecticut, Arnold received igh praise from the newspapers in his home colony. In July 1777, ie printer of the *Norwich Packet* described Arnold as being full of "heroic and magnanimous Spirit."[49] Arnold later commanded dvance battalions during the Battle of Saratoga in October 1777. fter receiving a serious wound at Saratoga, Arnold became the ommander of Philadelphia in June 1778. His actions in this post, rimarily his business deals designed to produce profits from war-elated supply movements, led to accusations of corruption by ocal leaders in Philadelphia. Arnold demanded a court-martial clear his name. He was convicted of two minor charges in nuary 1780 and this event resulted in Arnold's final frustration ith American leadership. Arnold had begun a potentially trea-onable correspondence with British authorities in May 1779 and is conviction pushed him to finalize ideas discussed in this cor-espondence.

The correspondence led to Arnold's attempt to turn West Point ver to the British in 1780. This event shocked the nation and roduced a torrent of abuse in the press that was unequaled in s day. The newspapers made Benedict Arnold into the ultimate aitor, a reputation that still holds today. Epithets applied to him icluded "Judas,"[50] "unparallelled traitor,"[51] "the meanest & basest f mankind,"[52] and "the basest villain on earth."[53] Reproaches and ecriminations flooded the public prints. The following acrostic, ublished in the *Boston Gazette* in November 1780, was only one f many barbs that flew Arnold's way:

**B**ORN for a curse to virtue and mankind!
**E**arth's broadest realms can't show so black a mind.
**N**ight's sable Veil, your crimes can never hide.
**E**ach is so great—they'st glut th' historic tide.
**D**efunct—your memory will ever live.
**I**n all the glare that Infamy can give!
**C**urses of ages will attend your name;
**T**RAITORS alone will glory in your shame.
**A**lmighty Justice sternly waits to roll
**R**ivers of sulphur, on your trait'rous soul—
**N**ature looks back, in conscious error, sad,
**O**n such a tarnish'd blot, that she has made!
**L**et HELL receive you rivetted in chains!
**D**amn'd to the hottest focus of its FLAMES.[54]

This poet proved very accurate in his prediction of Arnold's future reputation. Arnold's name has lived on precisely as the poet said it would. This reality reflects how vigorously Arnold was attacked in the press during the American Revolution. Thus, the newspapers helped shape public memory by creating a lasting negative image of Benedict Arnold.

Arnold wrote a letter to the American people to explain and justify his actions. Appearing originally in New York, printers throughout the United States carried the letter and the introduction that went with it, which had been written by the printers who originally printed the letter: "As the public may be anxious to see the feeble efforts of the basest villain on earth, to justify his conduct, we shall insert the following address . . . leaving it to our readers to make what criticisms on it they may think proper; only reminding them that it comes from a man, who, for a pecuniary reward, was about to sell his country, and the lives of thousands."[55] Clearly, the printers did not believe Arnold's justification for his actions.

Printers took great glee in reporting that Arnold's reception among the British Army was less than cordial. Anthony Haswell, ıe printer of the *Vermont Gazette,* reported in July 1781 that "it said Lord Cornwallis refused to see him, and that the officers in is Lordship's army (who are chiefly gentlemen) refused to serve ith him." The result of such reactions proved difficult for Arnold › bear: "In consequence of these public marks of contempt, poor enedict is driven to the old trade of 'horse-jockeying' and 'soul riving', which he followed for several years as a skipper in the Vest-Indies."[56] In August of that same year, the *American Journal* ırried a poem from a London paper that questioned whether rnold could be loyal to anyone:

Arnold; or, A Question answered.
Our troops by Arnold thoroughly were bang'd,
And poor St. Andre was by Arnold hang'd;
To George a Rebel, to the Congress Traitor,
Pray what can make the name of Arnold greater?
By one bold treason more to gain his ends,
Let him betray his new adopted friends.[57]

This poem clearly accused Arnold of cowardice for fleeing and aving his British contact, Major John Andre, to suffer alone. lthough no one doubted that Andre was a spy, the Patriots were ıll of praise for the gentlemanly manner in which he faced his xecution. An account published in the *New Hampshire Gazette* n October 14, 1780, stated: "Major Andre, Adjutant-General of ıe British Army, received the reward of his dear earned labours, ıe gallows, on Monday last. His unhappy fate was much regret- ed; though his life was justly forfeited by the law of nations. From is behaviour, it cannot be said, but that, if he did not die a good Christian, he did like a brave soldier."[58] A letter from the camp f the Continental Army published in the *Providence Gazette* in November 1780 declared: "Never, perhaps did a man suffer death vith more justice, or deserve it less."[59]

Many wished that the victim had been Arnold instead of Andre. In a letter originally published in the *New Jersey Journal* and later reprinted in the *American Journal* in late 1780, Sarah Warner attacked Arnold for his cowardice: "A friend of mine, my dear General, gave me a most pathetic account of the death of that unfortunate youth, Andre. His unhappy death drew tears from the eyes of every American officer, and altho' they, with silent pity, commended the decision of our best of commanders in ordering it, yet wept for a brave soldier, and curst a scoundrel. I will not tell you who, for fear I should offend you. It is said that had you half the bravery of Andre, he would have been alive; and there are some so malicious as to say, your fears have involved him in his unhappy catastrophe. For had you acted with the decision you pretended, that brave youth had still been alive."[60] In comparing Arnold to Judas Iscariot, the printer of the *New Hampshire Gazette* in August 1781 urged Arnold to imitate him even more: "Judas Iscariot betrayed his Master for thirty Pieces of Silver, but repenting of his Guilt, returned the Money into the Treasury, and went and hanged himself. . . . Judas Arnold received Five Thousand Pounds Sterling for his Treachery, and we find has lodged the Money in the British Funds, but he has not spirit enough to pursue the Character in the only part worthy of Imitation."[61] Such comparisons only added to the strong negative reaction to Arnold on the part of many Americans.

Many writers also saw desperation in the British bribery of Arnold. One essayist in the *Norwich Packet* in November 1780 concluded that "there is one reflection [that] results from this black business, that deserves notice, which is, that it shows the declining power of the enemy. An attempt to bribe is a sacrifice of military fame, and a concession of inability to conquer; as a proud people they ought to be above it, and as soldiers to despise it; and however ney may feel on the occasion, the world at large will despise them or it, and consider America superior to their arms."[62] Printers also sed the willingness of the British to resort to bribery as a further gn for the need for Americans to win their independence from tyrannical government that would depend on a traitor for help: It is said the traitor General Arnold receives the most flattering tention from his tyrannical majesty George the 3d, is often conulted by him in private, and particular regard is paid to his opinons in whatever regards the future prosecution of the American ar. [How truly little and despicable do kings appear, when, for e purpose of policy, they are forced to smile upon the meanest basest of mankind!]"[63]

In November 1780, the printer of the *Connecticut Courant* also sed Benedict Arnold's actions as a means to heap praise on merican patriots through a comparison between Arnold and the ilitiamen who had captured Andre:

> To his [Arnold's] conduct, that of the captors of Andre forms a striking contrast: He tempted their integrity with the offer of his watch, his horse, and any sum of money they should name. They rejected his offers with indignation: and the gold that could seduce a man high in the esteem and confidence of his country, who had the remembrance of past exploits, the motives of present reputation and future glory to prop his integrity, had no charms for three simple peasants, leaning only on their virtue and a sense of duty. While Arnold is handed down with execration to future times, posterity will repeat with reverence the names of Van Wert, Paulding and Williams.[64]

Such reports, along with the accusations aimed directly at Arold, served as encouragements for Americans to do their utmost for the war effort: "America has yet to learn one important lesson from the defection and treachery of General Arnold. To cultivate domestick and moral virtue as the only basis of true patriotism. Public virtue and private vice are wholly incompatible. A speculator in office, a drunkard, a debauchee, a sharper in business, and a man unfaithful to promises, and treacherous in private friendships, should never be trusted with any share of the power, honor, or treasure, of the United States"[65] Such appeals had been common since the beginning of the war. In June 1776, Isaiah Thomas printed the following encouragement to the readers of the *Massachusetts Spy:* "Let us not busy ourselves now about our private internal affairs, but with the utmost care and caution, attend to the grand American controversy, and assist her in her earnest struggle in support of her natural rights and freedom."[66] In June 1783, Benjamin Edes insisted in the *Boston Gazette* that independence would be valued more highly if it cost dearly:

> The independency of America will let the unified people of the globe know, that supported by their proper virtue, fortitude and valor, they courted danger as the best honor; that the dearer their Independence cost them, the more savored, the more revered it must be to immortal ages; that each memorial of their sufferings will forever occur as the inestimable badge and charter by which they purchased their freedom, and that every monument, sacred to the names of those Patriots who have died in the contest, will be considered as the Household Gods by whom they swore to be Free.[67]

Calls for increased endeavors accompanied both victory and defeat. The victory at Saratoga produced a need for more American exertions to encourage aid from France and Spain, while the de-

·at at Brandywine would reinvigorate and inspire Americans to
eep fighting until victory was achieved.

The newspapers urged their readers to continue fighting so ıat the war could be won, but they also reminded them not to ›rget the justness of their cause so that they would remember ʼhy the war was worth fighting: "Remember, my brethren, that ıe cause in which we are engaged is still the same—that the prize ʼhich we contend has not diminished, but increased its value, in roportion to the losses we have sustained. Let us therefore unitdly resolve, with firm reliance on the goodness of Almighty God, ıat tyranny and oppression shall not enter and possess our land, ll the body of the last freeman hath filled up the breach"[68] The Continental Congress expressed this idea best in 1778 in a call for nity and strength among the people: "It is to obtain these things ıat we call for your strenuous, unremitted exertions. Yet do not elieve that you have been or can be saved merely by your own rength. No! It is by the assistance of Heaven, and this you must ssiduously cultivate, by acts which Heaven approves. Thus shall ıe power and the happiness of these sovereign, free and independent States, founded on the virtue of their citizens, increase, exend and endure, until the Almighty shall blot out all the empires f the earth."[69] The printer of the *Independent Chronicle* concluded ı October 1780 that the future would confirm the justness of merican actions: "That Britain is guilty of waging the present var against America, not only without provocation, but in defince of entreaties the most tender, and submission the most huiliating, faithful history will in time evince."[70]

EIGHT

# VICTORY LEADS TO PEACE

The American victory at Saratoga in October 1777 convinced many people that an overall American victory was imminent. But that did not prove to be true, because the war dragged on for six more years. During this period, American military efforts did not fare well. Along with the treachery of Benedict Arnold came losses on the battlefield that many feared could lead to the dismembering of the colonies, if not a total loss in the fight for independence. Patriot newspaper printers tried to fight this growing despair by urging Americans to keep fighting because the ultimate victory would result in freedom and was worth the cost.

One outcome of the Battle of Saratoga was a change in British military strategy. In 1778, the focus of the British military effort moved southward. British leaders hoped to regain control of America one colony at a time. They took Savannah, Georgia, in late December 1778. In 1779, they turned their attention to South Carolina. Initially, they sought to support Loyalist forces throughout South Carolina. Finally, in December 1780, a British force from New York under the command of Sir Henry Clinton sailed for South Carolina. They landed near Charleston on February 11,

780, and laid siege to the city. On May 12, 1780, the American rmy of over 5,000 Continental regulars and local militia surndered. It would be the worst military reversal suffered by the Continental Army during the American Revolution.

During the siege, Patriot printers tried to keep their readers nformed about what was going on between the two armies that ced each other in South Carolina. Much of the information they rinted came from Loyalist newspapers because these were the nly published sources available from the area where the fighting was taking place. For example, on May 8, Benjamin Edes reprinted a piece from a Loyalist newspaper in the *Boston Gazette* hat reported the arrival of the British Army at Charleston. The tory stated that the British forces were in good shape and ready o win a victory over the American rebels they had cornered in Charleston: "Health and plenty prevailed throughout the British nd Hessian encampments, also in the fleet, and every department ied with each other in alacrity to promote his Majesty's service."[1] This report did not encourage the readers of the *Boston Gazette,* ut it did help them be better informed about the war.

Loyalist printers rejoiced over the victory at Charleston and oped that it would awaken Americans to the folly of their Revolution. For example, James Rivington reported the British victory nd hoped that it would shorten the war:

> How greatly would it have added to the lustre of his Majesty's arms, had this been a conquest over the natural and perfidious enemies of the British empire? Every brave Briton will feel a mixture of pain on being informed, that about 900 of his Majesty's deluded subjects perished in the siege. How happy, nevertheless, if the increase of the miseries of this country, shortens their duration, and the disobedient return to the blessings so often tendered by the

> clemency of their Sovereign, and so generally wished for by their fellow subjects, not only of the Parent country, but in all the other quarters of the globe?[2]

Rivington clearly hoped that the outcome at Charleston signaled that the British would ultimately win the war with their American colonies.

Patriot printers struggled to get news reports of the loss at Charleston and often reprinted Loyalist accounts to provide some information about the siege (as shown by the *Connecticut Courant*'s reprinting of Rivington's report). But their primary focus lay in convincing their readers that the loss was not a total disaster. Isaac Collins, the printer of the *New Jersey Gazette,* reported that the British military leaders were dismayed after the victory because the American garrison had been so small:

> The enemy we are told, were much surprized to find so small a number of continental troops in Charles-Town. Gen. Leslie, who was appointed to receive these troops after the surrender, said to Gen. Lincoln, "I take this, Sir, to be your first division." "This body, Sir," replied Gen. Lincoln, "contains my first and my last division; they are all the troops I have." The enemy were not a little chagrined, to find that they had spent so much time, and incurred so much loss against so small a garrison.[3]

Stories such as this report showed that losing engagements such as the siege of Charleston really did not hurt the American overall war effort.

Other Patriot printers focused on the impact of the loss on future efforts. Bennett Wheeler declared in the *American Journal* that the loss would produce good results: "With pleasure we obrve the noble Spirit which invigorated these States in Seventy x, again taking Possession of every Breast. The Loss of Charles- n, like that of Ticonderoga, instead of being a Misfortune, will, it presumed from present Appearances, turn out a real Advantage. ur illustrious Chief will shortly have an Army sufficient to ex- rpate the Britons from this Continent; and with the Assistance ur generous Ally has sent us it will, no Doubt, be soon accom- ished."[4] In reporting the arrival of General Benjamin Lincoln in oston following his parole by British authorities, an anonymous riter in the *New Hampshire Gazette* declared that the American ilitary effort would only benefit from the loss at Charleston: The gratitude and good sense of America will do General Lin- oln justice, while the surrender of a garrison which it became npossible he should any longer maintain, *will have the effect,* which isfortunes always have upon the virtuous and the brave, *to stimu- te their future exertions.*"[5] Losing at Charleston would only make mericans fight harder until victory was achieved.

The loss at Charleston was soon followed by another defeat Camden, South Carolina. General Horatio Gates, the "hero of aratoga," had been given command of the southern army. He arched his forces into South Carolina, intending to avenge the ss at Charleston. He marched into battle against the British on ugust 16, 1780, without making many definite plans. His de- endence on the untrained militia resulted in a disaster because ey fled in the face of the well-trained British regulars. Approxi- ately 1,900 Americans were killed and 1,000 taken prisoner. The ritish suffered 68 killed and 350 wounded. Gates himself fled the eld before the battle ended and thus ruined his career. The loss of nother southern army seemed almost more than the Americans ould bear. Many worried that the southern colonies were lost rever. In his official report, which was printed in the *Boston Ga-*

*zette* in late September 1780, Gates tried to calm such fears, stating that "Anxious for the public good, I shall continue my unwearied endeavours to stop the progress of the enemy, to reinstate our affairs, to recommence an offensive war, and recover our losses in these Southern States."[6]

Loyalist printers again rejoiced over the success of the British Army. James Rivington summarized the victory at Camden for the readers of his *Royal Gazette:* "An account was brought to town yesterday, that in the neighbourhood of Camden, on the borders of North Carolina, Earl Cornwallis having attacked the rebel army commanded by Mr. Gates, the enemy stood a charge from his Lordship's troops, which greatly deranged them. They were then pushed with the bayonet, and the British cavalry advancing, entirely broke, routed, and pursued them with great execution."[7] Hugh Gaine produced a more detailed report a week later that praised the British regulars and criticized the American militiamen:

> The Action happened about two o'Clock in the Morning of the 16$^{th}$ ult. when both Armies were manoeuvering, in order to obtain an Eminence, they unexpectedly fell in with each other; that the Royal Army discharged a very heavy Fire upon the Rebel Militia, who were in Front, which soon put them to the Rout; they then fell back on the Continental Troops, which threw them into Confusion, and they being immediately charged by the Royalists, were soon dispersed, and the whole Body, (General Gates, and his Suite, with about 50 of their Cavalry excepted) killed, wounded or taken Prisoners. Those who escaped were pursued many Miles from the Field of Action.[8]

The following week, Gaine rejoiced over the victory in the *New-York Gazette, and Weekly Mercury* and described it as "the perfect ictory gained on the 16th of August by Earl Cornwallis over the ebel army under Mr. Gates."[9]

Patriot printers once more sought to boost morale by down-laying the loss. The printer Samuel Loudon used the pages of his ewspaper the *New York Packet* to encourage his readers following ne loss. Loudon had grown up in Great Britain and immigrated New York City around 1760. He had fled the city just before ne British occupation and reestablished his print shop up the Iudson River in Fishkill, New York. In his account, Loudon first riefly described the battle:

> The contending armies engaged each other with the greatest fury, and the prospect, for some time, was extremely favourable to the American troops, who charged bayonets on the enemy, which obliged them to give ground, and leave some of their artillery in the possession of our advancing troops—but, unfortunately, at this critical moment the premature flight of militia terminated the conflict in favour of the enemy—an event which hath proved fatal to many of our brave countrymen of the regular troops, 4 or 500 of whom have been killed and taken.[10]

oudon then declared: "Notwithstanding this misfortune, Gen. Gates, hose Head Quarters are at Hillsborough, is collecting a force much iperior to the late army, and appears resolved to try the fortune f another day." An anonymous writer in the *Pennsylvania Gazette* eported in September that the loss had not been as great as origi-ally supposed:

> Since my last, advice is received from General Gates, informing that our loss of officers is but small, and upwards of 500 men made their escape. Very few of Sumpter's part have suffered; our greatest

> loss is the baggage and stores. The greatest honour is due to the Maryland and Delaware brigades; they killed and wounded upwards of 500 of the enemy, and made their retreat good.[11]

The Boston printer Nathaniel Willis also downplayed the losses in his report of the battle in the September 21 issue of the *Independent Chronicle:*

> By a gentleman of veracity, just arrived from Philadelphia, we are informed that a letter had been received there from Governor Nash of North-Carolina, giving an account of the late battle between General Gates and Lord Cornwallis, near Camden, much more favorable on the side of our forces than was at first represented. According to this account, General Gates's army received the attack of the enemy with great firmness, many of whom fell; and even the militia, were not broken till some time after the fight had been carried on by the push of the bayonet: After our line was broken, a line of Continental troops, amounting to about 900, and the South-Carolina militia, continued in good order, and fought bravely, but finding themselves overpowered, retreated, though still keeping in a body. The enemy's horse pursued our broken militia some miles, and upon their return, falling in with the body of Continental troops, the fight was renewed, and the greater part of the horse was slain. This account adds, that General Smallwood remained with the Continentals and was safe; that Baron Kalb was missing, and said to be wounded; that of all the American forces on the field, not more than 300 were missing; and that the number of killed in this action was greatest on the side of the enemy.[12]

These printers presented the loss at Camden as relatively minor and easy to overcome.

Clearly, both Patriot and Loyalist printers showed favoritism to ıe side of the conflict they supported and sought to portray their oops in the best light. They also strove to inspire their readers keep fighting until victory was achieved by emphasizing wins ıd downplaying losses. The back-and-forth nature of victory ıd defeat in the southern campaign provided many opportuni-es for both sides to print these types of materials. Reading only atriot or Loyalist reports makes it seem as though that side was early prevailing in the fighting, while reading both makes it hard see who was winning the war. By this time in the conflict all ıe printers, whether Patriot or Loyalist, had come to see one of ıeir primary roles as keeping people engaged in the conflict by oosting morale, and these types of one-sided reports played a ıajor role in that effort.

By late 1780, such reports by Patriot printers became very im-ortant because many Americans began to wonder if ultimate mil-ary victory was still possible. Lord Charles Cornwallis, the British ommander, moved into North Carolina following the Battle of amden to take that colony as well. He took Charlotte, North arolina, on September 26, 1781. As part of his move northward ıto North Carolina, Cornwallis sent a force of Loyalists under ıe command of Major Patrick Ferguson to the foothills of the lue Ridge Mountains. Ferguson hoped to organize the military fforts of the Loyalists into something more than random raids ıd assaults. Ferguson's efforts to hunt down and punish Patriot ıilitiamen angered many Americans and produced a reaction by esidents of western North Carolina and eastern Tennessee. The mericans organized into a military unit and forced Ferguson to etreat eastward. Ferguson took refuge on King's Mountain, thirty ıiles west of Charlotte on the North Carolina/South Carolina order. The battle between these two groups at King's Mountain took place on October 7, 1780. It did not last long. The Americans surrounded the Loyalists and slaughtered them because they had no means of retreat. When the battle was over, Major Ferguson was dead and more than three hundred of his men out of a force estimated at one thousand soldiers were either dead or wounded.

The Battle of King's Mountain proved to be a major turning point in the war. The American victory pushed Cornwallis to withdraw to Wilmington, North Carolina, on the East Coast and gave the Americans an enormous morale boost because they had finally won a battle against the British in the south. And Patriot newspaper printers throughout the country rejoiced over the victory because they knew what it meant for the American cause. When news of the victory reached Philadelphia, printers William and David Hall and William Sellers printed a letter from William Davison in the *Pennsylvania Gazette* that described the victory and closed with the following prediction: "This blow will certainly affect the British very considerably. The Brigade Major who gives us this was in the action. The above is true. The blow is great. I give you joy upon the occasion." The printers then added their own comment on what the victory at King's Mountain meant to the people of Philadelphia: "On the above important intelligence being circulated in the city, the chearful countenances of the honest and virtuous part of the community fully evinced the heart-felt satisfaction they experienced on the joyful occasion; whilst the malignant aspects of the disaffected sufficiently betrayed their chagrin and disappointment."[13] Davison reflected the hopes of many Americans that success in this battle meant that victory over Great Britain was within reach.

Throughout late 1780, the British and the Americans sniped at each other in the Carolinas. Both armies divided in an effort to catch the other side at a disadvantage. This action resulted in attles at Cowpens in South Carolina in January 1781 and Guilord Courthouse in North Carolina in March 1781. The Americans won the battle at Cowpens, but they retreated from the field : Guilford Courthouse. Despite the British victory at Guilford Courthouse, their casualties in these two battles were so great that was clear that the Americans had gained the upper hand in the var.

As had been true for Patriot printers following the American osses at Charleston and Camden, Loyalist printers tried to downlay the losses. A Loyalist report reprinted in the *Boston Gazette* in 781 declared that the British loss had not been that great and that heir forces would ultimately succeed:

> Though the numbers of killed and wounded on either side cannot as yet be well ascertained, there is great reason to believe our loss by no means so great as the enemy would fain insinuate; and, by all accounts, Col. Tarleton was never more distinguished for spirit and gallantry, than on this occasion. . . . We have the pleasure to assure the public, from undoubted authority, that Lord Cornwallis is now in pursuit of General Morgan, who after his late action with Col. Tarlton, took to the mountains, where he is likely also to meet with large numbers of Indians and embodied Loyalists, who, we are well informed, are actually in arms for us in those parts.[14]

The losses were only a minor setback and victory over the Americans would soon be achieved.

The newspapers carried numerous reports on these battles, uch as this brief one from an American officer printed in the *Pennsylvania Gazette* on February 14, 1781: "It is with pleasure congratulate you on a compleat victory obtained by General Morgan, with the militia and a detachment from this army, over

Col. Tarleton, at the Cow-pens, on the Broad River, the 17th instant. . . . This is but the prelude to the aera of 1781, the close of which, I hope, will prove memorable in the annals of history, as the happy period of Peace, Liberty, and Independence to America." In the same issue, the printers of the *Gazette* reprinted the official report from General Daniel Morgan to his commanding officer, General Nathanael Greene:

> The troops I have the honour to command have gained a compleat victory over a detachment from the British army, commanded by Lieut. Colonel Tarleton. The action happened on the 17th instant, about sunrise, at a place called the Cowpens, near Pacolet River. . . . Although our success was compleat, we fought only eight hundred men, and were opposed by upwards of one thousand of chosen British troops. . . . Such was the inferiority of our numbers, that our success must be attributed, under God, to the justice of our cause, and the bravery of our troops.[15]

Newspapers also carried the official reports of the battles that were sent to the Continental Congress. For example, the *Pennsylvania Gazette* reprinted General Nathanael Greene's official report about the Battle of Guilford Courthouse. He declared that, once he had his men ready, he had taken "the resolution of attacking the enemy, without loss of time, and made the necessary disposition accordingly; being persuaded that if we were successful, it would prove ruinous to the enemy, and if otherwise, it would only prove a partial evil to us." He then described the battle in some detail and reported on the losses suffered by the British: "From the best information I can get, the enemy's loss is very great, not less in killed and wounded than six hundred men, besides some few prisoners that we brought off." Greene then went on to praise his men:

> Our men are in good spirits, and in perfect readiness for another field day. . . . The firmness of the officers and soldiers, during the whole campaign, has been almost unparalleled. Amidst innumerable difficulties, they have discovered a degree of magnanimity and fortitude, that will for ever add a lustre to their military reputation.[16]

uch reports sought to focus American attention on the positive esults of the Continental Army's efforts in the South.

Many people believed that Cornwallis and the British Army ould be unable to recover from these defeats. One anonymous riter, in discussing the battle at Guilford Courthouse in a letter rinted in the *Connecticut Courant* in April 1781, compared the esults to the events that had earlier led to the American victory Saratoga:

> On the $15^{th}$ instant we met Lord Cornwallis, and a general action ensued; our force being mostly militia we were not able wholly to destroy my Lord and his army, but it is certain that we have killed and wounded seven or eight hundred of them. Our loss is about 50 killed and 220 wounded and missing; we are retired to this place to-day, the enemy remain near Guilford Court-House. I consider this action like that with Burgoyne, the $19^{th}$ of September 1777, he kept the field but it proved his ruin. . . . What a glorious opportunity now offers to put an end to the war—The enemy in this country by victories and defeats, have lost two thirds of their army since the taking of Charlestown, and a little exertion of the States would totally destroy them. I fear you will not make those exertions before you are scourged to it by the enemy—It is a very foolish way to ruin an enemy by allowing him to obtain expensive

> victories when we might so easily do it by defeats, though I am certain his ruin is inevitable.[17]

Since Saratoga was still seen as the greatest American victory in the war so far, such comparisons sought to increase American pride over the Southern successes.

The casualties at Cowpens and Guilford Courthouse forced Cornwallis to withdraw from the Carolinas and move north into Virginia in May 1781. Reports of his withdrawal, like the following account from the *Boston Gazette,* appeared in numerous Patriot publications: "By accounts from the southward we learn, That Earl Cornwallis has evacuated his post at New Gardens, leaving behind him all his sick and wounded, who have fell into our hands; that Gen. Greene is close in his rear, pushing him very hard; and in all human probability, will oblige him very soon to surrender. The action of the 15th so weakened Cornwallis, that it is doubtful whether he will risk another, if he can avoid it, while General Greene's resources of men are like the hydra's head."[18] Cornwallis went to Yorktown on the York River near the coast to make it easier for the British Royal Navy to resupply his forces and evacuate them if necessary. But this move also enabled Washington and his French allies to trap the British on the Virginia peninsula. Washington ordered 7,000 American and French troops to march to Virginia and the French fleet in Newport, Rhode Island, headed south with the heavy artillery that would be needed for a siege. The French fleet reached Virginia on August 26 and defeated the British on September 5 in the Battle of the Capes. By mid-September 1781, all the pieces were in place for the siege of Yorktown to begin. The American and French troops prevented Cornwallis from retreating by land while the French eet prevented rescue by sea. The siege of Yorktown ended with ıe British surrender on October 19, 1781.

The Patriot newspapers quickly reported the victory because ıany believed that this might be the final battle. William and avid Hall and William Sellers, the printers of the *Pennsylvania azette* in 1781, reported the American victory as soon as possible, ven though they had few details: "Early on Monday morning an xpress arrived in town, with the agreeable and very important ıtelligence of Lord Cornwallis and his army having surrendered n the 17th inst. We impatiently wait the arrival of his Excellency eneral Washington's dispatches, particularising this most intersting event."[19] And Washington's official report to the Contiental Congress about the victory at Yorktown soon appeared in rint in newspapers throughout the country. Besides conveying ıe results of the battle, Washington also praised his troops:

> I have the honour to inform Congress that a reduction of the British Army under the command of Lord Cornwallis is most happily effected. The unremitted ardour which actuated every officer and soldier in the combined army on this occasion has principally led to this important event, at an earlier period than my most sanguine hopes had induced me to expect. . . . The singular spirit of emulation which animated the whole army from the first commencement of our operations has filled my mind with the highest pleasure and satisfaction and has given me the happiest presages of success. . . . Your excellency and Congress will be pleased to accept my congratulations on this happy event.[20]

Printers also personally rejoiced in print over the news of the ictory. For example, Samuel Hall, the printer of the *Salem Gaette,* took great pleasure in reporting the news: "It is with the most singular satisfaction, that the Publisher of this Paper can, so soon after the commencement of its publication, congratulate his Readers on so great an event as the capture of Lord Cornwallis and his army.—He has inserted every particular yet come to hand.—The greatest joy and satisfaction were shown, in this and the neighbouring towns, on the receipt of this most interesting intelligence."[21] Hall had been a printer in New England for many years. He had learned the trade in New Hampshire as an apprentice of his uncle, Daniel Fowle. He originally established his printing business in Newport, Rhode Island, and then moved to Salem, Massachusetts, in 1768. He moved to Boston in 1776 after the British evacuated the city and then back to Salem in 1781. He clearly hoped that the victory at Yorktown would mark the end of the war and would bring peace for all (and possibly produce a more settled life for him and his family). Hall also knew that his readers would want to know everything about the victory at Yorktown so he printed everything he received.

The Loyalist newspaper printers once more tried to downplay the American victory. James Rivington declared that the Americans had sold their souls to the devil embodied in the nation of France:

> We can assure the public from recent information, that the whole Continental army is at this time in the actual *service* of his Most Christian Majesty Louis the Sixteenth, and are paid with French money, which has been for that purpose remitted to Mr. Washington, Lieutenant-General and Commander in Chief of all the French and Rebel forces in this country, so that every American soldier of this alliance is now become in every sense a *Frenchman*. The Congress have no sort of interference with his power, and they lately felt the humiliating mortification of perceiving General

> Washington *alone* entrusted with the cash received from France to pay the army. The people of America since their revolt from Great Britain, will have no other choice to make of a Ruler, as their Congress's command and influence now existed in the *Frenchified* Mr. Washington alone.[22]

uch comments sought to downplay the American victory by apealing to the long animosity between Great Britain and France ıat dated back centuries.

As part of their rejoicing, the Patriot newspaper printers also escribed the celebrations that took place in response to the ews of the victory at Yorktown. In Newport, Rhode Island, "The :hurch Bell was set a ringing and continued nearly all that night ıd next day, when the troops here were drawn up on the parade, here thirteen cannon were discharged in the morning and thireen at noon, besides a grand feu de joy from the musquetry. . . . number of patriotic toasts were drank by the officers of the my and gentlemen of the town."[23] Daniel Fowle described the elebration in his hometown of Portsmouth, New Hampshire: The above great and glorious intelligence was received in town ıe last evening, by express to Colonel Langdon, and immedi:ely announced to the public by the discharge of cannon, ringing f bells, illuminations, and every other token of joy that grateful earts could demonstrate. This morning was likewise usher'd in y the discharge of cannon from the fortresses and the shipping ı the harbour, the display of colours and the ringing of bells, c., which continue at this publication."[24] John Dunlap, printer of ıe *Pennsylvania Packet,* reported on the rejoicing in Philadelphia: The very great joy which the people of this city felt on the arival of the glorious news of the capture of lord Cornwallis and is whole force, immediately diffused itself through all parts of the country."[25] Such reports sought to show the unity of Americans in their joy over the news from Yorktown.

But not everyone was happy about the news of the American victory in Virginia. The Patriot newspapers seemed to enjoy telling their readers about the negative reactions and concerns of the Loyalists to the news about Yorktown. On November 20, 1781, Barzillai Hudson and George Goodwin, the printers of the *Connecticut Courant* in Hartford, reported:

> All the late New-York papers have at length confessed the surrender of Lord Cornwallis to be real. They have even condescended to insert the articles of capitulation verbatim from the Philadelphia gazettes. The women are in tears, the soldiery in a panic, the merchants selling off their goods for much less than the first cost in Europe, the tories are in the utmost consternation, and Benedict Arnold himself, it is said trembles like an aspen leaf—in the midst of this scene of distress and wretchedness, with a superior French fleet on the coast ready to swallow them, the demagogues of that city are publishing in their gazettes contents of rebel mails and criticisms upon poems written by the King of Prussia; which is full as ridiculous and stupid as if a criminal on his way to the gallows, and sitting on his coffin, should at the same time be amusing himself with Ben Johnson's jests, or writing strictures on the stile and language of the sheriff's warrant which condemns him to be hanged.[26]

Patriot printers hoped their Loyalist counterparts would admit that they had been wrong in their support of British authority.

Although many American leaders believed that the victory at Yorktown meant that the war would end soon, others worried that the British would not give up the fight. In a piece that origi-

ated in Boston and was reprinted in New Hampshire in Decem-
er 1781, an anonymous essayist urged Americans to continue to
e vigilant:

> Notwithstanding our late important successes it is very far from being certain that our enemies will seriously think of peace this winter. There are some strong appearances to the contrary. . . . Bitter as the pill of independence is, Britain, however, must swallow it at last; but vain hopes may probably induce her to continue the struggle. At the same time it is very far from being certain that an immediate peace would be for the advantage of America: Many are clearly of opinion that it would not; & that another campaign, if well prepared for, and vigorously prosecuted, would give us the advantages in a final settlement, infinitely more than sufficient to compensate the continuance of the war, so that, in every view of the matter, whether we consider the haughty and relentless disposition of our enemies, or our own interest, the affairs of this country ought certainly to go upon the expectation of another campaign, for which every exertion should be seasonably and vigorously made.[27]

ut printers also reported that some British leaders had admit-
ed that the war might be lost. For example, in December 1781,
enjamin Edes commented in the *Boston Gazette* that "since the
apture of Earl Cornwallis, his Lordship has been heard to say, the
mericans need not doubt, now, but that their Independency will
e established."[28] Patriot printers hoped that the British would
ealize that continued fighting would not be worth the effort.

Yorktown did prove to be the last of the fighting, primarily be-
ause the British were tired of the war. As the conflict had dragged
n year after year, more and more Britons expressed surprise that
heir nation continued the war effort when victory did not seem

possible or worth the cost. In 1782, an anonymous writer in the *Connecticut Courant* summed up the feelings of many in Great Britain who desired an end to the long hostilities: "It would ill become me to dictate to our Ministers, but humanity, love of country, and self-interest extort from me many an ardent wish for peace and an end to this diabolical unavailing war—Give the Americans their independence—give them anything—but give us peace."[29] Leaders in Great Britain became more concerned about the growing conflict with France than the loss of the American colonies. As a result, serious peace negotiations between the British and the Americans began in April 1782. The American peace commissioners were John Jay of New York, John Adams of Massachusetts, and Benjamin Franklin of Pennsylvania. Although they had promised their French allies that they would negotiate a peace together, the Americans were ready to disregard their arrangements with France because France and Spain had made agreements that seemed to undermine American interests. In particular, Spain and France had promised to continue fighting until Spain retook Gibraltar, an event that was very unlikely to happen. The British and Americans negotiated off and on from April until October. These talks resulted in them signing a preliminary agreement on November 30, 1782.

News of the preliminary treaty reached America in early 1783. Americans who had supported Great Britain worried what would happen to them, so Loyalist printers sought to reassure them. Hugh Gaine reported in the *New-York Gazette, and Weekly Mercury:* "By a particular article between Great-Britain and the United-States, liberty is given to the Loyalists to remain in America without molestation, or to dispose of their property, if it has not been *already* confiscated."[30] At the same time, Patriot printers rejoiced over the American victory. Isaiah Thomas declared, "It is with the greatest leasure we congratulate our readers on the certain prospect of speedy Peace: . . . it is reported that Congress have received the reliminary articles signed by his Britannick Majesty's Plenipo- entiary at Paris; and we may hourly expect further intelligence oncerning the happy termination of an eight year's war; which ill prove *That the noble efforts of a virtuous and united people can xtirpate Tyranny and establish liberty and Peace.*"[31] And Benjamin des stated:

> The independency of America will let the unified people of the globe know, that supported by their proper virtue, fortitude and valor, they courted danger as the best honor; that the dearer their Independence cost them, the more savored, the more revered it must be to immortal ages; that each memorial of their sufferings will forever occur as the inestimable badge and charter by which they purchased their freedom, and that every monument sacred to the names of those Patriots who have died in the contest, will be considered as the Household Gods by whom they swore to be Free.[32]

atriot printers emphasized that victory in the fight for indepen- ence really had been worth the effort.

It took almost another full year to finalize the treaty to end the merican Revolution, primarily because treaties had to be nego- ated between Great Britain, France, Spain, and the United States. reliminary treaties between Great Britain, France, and Spain were oncluded on January 20, 1783, and definitive treaties between all our countries were finally signed on September 3, 1783. Word of e signing of the treaties reached America in November. Fol- owing the receipt of this news, the British commander in chief, ir Guy Carleton, evacuated the city of New York and the Con- nental Army marched into the city on November 25, 1783. In reporting this event, the printers of the *Pennsylvania Gazette* stated: "We congratulate our fellow-citizens on this important day!—It loudly demands LAUS DEO from the United States in general, and from the late dispersed and exiled inhabitants of this city in particular.—May it not be the language of their lips only, but may it be engraven on their hearts, and expressed in their future lives!"[33] Patriot printers rejoiced over this event because they knew that the British withdrawal from New York City truly marked the end of the war.

But the Patriot printers could not resist doing more than just rejoicing over the victory. They also criticized the British regulars for their actions during the withdrawal. An anonymous writer in the *Pennsylvania Gazette* criticized them for property destruction:

> Yesterday gave us our city. To the honour of Britain, let it be published in every newspaper, that to add to their name (which has already been branded with every kind of infamy) they cut away the halliards from the flag-staff in the fort (formerly Fort George) and likewise greased the post, so that we were obliged to have a ladder to fix a new rope. Invention prevented any delay; for the glorious stripes were fixed in the sod, and discharge of thirteen fired. The city has been remarkably quiet. A few days will, I hope, produce a little scrutiny, when Tories take care.[34]

Another anonymous writer in the *Independent Chronicle* declared that the British actions showed that the Americans had a better character and attitude:

> The character of the British army exemplified, on their precipitate flight from this city, in cutting away the halliards of, and greasing the flag staff in the fort lately called Fort George, strongly marks the

> character of those people, and demonstrates their meanness of spirit, and indisposition to conciliate the affections of the Americans; men who have proved themselves their superior in every virtue, and who may without arrogance be denominated their Conquerors.[35]

hus, Americans had won the war because they fought hard and onorably until victory was achieved.

The Patriot printers also sought to convince their readers that merica's success was foreordained. The public prints insisted that od had chosen America for a special mission; its effort for independence was to be a shining example for the rest of the world to ollow. Many felt that another part of the British Empire, Ireland, ould be the first to follow the American model. Interest in Britn's troubles in Ireland increased, because "the Independence of ese States, & the Efforts of our Allies, have prepared the way for e Freedom of Ireland."[36] In 1782, a local essayist in the *Massachutts Spy* urged the Irish to quickly follow the American example:

> Now is the Time! Providence opened the pearly gate to America, she flew to enter, cut her way through the opposing legions of Britain, and hath taken her seat in the TEMPLE OF LIBERTY.— Shall Ireland pause, while the portals are open, and her American sister beckons her to come in and join the triumphant circle of the FREE! . . . ON God and yourselves depend. Let your own counsels make your laws, and your own swords defend them; then and not until then can you be free. . . . LET IRELAND AND AMERICA TAKE CARE OF THEMSELVES![37]

uch statements reflected a hope that America's victory over Brith tyranny would only be the first of many more to come in the ture.

The end of the fighting in 1781 and the peace treaty in 1783 promised fulfillment of these dreams of future greatness expressed in the Patriot newspapers. The press had played an integral part in the overall war effort by making it a national concern. The widespread reprinting of essays and letters along with accounts of actions in other colonies served to create a unity of ideas and feelings about the war on the part of many Americans. This proved particularly crucial throughout the country as the fighting jumped from place to place throughout the course of the war. The public prints performed a crucial task in convincing their readers that the war was everyone's fight even though the center of operations had shifted elsewhere. The overall result was the solidarity of purpose needed for a successful revolution. This solidarity had been reflected in the press as the newspapers presented a united front in the face of the enemy.

NINE

# CONCLUSION

The fighting in the American Revolution ended in 1781, but it took two more years to negotiate a peace treaty to finally end the conflict. Though the war lasted until 1783, almost everyone in America believed that the victory at Yorktown would be decisive in persuading the British to relinquish the American colonies. And this proved to be true. Most Americans breathed a sigh of relief that the fighting was apparently over. Even many of the Loyalists expressed some relief at the end of the conflict.

Patriot Americans rejoiced over their successful fight for independence, but they also expressed happiness over the fact that the sufferings and trials produced by the war had now ended. This proved true for printers who had suffered much during the Revolution. For many printers, their readership went up during the war and the circulations of their newspapers increased because of interest in military events, but the damages produced by the war were often greater than the benefits. Military operations disrupted publishing, emotional fervor created by the dangers and passions of the war restricted freedom of the press, news coverage was made complicated and difficult, printing materials were in short supply, and newspapers struggled to survive.

When the American Revolution began in 1775, thirty-seven newspapers appeared throughout the colonies. Only twenty of them survived until the end of the war. Printers founded thirty-three new publications during the war, of which fifteen survived the war, meaning that, in all, thirty-five newspapers were being published in the new country. Although a net loss of two newspapers over the course of the Revolution sounds minor, the numbers of starts and losses show a much larger impact from the war. During the course of the Revolution, seventy different newspapers were published. Readership had increased as people sought out newspapers in an effort to keep up with what was happening elsewhere. By the time independence was declared in July 1776, publication totals approached 40,000 printed copies sold to the public, and most issues were read by many people, meaning the actual readership would have been much larger.

But the fighting in the American Revolution also created many problems for printers. Some of these problems were new ones like dealing with new state government entities and officials trying to oversee what the newspapers published, while the war exacerbated some of the difficulties always present in running a print shop. Finding enough help to run the business could prove difficult and printers often advertised in the pages of their newspapers for apprentices and journeymen to work in the shop. The war made acquiring employees more difficult, as many young men went off to fight. Government officials sometimes excused printers and their employees from militia duty, but that did not always solve the problem. Advertisements for help continued throughout the war, but with little success. In April 1776, Samuel Hall moved his printing office from Cambridge to Boston after the British evacuated Massachusetts. As the printer of the *New England Chronicle,* Hall promised "constant Employ, good Wages, and punctual Payment" in his advertisement for journeymen printers. This promise apparently did not help him acquire the employees he needed for his business to succeed because he sold the business to Nathaniel Willis and Edward E. Powars in June 1776.[1]

Also, many of the necessary supplies for producing a newspaper were imported from Europe. The war cut off access to imported supplies of presses, types, ink, and paper from Great Britain. In 1778, Nathaniel Willis and Edward E. Powars, the printers of the *Independent Chronicle* in Boston, tried to explain the financial impact of the loss of access to imported supplies: "Our types (very costly in the cheapest times) and many other items which compose the apparatus of our office, are of foreign manufacture; therefore the great difficulty of procuring a new set (and our old will soon be unfit for service) and the prodigiously enhanced price of them, when obtained, must be obvious to all."[2] Americans attempted to produce the needed materials, but could not keep up with demand. Efforts to produce these supplies locally actually predated the Revolution. Christopher Sower Jr. of Germantown, Pennsylvania, built his own printing presses as early as 1750. But the domestic manufacture of presses grew slowly. By 1776, presses were being produced in Philadelphia, Pennsylvania, and Hartford, Connecticut. But it would not be until the 1790s that enough printing presses were produced in America to satisfy demand. A number of people also established type foundries in the decade prior to the Revolution, but with little success because the market was not large enough for the business to prosper. David Mitchelson tried in 1768 while Abel Buell tried in 1769 and again in 1781. All three efforts failed. In 1778, Isaiah Thomas complained in the *Massachusetts Spy* that "printing utensils are no where to be procured in this country at present, types in particular, are not made in America."[3] Maintaining enough type to run the print shop became increasingly difficult throughout the Revolution.

The necessary paper and ink supplies also proved difficult to obtain. Printers had begun to make their own ink long before the nonimportation agreements began in 1765, but it never became more than a cottage industry for satisfying the needs of an individual shop. Most printers believed it was too much trouble and took too much time to produce the amount of ink they needed for all their printing work, so they desired to keep importing it from elsewhere if at all possible and only produced enough to keep their presses running when imports were not available. Paper mills had existed in the American colonies since the late 1600s and more had been built in the intervening years, but the quality was poor compared with imported paper, and the mills could not produce enough to meet the needs of American printers, so a substantial amount had to be imported. However, importations of paper from Great Britain had been greatly reduced following the adoption of the Stamp Act in 1765, and were totally cut off with the advent of the Revolution in 1775. Local production of paper became essential if print shops were to remain in operation. For example, in December 1775, Ebenezer Watson had to suspend publication of the *Connecticut Courant* for lack of paper. To prevent a recurrence, Watson, like many printers, began to take an active interest in papermaking ventures in order to secure a steady supply. He built a paper mill in 1776 in partnership with Austin Ledyard, and announced the new mill in his newspaper, soliciting donations of rags from his readers to be used for making paper.[4]

As the Revolution got underway, many other printers urged their readers to save rags for making paper in order to contribute to the fight for independence. In January 1777 the *Connecticut Journal* carried the following plea: "The inducement therefore must arise from the love of our country, and the benefit that individuals will receive, in a full enjoyment of freedom and property in common with the whole community in general."[5] John Trumbull, printer of the *Norwich Packet* in Connecticut, worried that the lack of paper caused by the scarcity of rags would mean that "the Press, that useful vehicle of instruction and amusement" would cease to function.[6] In particular, printers appealed to women to save rags as an easy way for them, as noncombatants, to contribute to the success of the war effort. Isaiah Thomas ran a recurring advertisement in the *Massachusetts Spy*:

> Earnestly requested that the fair Daughters of Liberty in this extensive Country, would not neglect to serve their country, by saving for the Paper-Mill at Sutton, all Linen and Cotton-and-Linen Rags, be they ever so small, as they are equally good for the purpose of making paper, as those that are larger. A bag hung at one corner of a room would be the means of saving many which would be otherwise lost. If the Ladies should not make a fortune by that piece of economy, they will at least have the satisfaction of knowing that they are doing an essential service to the community.[7]

Such efforts would help keep the presses running and the newspapers being published so that people throughout the colonies could know how the war effort was going.

Printers often reduced the size of their newspaper or did not publish at all because of the lack of the necessary supplies. A variety of problems, not always related to the Revolution, could delay production or result in a smaller edition of a newspaper. A common problem was bad weather, which made acquiring paper or news from elsewhere very difficult. Newspaper printers often commented that their publication was smaller because of a paper shortage caused by the lack of delivery during a time of bad weather.[8] In early 1780, Isaiah Thomas described the overall impact of the bad weather on the printing business in New England: "The Printers of News-Papers in Boston and Hartford, have published only half a sheet weekly, for four or five weeks past. The inclement season having prevented their getting a supply of paper from the mills: The same difficulty with regard to paper attends the publisher of the *Massachusetts Spy*."[9]

When problems like this occurred, printers apologized for the size and appearance of their newspapers. A number of papers in New England had trouble acquiring enough paper to publish in the fall of 1775 because of the cessation of trade with Great Britain. In September, Ebenezer Watson expressed regret over the state of his paper, but declared that it was better to print what he could rather than not to publish at all because "half a loaf, however, is better than no bread."[10] Less than a month later, Daniel Fowle, printer of the *New Hampshire Gazette* in Portsmouth, reached a similar conclusion, stating that "brown Bread with Liberty, will please more, than white with Slavery."[11] Eighteenth-century newspaper printers clearly wanted to print a quality product if at all possible, but the Revolution produced many publication problems that often could not be overcome.

The Revolution also exacerbated problems that printers faced in acquiring information to print. The normal sources of sharing newspapers sometimes failed because of mail delivery issues. The printers thus sought other sources of news, primarily by urging their readers to share any information they received so that the news could easily be shared with others through the newspapers. For example, in October 1775, the *Boston News-Letter* carried the following notice: "The Publisher would be extremely obliged to Gentlemen, into whose Hands Papers or Articles of Intelligence may accidentally fall, if they would be so kind as to favor him with them: They would thereby not only oblige the Printer, but afford the greatest Satisfaction to the Public."[12] All printers, both Patriots and Loyalists, hoped that such information would fill the news void created by the war.

The war also exacerbated the printers' precarious financial situation. Increasing costs because of scarcity and inflation caused by the Revolution pushed many printers to print regular calls in their newspapers urging their subscribers to pay their bills. In April 1775, Samuel Hall, printer of the *Essex Gazette* in Salem, Massachusetts, published the following request: "Our Customers are desired to consider the Difficulties with which we, in common with our country, are now involved; and that we cannot continue our Business without regular and punctual Payments. We shall be obliged to discontinue sending the Gazette to all who are indebted for more than one Year, unless they make immediate Payment."[13] Apparently, his customers did not comply with this request because, in May 1775, Hall ceased printing the *Essex Gazette* and began publishing the *New England Chronicle* in Cambridge, Massachusetts. He hoped that the move would improve his financial position by increasing his subscribers because he would now have easier access to more information regarding the British occupation of Boston since he was now just across the river from Boston.

On several occasions, Isaiah Thomas also requested that his customers pay their bills so that he could continue in business. In 1781, he criticized those readers who only subscribed during the summer months because there was no news during the winter because of mail delays. To do so was to endanger the continuation of the newspaper because the printer could not pay his bills. This criticism produced a poetic agreement in the *Pennsylvania Journal* that was reprinted in the *Newport Mercury:*

> Says Thomas, our neighbors have wrote to the Printer,
> To stop sending newspapers during the winter;
> For living is hard, and provisions are dear,
> And there's seldom much news at this time of the year;
> But in summer the papers more news will contain,
> And then or in spring we may take them again.
> Says John, neighbour Thomas, your scheme makes me smile;
> But how is the Printer to live the meanwhile?
> If times are so hard, as you do not deny,
> The Printer, unless he's supported, must die.
> Till summer or spring, he can never survive,
> Unless through the winter you keep him alive,
> And if you once starve him, it will be in vain
> To expect that he will ever serve you again.
> Says Thomas, indeed we did none of us think,
> That Printers could feel, or could want meat or drink,
> Or like other people would cloathing require,
> Or wood for the warming themselves with a fire;
> And if none of these wants any trouble could pause,
> They might live as the bears do by sucking their claws.[14]

Getting subscribers to pay their bills could be a very frustrating process at any time, but the financial strains produced by the Revolution only made it more necessary to receive subscription payments in order to offset the other costs produced by the war.

Of course, the actual fighting in the Revolution also had an impact on printers, as the communities they lived in were affected by the activities of the armies nearby. For example, in December 1776, both the *Connecticut Gazette* in New London and the *Providence Gazette* in Rhode Island appeared on only a half sheet of paper because of a lack of paper. The appearance of British ships off the coast made it impossible to acquire the needed paper from the usual paper mills in other communities. In the case of New London, there was no actual attack at that time. The area around Providence, however, witnessed several British raids.[15]

Coastal towns dealt with such concerns throughout the war. In the summer of 1779, Thomas and Samuel Green, printers of the *Connecticut Journal* in New Haven, declared that "the confusion in the town, since our visit from the enemy, the disorder our office was put in &c. has prevented our publishing till to-day. The first side of this paper was printed before the enemy's approach."[16] The issue in question was dated July 7, but it did not actually appear until July 21. The Greens were very happy that they were able to finish their production because that did not always prove to be true when the fighting got close by.

A number of printers also had to move their offices in the face of the approach of the enemy. For Patriot printers, this first happened in Boston as printers sought to keep printing their newspapers after the Battles of Lexington and Concord. Isaiah Thomas moved his printing press from Boston to Worcester. He had actually been approached about publishing a newspaper in Worcester earlier in 1775 and had been making plans to issue the *Worcester Gazette* while continuing the *Massachusetts Spy* in Boston. But the fighting changed his plans and he moved the *Spy:* "I accordingly removed my Printing Utensils to this Place, and escaped myself from Boston on the memorable 19th of April 1775, which will be remembered in the future as the Anniversary of the Battle of Lexington." He requested the help of the people of Worcester in his efforts to continue the paper in order to provide them information about the war: "I beg the Assistance of all the Friends to our righteous cause to circulate this Paper.—They may rely that the utmost of my poor Endeavours shall be used to maintain those Rights and Priviledges for which we and our Fathers have bled! and that all possible care will be taken to procure the most interesting and authentic Intelligence."[17]

Benjamin Edes and John Gill, printers of the *Boston Gazette,* ended their partnership because of the growing conflict. Edes chose to move the *Gazette* to Cambridge in hopes of continuing to publish it in a safer environment. Both Gill and Edes's son Peter remained in Boston and were arrested and put in jail. Peter Edes kept a diary during his time in prison. He was arrested on June 19, 1775, and finally released on October 3, 1775. On August 4, 1775, Edes recorded that "Mr. John Gill, Printer, was brought to gaol and put in our room.—He is charged with printing sedition, treason, and rebellion."[18] Others also took note of what happened to Edes and Gill. James Warren made reports to John Adams in Philadelphia in several letters over the course of the summer of 1775. On May 7, he stated, "By the way I have just heard that Edes has stole out. I wish his partner was with him." Two months later, Warren told Adams that General Thomas Gage had imprisoned Gill and several others until two men loyal to Great Britain were released from jail in Concord and allowed to return to Boston. A deal was worked out between British and Massachusetts leaders and Warren reported in an October letter that Gill had been released.[19]

The fighting at Lexington and Concord also produced the demise of the *Boston Evening-Post,* printed by Thomas and John Fleet. They ceased publication less than a week after the battles occurred, declaring that "the Printers of the Boston Evening-Post hereby inform the Town that they shall desist publishing their Papers after this Day, till Matters are in a more settled state."[20] They hoped to revive the newspaper when things calmed down, but that never happened.

Other Patriot printers faced similar problems. In November 1775, Daniel Fowle moved his press out of Portsmouth, New Hampshire, because of the approach of British forces: "The Printing Press is removed to Greenland, about Six Miles from Portsmouth . . . where any Persons may be supplied with this Paper, that the Course of Intelligence may not be wholly stoped."[21] In late

November 1776, Solomon Southwick buried his press and type in Newport, Rhode Island, and fled just before the British landed and took control of the town. In 1776, John Holt moved his operation from New York City to Kingston and then to Poughkeepsie to avoid the British Army as it took control of that area. When the British captured Charleston in May 1780, Peter Timothy shut down the *Gazette of the State of South-Carolina.* In August, Timothy was arrested with a number of others in Charleston and exiled to St. Augustine, Florida, because they were suspected of plotting to burn the city.

But Patriot printers were not the only ones to face problems because of military activities. And, once more, the problems began in Boston, Massachusetts. A number of newspaper printers had chosen to stay in Boston after the battles of Lexington and Concord because they remained loyal to Great Britain. Margaret Draper and John Howe continued to publish the *Boston News-Letter*—their newspaper was the only one printed in Boston while the city was besieged by the Continental Army. When the British evacuated Boston in March 1776, Draper and Howe had to flee. Draper left with the British Army and went to Halifax, Nova Scotia, and then on to Great Britain. She received a British government pension for the rest of her life because of her support of the British cause in her newspaper in Boston. Howe also left with the Royal Army in March 1776. In January 1777, he went to Newport, Rhode Island, following the British occupation of that port town. There, he established the *Newport Gazette,* which he printed until the British withdrew in October 1779. He then went to Halifax where he began to print the *Halifax Journal* and became the official printer to the local government.

Another Boston printer, John Hicks, also left with the British in March 1776. His experience shows the complications produced by the fighting in Massachusetts in 1776. His father had fought with the militia at Lexington and Concord and had died in the fighting as the colonials attacked the British forces retreating back to Boston. It is unclear whether Hicks was already a Loyalist prior to the fighting, but he clearly sided with Great Britain from that point on. He and Nathaniel Willis had partnered in the publication of the *Massachusetts Gazette and Boston Post-Boy.* Hicks first went to Halifax and then on to England. He later returned to America and partnered with a number of different printers in New York and South Carolina. He returned to Massachusetts about 1785 and spent the rest of his life in Newton.

Other Loyalist printers faced similar crises. Robert Luist Fowle, the nephew and business partner of Daniel Fowle in Portsmouth, New Hampshire, fled to New York City in 1777 to seek the protection of the British Army. He later went to England and received a British pension, but he was able to return to New Hampshire in 1782 after the end of the fighting. Alexander and James Robertson, both from Edinburgh, Scotland, had originally established their American printing business in New York City in 1768 and then moved up the Hudson River to Albany in 1771. They also set up a print shop in Norwich, Connecticut, in 1772. They moved their business back to New York City in 1777 to be closer to the British Army. Alexander remained in New York for the remainder of the war and moved to Nova Scotia when the British evacuated the city. James began to move around with the British Army from New York to Philadelphia to Charleston. He established a Loyalist newspaper in each city that supported the British war effort. Both of these men moved where they did because they could only continue to print under the protection of British authorities. Alexander died in Nova Scotia in 1784 while James returned to Edinburgh after the end of the war.

The most hated Loyalist printer was James Rivington of New York. Because he was very blunt in his criticisms of the revolt against Great Britain, Rivington became the focus of anti-Loyalist feelings and actions on the part of many Americans. Anti-Rivington feelings got so strong in neighboring Connecticut that he was hung in effigy in New Brunswick in April 1775. Patriot newspaper printers took great joy in reviling Rivington and hoped that he would suffer some terrible fate. Rivington had begun publishing the *New-York Gazetteer* in 1773, but had to cease in November 1775 when some armed men from Connecticut destroyed his printing equipment. At that point, Rivington went to Great Britain where he received an appointment as the official printer for the colony of New York. He returned in late 1777 and established the *Royal Gazette,* which he published until the British evacuated the city. Other newspaper printers republished materials from Rivington's paper because sources were so scarce, but they always urged readers to be careful not to believe everything that came from "James Rivington's Loyal, Royal, Lying (what do ye call it) Gazette."[22] Patriot printers also expressed surprise at Rivington's fate when the war ended: "It is reported as an undoubted fact, that Mr. James Rivington, Printer, at New York, was, as soon as our troops entered the city, protected in person, and property, by a guard, and that he will be allowed to reside in the country, for reasons best known to the great men at the helm."[23] This report appeared in a number of newspapers because the printers were surprised that Rivington was not immediately arrested. Reports of Rivington having served as a spy for George Washington surfaced in the years after the Revolution.

Printers on both sides also experienced problems as public officials sought to guide the content of local newspapers to influence readers to support their side in the conflict. There was a lively discussion about the freedom of the press, and how far it should go. For example, Francis Hopkinson, a signer of the Declaration of Independence and member of the Continental Congress, argued that newspapers had to play a constructive role in supporting the fight for independence: "When this privilege is manifestly abused, and the press becomes an engine for sowing the most dangerous dissensions, for spreading false alarms, and undermining the very foundations of government, ought not that government upon the plain principles of self-preservation to silence, by its own authority, such a daring violator of its peace, and tear from its bosom the serpent that would sting it to death?"[24]

Printers found themselves facing all sorts of restrictions from public officials because of materials they published in their newspapers. In January 1776, Daniel Fowle was summoned to appear before the New Hampshire legislature because he had published an essay opposing independence in the *New Hampshire Gazette.* The legislature reprimanded him for this action. He then suspended the newspaper. Benjamin Dearborn revived the paper in May 1776 under the new title of *Freeman's Journal.* Fowle became involved in the production of the paper again in December 1776. Not long after beginning publication, Dearborn tried to defend the actions of Fowle and other newspaper printers by praising the freedom of the press. In doing so, he summed up the feelings of many newspaper printers on this issue:

> The liberty of the Press has ever been held as one of the most sacred rights of a free people, and when we are abridged of that invaluable priviledge, farewell to Peace, Liberty, and Safety, farewell to Learning Knowledge and Truth, farewell all that is dear to us; we must ever after grope in darkness, thick darkness, that may even be felt: may Heaven forbid such a deprivation, and long continue to us this invaluable blessing.[25]

Shortly after the war ended, Isaiah Thomas declared that "the Press is the great Palladium of Liberty, every man may express his sentiments—every man may be acquainted with what his rulers are doing—to what use publick property is put, and guard against the encroachments of Tyranny, &c."[26]

But others were not so free with their praise for the free press. In 1776, Robert Luist Fowle concluded that "sometimes it so happens; that it is thought and may be best, not to allow the full Liberty of the Press, in the strictest Sense of the Words, least some Disaffected Persons might abuse it."[27] The following year General Arthur St. Clair, in a letter to the *Boston Gazette,* declared:

> The liberty of the press is a priviledge that a free people, and who mean to preserve their freedom, ought to guard with the most watchful jealousy; at the same time they should be careful to prevent the press from becoming licentious. When it is perverted to the circulating falsehood, and thereby raising, and keeping up unreasonable prejudices in the minds of the people, or to the murder of characters, it becomes a nuisance: and when publications which have such tendency, particularly the latter, are generally relished, it is an evidence that the people have lost part at least of that virtue without which liberty cannot long subsist.[28]

Such statements constituted one of the first discussions in American history about what constituted freedom of the press. The issue did not get settled during the American Revolution (and some would argue that it still has not been fully settled). Both Patriot and Loyalist printers faced restrictions on what they could print and tried to argue that a free press meant that they could publish anything they thought necessary. The Loyalist printers suffered the most in this debate and most of them were forced out of business because they failed to adequately support the American cause in the Revolution.

Printers supporting the British cause faded away, but, overall, the Patriot printers as a group managed to keep producing some newspapers even in the face of all of these obstacles. Specific printers and newspapers came and went, but publications supporting the Patriot cause continued to be published throughout the war. Their newspapers played a vital role in the success of the American Revolution. Obviously, during the years of actual fighting, the press provided information about the war. But more than any other institution, the press encouraged the people to support the war effort, becoming the primary morale boosters throughout the Revolutionary era. Printers such as Benjamin Edes and Isaiah Thomas used a variety of means to lift public confidence in the drive for independence. Throughout the war, essays and news stories emphasized the tyranny and corruption of the British and glory and justness of the American cause. Patriot newspapers sought to destroy any lingering ties to Great Britain as well as point out American successes and future prospects. Printers filled their productions with material on the justness of the American cause and the success of the Continental Army in battle. Newspapers also worked to increase public resolve by urging all readers to put the war above all other concerns.

Newspaper printers urged their readers to depend on their publications as a primary source of information about events in America during the war. In the summer of 1776, William Stearns and Daniel Bigelow, printers of the *Massachusetts Spy* in Worcester at the time, summarized the feelings of all the Patriot printers: "At a time when Our All is at stake; when no less than the fate of the States of America is in agitation, then (of all times) the means of conveying intelligence ought to be encouraged."[29] At about the same time, Edward E. Powars and Nathaniel Willis took over the production of the *New England Chronicle* in Boston from Samuel Hall and they promised their readers that they would continue to publish the same types of information: "They may be assured, that the character it has hitherto sustained, in exposing, condemning and execrating the jesuitical and infernal machinations of tories and tyrants, and in rendering due praise and honour to the manly and virtuous supporters of the Glorious Cause of America, we shall, with assiduity and zeal, endeavour to preserve."[30]

Loyalists also recognized the potential impact of newspapers in the conflict. In November 1776, Ambrose Serle, who was secretary to Lord Richard Howe and also in charge of the Loyalist press in New York during the Revolution, wrote a letter to Lord William Dartmouth, the lord privy seal, in which he discussed the newspapers and their impact: "Among other Engines, which have raised the present Commotion next to the indecent Harangues of the Preachers, none has had a more extensive or stronger Influence than the Newspapers of the respective Colonies. One is astonished to see with what Avidity they are sought after, and how implicitly they are believed, by the great Bulk of the People." After describing how popular newspapers were among American readers, Serle went on to urge British authorities to take advantage of the potential impact: "Government may find it expedient, in the Sum of things, to employ this popular Engine."[31]

Newspapers were an important source of information because "newspapers are the histories of the day" because they provided the most readily available source of information about current events in distant locales.[32] According to Powars and Willis, the newspapers had been essential for American freedom and independence: "If the despotic measures and deep-laid plots of a British court had not been freely canvassed and laid open by means of these publications, we might, before this time, have been fast bound by the chains of tyranny."[33] Patriot printers sought to be "a scourge to tyranny"[34] through what they published in their newspapers. And many of their readers believed they succeeded in this goal. For example, "Senex" stated in 1782 that the *Boston Gazette* had been a "most valuable Paper, which has done more Service in support of the Public Cause, than some Thousands that has been spent in support of the War."[35]

Patriot newspaper printers deserved such praise because they did keep their readers informed. During the war, printers filled their newspapers with stories and essays about the fighting. While obviously seeking to help their readers remain knowledgeable about the war, printers also hoped to keep their readers engaged as well. Newspaper efforts to encourage support and involvement and to boost morale went on for years, for the war proved to be a long one. As it came to a close, Benjamin Franklin praised newspapers in general for their usefulness because they provided a means of communicating with great numbers of people that had not existed in the past:

> The ancient Roman and Greek orators could only speak to the number of citizens capable of being assembled within the reach of their voice. Their *writings* had little effect, because the bulk of the people could not read. Now by the press we can speak to nations; and good books and well written pamphlets have great and general influence. The facility, with which the same truths may be repeatedly enforced by placing them daily in different lights in *newspapers,* which are everywhere read, gives a great chance of establishing them. And we now find, that it is not only right to strike while the iron is hot, but that it may be very practicable to heat it by continually striking.[36]

Although Franklin was talking about the impact of all newspapers in increasing communication in the eighteenth century, a major example he would have been familiar with was the newspapers that had supported the Revolution. They had clearly kept striking the iron while it was hot (to use Franklin's metaphor), through both defeat and victory, by their nonstop discussion of the war.

But printers could not print everything. They used the pages of their weekly productions to keep their customers informed about events occurring in America and the rest of the world, but choices had to be made about what went into each paper. In making these choices, the printer made a statement about what issues were important. By emphasizing some topics and downplaying or ignoring others, a printer instructed readers in what they should be thinking about, a concept known to modern-day journalists as "agenda-setting." Journalism scholars debate whether newspapers originate the public agenda, but they agree that the press affects what people talk about through the attention given certain events and topics. The press during the American Revolution fits this model. Through the emphasis placed on various issues, the newspapers played an important role in shaping the agenda of public discussion. As had been true before the Revolution began, printers continued to report on news and events that had nothing to do with the war such as political actions by local governments, problems such as fires and Indian attacks, and local events such as weddings and funerals. But their continual reports on the fighting made it possible for Americans to see the war as a really important issue that they needed to keep up to date about, and people turned to the newspapers to acquire that needed information. As a result, newspaper printers impacted how Americans viewed the conflict with Great Britain and the fight for independence.

The press played an important role during the American Revolution by keeping Americans engaged in the war even when the fighting occurred in distant locales. Some writers used the newspapers to stir up the people's passions against Great Britain, but the press served primarily to keep Americans informed about the progress of the fight with Great Britain. From the moment that the colonials received word of Britain's new taxes in 1764 until news of the peace treaty arrived in 1783, newspapers constituted the major source of information about events and developments in the conflict with Great Britain. In 1783, "Consideration" wrote in the *Vermont Gazette* that "without knowledge among the people, liberty and public happiness cannot exist long in any country; and this necessary knowledge cannot be obtained in any other way than by a general circulation of publick papers."[37] Without the press, many Americans would have known practically nothing about what was happening and could have lost their interest in the outcome of the fight for independence. For example, large-scale fighting ended in New England when the British Army withdrew from Boston in March 1776. But the people remained interested in what was going on in the war with Great Britain for a number of reasons (such as the fact that they had relatives fighting in the various battles throughout America). But newspaper printers also sought to keep their readers interested in the war by printing as much information about the fighting as they could get. Knowledge produces involvement. Patriot printers worked hard to make sure that a loss of interest in the outcome of the Revolution did not occur among the readers of their newspapers.

Patriot newspaper printers sought to keep their readers informed about the events of the war, but they also sought to keep people encouraged about the Revolution. In December 1776, Stearns and Bigelow stated that they hoped the materials they printed in the *Massachusetts Spy* would provide "encouragement to the Public (within their sphere) with respect to the unnatural controversy now subsisting, to keep up a most vigorous opposition to the engines of slavery and bloody oppression."[38] They often put such a positive spin on the reports they published. Military victories and successes were extolled while defeats and setbacks were downplayed and minimized. For example, printers lavished praise on George Washington and the Continental Army for the relatively small victory at Trenton in December 1776 while passing off the loss of a 5,000-man army at Charleston in May 1780 as a minor setback that would quickly be overcome. Printers also wrote off the loss of another southern army at Camden in August 1780 as an unimportant loss while rejoicing over the victory at King's Mountain in October 1780. The Battle of King's Mountain did end up being a major turning point in the war, but newspaper printers did not know that initially. They just focused on the fact that the American forces had beaten the British because that was what they were most concerned about at the moment. Through such strategically biased reporting, newspaper printers helped to boost morale and keep people engaged in the war even when the actual events took place hundreds of miles away.

The public view of newspapers changed during the Revolution as more and more people read them on a regular basis. Almost everyone wanted to find out as much as they could about what was happening in the conflict with Great Britain and the newspapers provided the most available and accessible source of information. So everyone turned to the news sheets to find out what was going on. No longer were the newspapers just purveyors of news and information to the wealthy; now the newspapers belonged to everyone. Much of this change resulted because of the part played by the press in bringing about a successful separation from Great Britain by keeping Americans informed and engaged.

Many people, both contemporaries and historians, have praised the public prints for their efforts on behalf of American independence. Historians of American journalism and the American Revolution, from Isaiah Thomas to Frank Luther Mott to Arthur Schlesinger to Bernard Bailyn, have all praised the newspapers for the role they played in winning independence. But the views of contemporaries can be more enlightening. One essayist, looking back at the Revolution in 1785, exclaimed, "What inflamed with a holy enthusiasm of liberty such numbers of intrepid patriots as dared death in defence of America, during the late sanguinary contest? In a word, to what does this country owe the establishment of her independence? Surely to the illumination of the understanding" that came from reading newspapers.[39] Truly, the Patriot papers published during the Revolution have always been considered influential. But the growing impact of the newspapers during the Revolution helped set the stage for the press to help engender other political changes as the United States moved toward a more democratic political system in the early nineteenth century.

The American colonies had always been a more egalitarian society than those of Europe. Based on the ideas commonly accepted in the eighteenth century, there was only one class of people in America, what contemporary political thinkers called the democratical element. No legally recognized privileged or upper class existed. The press has been referred to as the "fourth estate" because European society was generally divided into royalty, nobility, and commoners. But in eighteenth-century America, it actually constituted a "second estate" because the citizens were all legally part of one group and the press came next. The press complemented the popular element by providing a major source of political information. American newspapers therefore constituted a somewhat unusual institution, unlike any other in the Western world, because of their increasing impact. More and more, newspapers reached out to inform an ever-growing group of readers about their country and the world they lived in. These sources of information became increasingly important as the United States instituted a new form of government in the 1790s and as the nation moved toward a more democratic system in the first half of the nineteenth century.

The press became increasingly open to egalitarian ideas during the second half of the eighteenth century; it reflected developments in the political arena as more and more people not only voted, but also became more directly involved in government, instructing their representatives and seeking offices previously held by their social betters. The public prints likewise contributed to political change. By proclaiming that newspapers were essential for people to keep informed about the doings of their rulers, they implied that all had a right to participate in government to protect their liberties. Historian Gordon Wood asserted that the Revolutionary era produced "a democratization of the mind" whereby public opinion replaced the social and intellectual elite as the guiding force in political circles.[40] Newspapers played an important part in this change by helping shape American public opinion. The American press was far ahead of that in Europe at this time. Even in Britain, hailed by continental thinkers such as Montesquieu as the most enlightened of nations, the press amounted to little more than scandal sheets or government political organs and there really was no widespread outlet for the expression of opinions about politics. But the reality was different in America, beginning in the eighteenth century and continuing ever since then. As both reflectors and formers of public opinion, American newspapers—"this popular engine"—have played an essential role in the democratic evolution of the United States ever since the Revolutionary era.

Newspapers have been an important source of information for Americans for a long time. This proved true for the first time during the American Revolution. There is little doubt that newspapers played an important (and probably an essential) role during the war. When people wanted information about how the war was going elsewhere, they turned to their local newspaper. Their reports were not always accurate, but printers hoped they would boost morale by helping to maintain interest in, and support for, the war effort. By publishing accounts from throughout the colonies, the newspapers helped foster a sense of unity and solidarity of purpose that was essential if Americans were going to win their fight for liberty and independence.

Contemporaries on both sides of the conflict believed that the newspapers played an essential role in the outcome of the war. Both Benjamin Franklin and Ambrose Serle described the press as sort of a machine that should be used extensively to advance the cause. And most Americans concluded that the efforts of Patriot newspaper printers to keep readers informed about the war helped ensure ultimate success by boosting people's morale and rallying Americans to the cause until victory was achieved.

Throughout history, revolutions have generally been won when the people involved have continued to fight until victory was achieved. This was difficult to do in America because the fighting was so spread out and many people were not directly affected throughout the entire war. For the Patriots involved in the American Revolution, the weekly news sheets published throughout America were an essential part of the fight. By keeping people informed about the war's progress, newspapers made winning independence possible.

Americans still rejoice over the fact that the freedom described in the Declaration of Independence became reality because the war was won. They should also rejoice over the information essential to victory that was spread across the country by the newspapers and be thankful to the printers who worked hard to acquire and publish that information. Newspapers were essential in the fight to win independence and thus were essential in the creation of the United States.

# NOTES

## CHAPTER ONE

1. Much of this historiographical discussion first appeared in Carol Sue Humphrey, "The Revolutionary Press: Source of Unity or Division?" *American Journalism* 6 (Fall 1989): 245–56. Many thanks to Jim Martin, editor of *American Journalism,* for permission to use this material.

2. Jeremy Belknap, *The History of New-Hampshire* 2 (Boston: Printed for the author by I. Thomas and E.T. Andrews, 1791): 327.

3. David Ramsay, *The History of the American Revolution* 2 (Philadelphia: R. Aitken, 1789): 319.

4. Isaiah Thomas, *The History of Printing in America* (Worcester, Mass.: Isaiah Thomas, Jr., 1810; reprint, Barre, Mass.: Imprint Society, 1970), 137.

5. Joseph T. Buckingham, *Specimens of Newspaper Literature* 1 (Boston: C. C. Little and J. Brown, 1850): 192.

6. Frederic Hudson, *Journalism in the United States, from 1690 to 1872* (New York: Harper and Brothers, 1873), 102; James Melvin Lee, *History of American Journalism* (Boston: Houghton Mifflin, 1923), 82–99; Willard Grosvenor Bleyer, *Main Currents in the History of American Journalism* (Boston: Houghton Mifflin, 1927), 76, 98; and Robert W. Jones, *Journalism in the United States* (New York: E. P. Dutton and Company, 1947), 145.

7. Frank Luther Mott, *American Journalism: A History, 1690–1960,* 3rd ed. (New York: Macmillan, 1962), 107; and "The Newspaper Coverage of Lexington and Concord," *New England Quarterly* 16 (December 1944): 489–505.

8. Albert Carlos Bates, "Fighting the Revolution With Printer's Ink in Connecticut: The Official Printing of that Colony From Lexington to the Declaration," *Papers of the New Haven Colony Historical Society* 9 (1918):129–60; Rollo G. Silver, "Government Printing in Massachusetts, 1751–1801," *Studies in Bibliography* 16 (1963): 161–200; Rollo G. Silver,

"Aprons Instead of Uniforms: The Practice of Printing, 1776–1787," *Proceedings of the American Antiquarian Society* 87 (1977): 111–94; and C. M. Thomas, "The Publication of Newspapers During the American Revolution," *Journalism Quarterly* 9 (1932): 373.

9. Jim A. Hart, *The Developing Views on the News: Editorial Syndrome, 1500–1800* (Carbondale: Southern Illinois University Press, 1970), 167; and John M. Harrison, "The War of Words: The Role of Our First Editorial Writers in Making a Revolution," in *Newsletters to Newspapers: Eighteenth-Century Journalism,* ed. by Donovan H. Bond and W. Reynolds McLeod (Morgantown: School of Journalism, West Virginia University, 1977), 207.

10. Alfred McClung Lee, "Dunlap and Claypoole: Printers and News Merchants of the Revolution," *Journalism Quarterly* 11 (1934): 160–78; Sidney I. Pomerantz, "The Patriot Newspaper and the American Revolution," in *The Era of the American Revolution,* ed. Richard B. Morris (New York: Columbia University Press, 1939), 331; and Robert M. Ours, "James Rivington: Another Viewpoint," in Bond and McLeod, 230.

11. Arthur M. Schlesinger Sr., "Colonial Newspapers and the Stamp Act," *New England Quarterly* 8 (1935): 63–83; and *Prelude to Independence: The Newspaper War on Great Britain, 1764–1776* (New York: Alfred A. Knopf, 1958), viii, 285, 287.

12. Philip Davidson, *Propaganda in the American Revolution, 1763–1783* (Chapel Hill: University of North Carolina Press, 1941), xv, 410.

13. Carl Berger, *Broadsides and Bayonets: The Propaganda War of the American Revolution,* rev. ed. (San Rafael, Calif.: Presidio Press, 1976 [1961]), 199; Ralph A. Brown, "The *Pennsylvania Ledger:* Tory News Sheet," *Pennsylvania History* 9, (1942): 168–69; Ralph A. Brown, "The *Newport Gazette,* Tory News Sheet," *Rhode Island History* 13 (1954): 97–108 and 14 (1955): 11–20; and Ralph A. Brown, "New Hampshire Editors Win the War," *New England Quarterly* 12 (1939): 35–51.

14. Edwin Emery and Michael Emery, *The Press and America: An Interpretive History of the Mass Media,* 6th ed. (Englewood Cliffs, N.J.: Prentice-Hall, 1988), 47, 58.

15. Robert D. Harlan, "David Hall and the Stamp Act," *Papers of the Bibliographical Society of America* 61 (1967): 13–37; Alfred L. Lorenz, *Hugh Gaine: A Colonial Printer-Editor's Odyssey to Loyalism* (Carbondale: South-

ern Illinois University Press, 1972), 142, 145; Dwight L. Teeter, "John Dunlap: The Political Economy of a Printer's Success," *Journalism Quarterly* 52 (1975): 3–8, 55; William F. Steirer Jr., "A Study in Prudence: Philadelphia's Revolutionary Journalists," *Journalism History* 3 (1976): 16.

16. Robert A. Rutland, *The Newsmongers: Journalism in the Life of the Nation, 1690–1972* (New York: The Dial Press, 1973), 34; Susan Henry, "Margaret Draper, Colonial Printer Who Challenged the Patriots," *Journalism History* 1 (1974): 141–44; Norma Schneider, "Clementina Rind: 'Editor, Daughter, Mother, Wife,'" *Journalism History* 1 (1974): 137–40; Charles L. Cutler, *Connecticut's Revolutionary Press* (Chester, Conn.: Pequot Press, 1975), 7, 20, 28; William F. Steirer, "Riding 'Everyman's Hobby Horse': Journalism in Philadelphia, 1764–1794," in Bond and McLeod, 268; and Thomas C. Leonard, *The Power of the Press: The Birth of American Political Reporting* (New York: Oxford University Press, 1986), 36.

17. This group of historians is sometimes called the neoconservative school, for its emphasis on the Revolution as essentially a conservative movement.

18. Edmund S. Morgan and Helen M. Morgan, *The Stamp Act Crisis: Prologue to Revolution* (Chapel Hill, N.C.: Published for the Institute of Early American History and Culture at Williamsburg, Va., by the University of North Carolina Press, 1953).

19. Bernard Bailyn, *The Ideological Origins of the American Revolution* (Cambridge, Mass.: Belknap Press of Harvard University Press, 1967), 19–21.

20. Maurice R. Cullen, "Middle-Class Democracy and the Press in Colonial America," *Journalism Quarterly* 46 (1969): 531–35; Francis G. Walett, "The Impact of the Stamp Act on the Colonial Press," in Bond and McLeod, 157–69; and Bill F. Chamberlin, "Freedom of Expression in Eighteenth-Century Connecticut: Unanswered Questions," in Bond and McLeod, 257.

21. Sidney Kobre, "The Revolutionary Colonial Press—A Social Interpretation," *Journalism Quarterly* 20 (1943): 194, 202; and *Development of American Journalism* (Dubuque, Iowa: W. C. Brown Company, 1969), 53–100.

22. Janice Potter and Robert M. Calhoon, "The Character and Coherence of the Loyalist Press," in *The Press and the American Revolution,*

ed. by Bernard Bailyn and John B. Hench (Worcester, Mass.: American Antiquarian Society, 1980), 250; Paul Langford, "British Correspondence in the Colonial Press, 1763–1775: A Study in Anglo-American Misunderstanding Before the American Revolution," in Bailyn and Hench, 273–314; Robert M. Weir, "The Role of the Newspaper Press in the Southern Colonies on the Eve of the Revolution: An Interpretation," in Bailyn and Hench, 116; and Stephen Botein, "Printers and the American Revolution," in Bailyn and Hench, 11–58.

23. Willi Paul Adams, "The Colonial German-Language Press and the American Revolution," in Bailyn and Hench, 153, 219.

## CHAPTER TWO

1. *Boston News-Letter,* August 28, 1721.
2. *Pennsylvania Gazette* (Philadelphia), October 2, 1729.
3. *New-York Gazette, or Weekly Post-Boy,* January 22, 1750.
4. Entry for August 20, 1774, John Adams. *Diary and Autobiography of John Adams.* Edited by Lyman H. Butterfield. 4 vols. (Cambridge, Mass.: Belknap Press of the Harvard University Press, 1961) 2:103.
5. See, for example, *Maryland Gazette* (Annapolis), March 21 and 28, 1754; and *Boston Gazette,* April 16–May 21, 1754.
6. *Pennsylvania Gazette* (Philadelphia), May 9, 1754.
7. *Boston Gazette,* July 23, 1754.
8. *Boston Evening-Post,* March 15, 1757.
9. Reprinted in the *Maryland Gazette* (Annapolis), August 12, 1756.
10. *Boston Evening-Post,* September 22, 1760.
11. *Boston Gazette,* August 6, 1759.
12. Frank Luther Mott, *American Journalism: A History, 1690–1960,* 3rd ed. (New York: Macmillan, 1962), 52.

## CHAPTER THREE

1. *Boston Gazette,* May 12, 1766.
2. Ibid., October 7, 1765.

3. *New Hampshire Gazette* (Portsmouth), May 17, 1765.

4. P. H. Giddens, "Maryland and the Stamp Act Controversy," *Maryland Historical Magazine* 27 (1932), 83; Louis Turner Griffith and John Erwin Talmadge, *Georgia Journalism, 1763–1950* (Athens: University of Georgia Press, 1951), 5.

5. *Newport* (R.I.) *Mercury,* June 24, 1765.

6. Letter to the Ministry in London, August 15, 1765, *British Papers Relating to the American Revolution* (Sparks Collection, Harvard College Library, Cambridge, Mass.), 1: 43.

7. *Boston Gazette,* January 27, 1766, Supplement.

8. *Providence* (R.I.) *Gazette,* August 24, 1765.

9. John Adams, "A Dissertation on the Canon and Feudal Law," *Boston Gazette,* August 26, 1765.

10. *New London* (Conn.) *Gazette,* November 1, 1765.

11. *Boston Gazette,* October 7, 1765.

12. Ibid., October 14, 1765.

13. *Boston Evening-Post,* November 4, 1765.

14. *Constitutional Courant* (Woodbridge, N.J.), September 21, 1765.

15. *Pennsylvania Journal and Weekly Advertiser* (Philadelphia), October 31, 1765.

16. *New-York Gazette, or Weekly Post-Boy,* November 7, 1765.

17. Newspapers in Canada and the Caribbean colonies did appear on stamped paper as required by British law.

18. *South Carolina Gazette; and Country Journal* (Charleston), December 17, 1765.

19. Ibid., January 14, 1766.

20. Ibid., February 4, 1766.

21. David Ramsay, *The History of the American Revolution* (Philadelphia: R. Aitken, 1789), 1:61–62.

22. *Virginia Gazette* (Williamsburg: Rind), May 16, 1766.

23. "The Pennsylvania Farmer" (John Dickinson), *Pennsylvania Chronicle* (Philadelphia), December 9, 1767.

24. Colden to Lord Shelburne, November 23, 1767, *The Colden Letter Books,* Collections of the New York Historical Society, 9–10 (1876–77), 2:135.

25. Bernard to Lord Shelburne, August 24, 1767, *British Papers Relating*

*to the American Revolution* (Sparks Collection 1, Harvard College Library, Cambridge, Mass.), 74.

26. *Boston Gazette,* September 14, 1767.

27. *Pennsylvania Chronicle* (Philadelphia), November 11, 1767.

28. Ibid., February 15, 1768.

29. *Boston Evening-Post,* December 12, 1768.

30. See, for example, "Journal of Occurrences," June 22, 1769. Quoted in Oliver Morton Dickerson, comp. *Boston Under Military Rule, 1768–1769 as Revealed in a Journal of the Times* (Boston: Chapman and Grimes, 1936), viii.

31. "Journal of Occurrences," October 28, 1768. Quoted in Dickerson, 13.

32. *Boston Chronicle,* December 21, 1767.

33. Ibid., June 1, 1769.

34. Ibid., September 25, 1769.

35. *Boston Gazette,* August 28, 1769; January 15 and 30, 1770.

## CHAPTER FOUR

1. *Boston Gazette,* March 12, 1770.

2. Ibid.

3. Ibid.

4. Ibid.

5. *Pennsylvania Gazette* (Philadelphia), March 22, 1770.

6. *Virginia Gazette* (Williamsburg: Rind), March 29, 1770.

7. *Boston Chronicle,* March 8, 1770.

8. Ibid.

9. *New-York Gazette, and Weekly Mercury,* April 2, 1770.

10. Ibid., December 17, 1770.

11. *Boston Gazette,* March 12, 1770.

12. Ibid., November 5, 1770; *Massachusetts Spy* (Boston), December 7, 1770.

13. *Massachusetts Spy* (Boston), March 7, 1771.

14. *Boston Gazette,* December 10, 1770.

15. Ibid., December 31, 1770.

16. Ibid., January 28, 1771.
17. Ibid., December 17, 1770.
18. Ibid., January 7, 1770.
19. Ibid., December 17, 1770.
20. Ibid., January 21, 1770.
21. Ibid., October 7, 1771.
22. Speech of December 27, 1770, reported in the *Massachusetts Gazette and Boston Post-Boy,* April 22, 1771.
23. *Massachusetts Spy* (Boston), November 22, 1771.
24. Ibid., July 30, 1772.
25. *Pennsylvania Gazette* (Philadelphia), December 8, 1773.
26. *Boston Gazette,* October 25, 1773.
27. *Pennsylvania Chronicle* (Philadelphia), November 15, 1773.
28. *Massachusetts Spy* (Boston), November 11, 1773.
29. *Boston Gazette,* December 20, 1773.
30. *Boston News-Letter,* December 23, 1773.

## CHAPTER FIVE

1. *South Carolina Gazette* (Charleston), June 13, 1774.
2. *Georgia Gazette* (Savannah), July 27, 1774.
3. *Virginia Gazette* (Williamsburg: Purdie and Dixon), August 11, 1774.
4. *North Carolina Gazette* (New Bern), September 2, 1774.
5. *New-York Gazette, and Weekly Mercury,* May 16, 1774.
6. *Boston News-Letter,* November 17, 1774.
7. *Boston Gazette,* September 27, 1773.
8. Ibid., December 27, 1773.
9. *New York Journal,* December 15, 1774.
10. *New-York Gazetteer,* August 25, 1774.
11. *Pennsylvania Journal* (Philadelphia), August 31, 1774.
12. *Boston Gazette,* May 30, 1774.
13. *New-York Journal,* June 30, 1774.
14. *New-York Gazetteer,* July 7, 1774.
15. *New Hampshire Gazette* (Portsmouth), July 22, 1774.
16. *New-York Journal,* August 4, 1774.

17. Ibid.

18. *Virginia Gazette* (Williamsburg: Purdie and Dixon), October 6, 1774.

19. *South Carolina Gazette* (Charleston), as quoted in the *Virginia Gazette* (Williamsburg: Pinkney), December 15, 1774.

20. *Pennsylvania Packet* (Philadelphia), November 14, 1774, reprinted in the *New York Journal,* November 24; *Virginia Gazette* (Williamsburg: Purdie and Dixon), November 24; *Connecticut Journal* (New Haven), November 25; *Massachusetts Gazette and Boston Post-Boy,* November 28; *New-York Gazetteer,* December 1; *Providence* (R.I.) *Gazette,* December 7; *Massachusetts Spy* (Boston), December 8; and *Essex Gazette* (Salem, Mass.), December 20.

21. *South Carolina Gazette* (Charleston), November 11, 1774.

22. *New-York Gazetteer,* January 1, 1775.

23. *North Carolina Gazette* (Wilmington), February 12, 1765.

24. *New-York Journal,* January 5, 1775.

25. *New-York Gazetteer,* September 2, 1774.

26. Ibid., December 15, 1774.

27. *Boston News-Letter,* April 20, 1775.

28. *Essex Gazette* (Salem, Mass.), April 25, 1775.

29. *Essex Journal* (Newburyport, Mass.), April 26, 1775.

30. *Providence* (R.I.) *Gazette,* April 22, 1775.

31. *Pennsylvania Gazette* (Philadelphia), April 27, 1775, Postscript.

32. *New-York Gazette, and Weekly Mercury,* May 22, 1775.

33. *New-York Gazetteer,* April 27, 1775.

34. Ibid., May 25, 1775.

35. *Massachusetts Spy* (Worcester), May 3, 1775.

36. Ibid., May 10, 1775.

37. *Newport* (R.I.) *Mercury,* May 8, 1775.

## CHAPTER SIX

1. *Pennsylvania Packet* (Philadelphia), June 26, 1775.

2. Ibid., July 3, 1775.

3. *Pennsylvania Gazette* (Philadelphia), June 28, 1775.
4. *Virginia Gazette* (Williamsburg: Dixon and Hunter), July 15, 1775.
5. *Pennsylvania Gazette* (Philadelphia), July 12, 1775.
6. *Connecticut Courant* (Hartford), July 10, 1775.
7. *Virginia Gazette* (Williamsburg: Dixon and Hunter), July 22, 1775.
8. *Boston Gazette,* June 19, 1775.
9. *Virginia Gazette* (Williamsburg: Dixon and Hunter), July 15, 1775.
10. *Connecticut Courant (*Hartford), June 26. 1775.
11. *New England Chronicle* (Cambridge, Mass.), September 28, 1775.
12. *Pennsylvania Packet* (Philadelphia), January 2, 1775.
13. *New-York Gazette, and Weekly Mercury,* April 1, 1776.
14. *New Hampshire Gazette* (Portsmouth), September 12, 1775.
15. *Virginia Gazette* (Williamsburg: Pinkney), December 20, 1775.
16. *Pennsylvania Journal* (Philadelphia), October 18, 1775.
17. *Virginia Gazette* (Williamsburg: Pinkney), February 3, 1776.
18. *New-York Gazette, or Weekly Post-Boy,* April 11, 1768.
19. *Boston Gazette,* October 11, 1773.
20. *Pennsylvania Ledger* (Philadelphia), March 16, 1776.
21. *New-York Gazette, and Weekly Mercury,* April 8, 1776.
22. *Pennsylvania Packet* (Philadelphia), February 12, 1776.
23. *New-York Gazette, and Weekly Mercury,* January 24, 1776.
24. *Virginia Gazette* (Williamsburg: Dixon and Hunter), April 20, 1776.
25. *Pennsylvania Journal* (Philadelphia), March 6, 1776.
26. *Pennsylvania Evening Post* (Philadelphia), February 17, 1776.
27. *Constitutional Gazette* (New York), May 8, 1776.
28. *Boston Gazette,* April 14, 1776.
29. *New York Packet,* March 7, 1776.
30. *Connecticut Courant* (Hartford), April 22, 1776.
31. *Virginia Gazette* (Williamsburg: Purdie), May 17, 1776.
32. *Pennsylvania Evening Post* (Philadelphia), July 2, 1776.
33. *Massachusetts Spy* (Worcester), July 10, 1776.
34. *New Hampshire Gazette* (Portsmouth), July 13, 1776.
35. *Virginia Gazette* (Williamsburg: Dixon and Hunter), August 10, 1776.
36. Ibid., July 26, 1776.
37. *Pennsylvania Evening Post* (Philadelphia), August 15, 1776.

## CHAPTER SEVEN

1. *New-York Gazette, and Weekly Mercury,* December 30, 1776.

2. *Virginia Gazette* (Williamsburg: Dixon and Hunter), January 10, 1777.

3. *Virginia Gazette* (Williamsburg: Purdie), October 31, 1777.

4. *Boston Gazette,* November 10, 1777.

5. *Royal Gazette* (New York), October 25, 1777.

6. *Virginia Gazette* (Williamsburg: Dixon and Hunter), October 24, 1777.

7. Ibid.

8. *New-York Gazette, and Weekly Mercury,* October 20, 1777.

9. John Adams to Nathanael Greene, May 9, 1777, *The Papers of General Nathanael Greene,* edited by Richard K. Showman, Dennis Michael Conrad, and Roger N. Parks, 13 vols. (Chapel Hill: Published for the Rhode Island Historical Society by the University of North Carolina Press, 1976–2005) 2:75.

10. *Connecticut Gazette* (New London), June 29, 1781.

11. George Washington to the President of the Continental Congress, May 5, 1777, *The Writings of George Washington, 1745–1799,* edited by John C. Fitzpatrick, 39 vols. (Washington, D.C.: United States Government Printing Office, 1931–44) 8:17.

12. John Carter to Joseph Trumbull, March 6, 1776, Connecticut Historical Society.

13. *New Hampshire Gazette* (Exeter), July 6, 1776.

14. *Massachusetts Spy* (Worcester), July 10, 1776.

15. *Connecticut Courant* (Hartford), April 22, 1776.

16. *Pennsylvania Journal* (Philadelphia), December 19, 1776.

17. *Boston Gazette,* June 2, 1777.

18. Ibid., August 25, 1777.

19. Ibid., September 29, 1777.

20. Ibid., April 20, 1778.

21. Ibid., February 19, 1776.

22. "A Dialogue Between the Devil, and George III, Tyrant of Britain." Pamphlet first printed in Boston in 1782. Reprinted in the *Maryland Chronicle* (Fredericktown), June 27, 1787.

23. *Boston Gazette,* January 22, 1776.

24. Thomas Paine, *The Crisis No. 4.* Originally published as a pamphlet, but reprinted in numerous newspapers (including the *Connecticut Gazette* [New London], October 3, 1777).

25. *Connecticut Journal* (New Haven), August 23, 1775.

26. *Boston Gazette,* December 10, 1779.

27. *New Jersey Journal* (Chatham), September 4, 1780. Reprinted in the *Independent Chronicle* (Boston), October 12, 1780.

28. *Massachusetts Spy* (Worcester), January 23, 1777.

29. *Newport* (R.I.) *Mercury,* March 25, 1776.

30. *Providence* (R.I.) *Gazette,* January 10, 1778.

31. *American Journal* (Providence, R.I.), July 15, 1779.

32. *Salem* (Mass.) *Gazette,* December 6, 1781.

33. *Boston Gazette,* August 14, 1775.

34. *Providence* (R.I.) *Gazette,* January 25, 1777.

35. *Continental Journal* (Boston), April 17, 1783.

36. *Newport* (R.I.) *Mercury,* June 19, 1775.

37. *Connecticut Courant* (Hartford), April 8, 1776.

38. *Continental Journal* (Boston), June 19, 1783.

39. *Newport* (R.I.) *Gazette,* May 27, 1777.

40. Ibid.

41. Ibid., July 5, 1777.

42. *American Journal* (Providence, R.I.), December 16, 1779.

43. *Virginia Gazette* (Williamsburg: Dixon and Hunter), September 14, 1776.

44. *American Journal* (Providence, R.I.), December 16, 1779.

45. *Independent Chronicle* (Boston), July 10, 1777.

46. *Independent Ledger* (Boston), August 24, 1778.

47. *New Hampshire Gazette* (Portsmouth), July 30, 1781.

48. *Providence* (R.I.) *Gazette,* March 29, 1777.

49. *Norwich* (Conn.) *Packet,* July 28, 1777.

50. *New Hampshire Gazette* (Portsmouth), August 21, 1781.

51. *Boston Gazette,* November 13, 1780.

52. *Continental Journal* (Boston), May 9, 1782.

53. *Massachusetts Spy* (Worcester), November 2, 1780.

54. *Boston Gazette,* November 13, 1780.

55. *Massachusetts Spy* (Worcester), November 2, 1780; *Boston Gazette,* November 6, 1780, Supplement; *American Journal* (Providence, R.I.), November 13, 1780, Extraordinary.

56. *Vermont Gazette* (Westminister), July 9, 1781.

57. *American Journal* (Providence, R.I.), August 15, 1781.

58. *New Hampshire Gazette* (Portsmouth), October 14, 1780.

59. *Providence* (R.I.) *Gazette,* November 29, 1780.

60. *American Journal* (Providence, R.I.), November 25, 1780.

61. *New Hampshire Gazette* (Portsmouth), August 20, 1781.

62. *Norwich* (Conn.) *Packet,* November 21, 1780.

63. *Connecticut Courant* (Hartford), May 7, 1782.

64. Ibid., November 7, 1780.

65. *Providence* (R.I.) *Gazette,* October 6, 1781.

66. *Massachusetts Spy* (Worcester), June 28, 1776.

67. *Boston Gazette,* June 9, 1783.

68. *Providence* (R.I.) *Gazette,* May 17, 1777.

69. *Independent Chronicle* (Boston), May 28, 1778.

70. Ibid., October 12, 1780.

## CHAPTER EIGHT

1. *Boston Gazette,* May 8, 1780, Supplement.

2. Reprinted in the *Connecticut Courant* (Hartford), June 6, 1780—Stated to be from the May 29, 1780, extraordinary issue of the *Royal Gazette* (New York).

3. *New Jersey Gazette* (Trenton), July 19, 1780.

4. *American Journal* (Providence, R.I.), July 12, 1780.

5. *New Hampshire Gazette* (Portsmouth), July 22, 1780.

6. *Boston Gazette,* September 25, 1780.

7. *Royal Gazette* (New York), September 6, 1780.

8. *New-York Gazette, and Weekly Mercury,* September 11, 1780.

9. Ibid., September 18, 1780.

10. *New York Packet* (Fishkill), September 14, 1780.

11. *Pennsylvania Gazette* (Philadelphia), September 20, 1780.

12. *Independent Chronicle* (Boston), September 21, 1780.

13. *Pennsylvania Gazette* (Philadelphia), October 25, 1780.
14. *Boston Gazette,* March 12, 1781.
15. *Pennsylvania Gazette* (Philadelphia), February 14, 1781.
16. Ibid., April 4, 1781.
17. *Connecticut Courant* (Hartford), April 10, 1781.
18. *Boston Gazette,* April 30, 1781.
19. *Pennsylvania Gazette* (Philadelphia), October 24, 1781.
20. *Freeman's Journal* (Philadelphia), October 31, 1781.
21. *Salem* (Mass.) *Gazette,* November 1, 1781.
22. *Royal Gazette* (New York), November 7, 1781.
23. *Newport* (R.I.) *Mercury,* October 27, 1781.
24. *New Hampshire Gazette* (Portsmouth), October 27, 1781.
25. *Pennsylvania Packet* (Philadelphia), November 3, 1781.
26. *Connecticut Courant* (Hartford), November 20, 1781.
27. *New Hampshire Gazette* (Portsmouth), December 22, 1781.
28. *Boston Gazette,* December 10, 1781.
29. *Connecticut Courant* (Hartford), July 2, 1782.
30. *New-York Gazette, and Weekly Mercury,* February 17, 1783.
31. *Massachusetts Spy* (Worcester), February 27, 1783.
32. *Boston Gazette,* June 9, 1783.
33. *Pennsylvania Gazette* (Philadelphia), December 3, 1783.
34. Ibid., December 3, 1783.
35. *Independent Chronicle* (Boston), December 18, 1783.
36. *Connecticut Journal* (New Haven), March 15, 1780.
37. *Massachusetts Spy* (Worcester), August 1, 1782.

## CHAPTER NINE

1. *New England Chronicle* (Boston), June 20, 1776.
2. *Independent Chronicle* (Boston), March 12, 1778.
3. *Massachusetts Spy* (Worcester), February 12, 1778.
4. *Connecticut Courant* (Hartford), November 14, 1776.
5. *Connecticut Journal* (New Haven), January 30, 1777.
6. *Norwich* (Conn.) *Packet,* March 30, 1778.
7. *Massachusetts Spy* (Worcester), November 26, 1778.

8. See, for example, *Massachusetts Spy* (Worcester), December 25, 1777; *Boston Evening-Post,* January 8–February 26, 1780; *Boston Gazette,* January 10, 1780; *Independent Ledger* (Boston), January 17, 1780.

9. *Massachusetts Spy* (Worcester), February 3, 1780.

10. *Connecticut Courant* (Hartford), September 11, 1775.

11. *New Hampshire Gazette* (Portsmouth), October 3, 1775.

12. *Boston News-Letter,* October 26. 1775.

13. *Essex Gazette* (Salem, Mass.), April 25, 1775.

14. *Newport* (R.I.) *Mercury,* March 3, 1781.

15. *Connecticut Gazette* (New London), December 6, 1776; *Providence* (R.I.) *Gazette,* December 14, 1776.

16. *Connecticut Journal* (New Haven), July 7 (21), 1779.

17. *Massachusetts Spy* (Worcester), May 3, 1775.

18. Peter Edes's Diary, Massachusetts Historical Society.

19. James Warren to John Adams, May 7, August 9, October 20, 1775. "The Warren-Adams Letters, Being Chiefly a Correspondence among John Adams, Samuel Adams, and James Warren, 1743–1777," *Collections of the Massachusetts Historical Society,* 72 (1917): 49, 100, 151.

20. *Boston Evening-Post,* April 24 1775.

21. *New Hampshire Gazette* (Portsmouth), November 2, 1775.

22. *Boston Gazette,* June 15, 1778.

23. *Massachusetts Gazette* (Springfield), December 16, 1783.

24. *Pennsylvania Evening Post* (Philadelphia), November 16, 1776.

25. *Freeman's Journal* (Portsmouth, N. H.), May 25, 1776.

26. *Massachusetts Spy* (Worcester), October 16, 1783.

27. *New Hampshire Gazette* (Exeter), June 1, 1776.

28. *Boston Gazette,* August 25, 1777.

29. *Massachusetts Spy* (Worcester), June 21, 1776. Isaiah Thomas had leased the *Spy* to Stearns and Bigelow for a year following the withdrawal of the British from Boston in March 1776.

30. *New England Chronicle* (Cambridge, Mass.), June 13, 1776.

31. Ambrose Serle to Lord Dartmouth, November 26, 1776. Reproduced in Benjamin F. Stevens, *Facsimiles of Manuscripts in European Archives Relating to America, 1773–1783.* 24 vols. (London: Malby and Sons, 1889–95) 24:2046.

32. Letter from Historicus, *New York Packet* (Fishkill), June 24, 1779.

33. *Independent Chronicle* (Boston), March 12, 1778.

34. *Boston Gazette,* February 22, 1779.

35. Ibid., May 6, 1782.

36. Benjamin Franklin to Richard Price, June 13, 1782, *Benjamin Franklin: Writings,* ed. J. A. Leo Lemay (New York: The Library of America, 1987), 1049–50.

37. *Vermont Gazette* (Bennington), October 2, 1783.

38. *Massachusetts Spy* (Worcester), December 11, 1776.

39. *American Herald* (Boston), August 22, 1785; *Salem* (Mass.) *Gazette,* August 23, 1785; *American Mercury* (Hartford, Conn.), August 29, 1785; *Falmouth* (Maine) *Gazette,* September 3, 1785.

40. Gordon S. Wood, "The Democratization of Mind in the American Revolution," in *Leadership in the American Revolution,* edited by Don Higginbotham, Library of Congress Symposia on the American Revolution (Washington, D.C.: Library of Congress, 1974), 63–89.

# BIBLIOGRAPHY

## PRIMARY SOURCES

Adams, John. *Diary and Autobiography of John Adams.* Edited by Lyman H. Butterfield. 4 vols. Cambridge, Mass.: Belknap Press of the Harvard University Press, 1961.

*American Herald* (Boston), 1784–88.

*American Journal* (Providence, R.I.), 1779–81.

*American Mercury* (Hartford, Conn.), 1785.

*Boston Chronicle,* 1767–70.

*Boston Evening-Post,* 1757–75, 1778–80.

*Boston Gazette,* 1754–83.

*Boston News-Letter,* 1721, 1773–75.

*Boston Post-Boy,* 1734–75.

*British Papers Relating to the American Revolution.* Sparks Collection, Harvard College Library, Cambridge, Mass.

Colden, Cadwallader. *The Colden Letter Books.* Collections of the New York Historical Society, vols. 9–10, 1876–77.

*Connecticut Courant* (Hartford), 1775–82.

*Connecticut Gazette* (New London), 1776–81.

*Connecticut Journal* (New Haven), 1774–80.

*Constitutional Courant* (Woodbridge, N.J.), 1765.

*Constitutional Gazette* (New York), 1776.

*Continental Journal* (Boston), 1782–83.

Dickerson, Oliver Morton, comp. *Boston Under Military Rule, 1768–1769 as Revealed in a Journal of the Times.* Boston: Chapman and Grimes, 1936.

*Essex Gazette* (Salem, Mass.), 1774–75.

*Essex Journal* (Newburyport, Mass.), 1775.

*Falmouth* (Maine) *Gazette,* 1785.

Franklin, Benjamin. *Benjamin Franklin: Writings.* Edited by J.A. Leo Lemay. New York: The Library of America, 1987.
*Freeman's Journal* (Portsmouth, N. H.), 1776.
*Freeman's Journal* (Philadelphia), 1781.
*Georgia Gazette* (Savannah), 1774.
Greene, Nathanael. *The Papers of General Nathanael Greene.* Edited by Richard K. Showman, Dennis Michael Conrad, and Roger N. Parks. 13 vols. Chapel Hill: Published for the Rhode Island Historical Society by the University of North Carolina Press, 1976–2005.
*Independent Chronicle* (Boston), 1777–83.
*Independent Ledger* (Boston), 1780–82.
*Maryland Chronicle* (Fredericktown), 1786–88.
*Maryland Gazette* (Annapolis), 1754–56.
*Massachusetts Gazette* (Springfield), 1783.
*Massachusetts Gazette and Boston Post-Boy,* 1771–74.
*Massachusetts Spy* (Boston), 1770–75.
*Massachusetts Spy* (Worcester), 1775–83.
*New England Chronicle* (Cambridge, Mass.), 1775–76.
*New Hampshire Gazette* (Exeter), 1776.
*New Hampshire Gazette* (Portsmouth), 1765–81.
*New Jersey Gazette* (Trenton), 1780.
*New Jersey Journal* (Chatham), 1780.
*New London* (Conn.) *Gazette,* 1765.
*Newport* (R.I.) *Mercury,* 1765, 1775–81.
*New-York Gazette,* 1725–44.
*New-York Gazette, and Weekly Mercury,* 1770–83.
*New-York Gazette, or Weekly Post-Boy,* 1750, 1765–68.
*New-York Gazetteer,* 1774–75.
*New-York Journal,* 1774–75.
*New York Packet,* 1776.
*New York Packet* (Fishkill), 1777–80.
*North Carolina Gazette* (New Bern), 1774.
*North Carolina Gazette* (Wilmington), 1765.
*Norwich* (Conn.) *Packet,* 1777–80.
*Pennsylvania Chronicle* (Philadelphia), 1767–73.
*Pennsylvania Evening Post* (Philadelphia), 1776.

*Pennsylvania Gazette* (Philadelphia), 1729, 1754, 1770–83.
*Pennsylvania Journal* (Philadelphia), 1774–76.
*Pennsylvania Journal and Weekly Advertiser* (Philadelphia), 1765.
*Pennsylvania Ledger* (Philadelphia), 1776.
*Pennsylvania Packet* (Philadelphia), 1774–81.
*Providence* (R.I.) *Gazette,* 1765–81.
*Royal Gazette* (New York), 1777–83.
*Salem* (Mass.) *Gazette,* 1781–85.
*Salem* (R.I.) *Gazette,* 1781.
*South Carolina Gazette* (Charleston), 1774.
*South Carolina Gazette; and Country Journal* (Charleston), 1765–66.
Stevens, Benjamin F. *Facsimiles of Manuscripts in European Archives Relating to America, 1773–1783.* 24 vols. London: Malby and Sons, 1889–95.
*Vermont Gazette* (Bennington), 1783.
*Vermont Gazette* (Westminister), 1781.
*Virginia Gazette* (Williamsburg: Dixon and Hunter), 1776–77.
*Virginia Gazette* (Williamsburg: Pinkney), 1774–76.
*Virginia Gazette* (Williamsburg: Purdie), 1776–77.
*Virginia Gazette* (Williamsburg: Purdie and Dixon), 1774–75.
*Virginia Gazette* (Williamsburg: Rind), 1766–70.
"The Warren-Adams Letters, Being Chiefly a Correspondence Among John Adams, Samuel Adams, and James Warren, 1743–1777." *Collections of the Massachusetts Historical Society* 72 (1917).
Washington, George. *The Writings of George Washington, 1745–1799.* Edited by John C. Fitzpatrick. 39 vols. Washington, D. C.: United States Government Printing Office, 1931–44.

## SECONDARY SOURCES

Adams, Willi Paul. "The Colonial German-Language Press and the American Revolution," in *The Press and the American Revolution,* edited by Bernard Bailyn and John B. Hench, 151–228. Worcester, Mass.: American Antiquarian Society, 1980.
Bailyn, Bernard. *The Ideological Origins of the American Revolution.* Cambridge, Mass.: Belknap Press of Harvard University Press, 1967.

Bates, Albert Carlos. "Fighting the Revolution with Printer's Ink in Connecticut: The Official Printing of That Colony from Lexington to the Declaration." *Papers of the New Haven Colony Historical Society* 9 (1918):129–60.

Belknap, Jeremy. *The History of New-Hampshire.* Boston: Printed for the author by I. Thomas and E.T. Andrews, 1791.

Berger, Carl. *Broadsides and Bayonets: The Propaganda War of the American Revolution,* rev. ed. San Rafael, Calif.: Presidio Press, 1976 (1961).

Bleyer, Willard Grosvenor. *Main Currents in the History of American Journalism.* Boston: Houghton Mifflin, 1927.

Bond, Donovan H., and W. Reynolds McLeod. *Newsletters to Newspapers: Eighteenth-Century Journalism.* Morgantown: School of Journalism, West Virginia University, 1977.

Botein, Stephen. "Printers and the American Revolution," in *The Press and the American Revolution,* edited by Bernard Bailyn and John B. Hench. Worcester, Mass.: American Antiquarian Society, 1980, 11–57.

Brown, Ralph A. "New Hampshire Editors Win the War." *New England Quarterly* 12 (1939): 35–51.

———. "The *Newport Gazette,* Tory News Sheet." *Rhode Island History* 13 (1954): 97–108 and 14 (1955): 11–20.

———. "The *Pennsylvania Ledger:* Tory News Sheet." *Pennsylvania History* 9 (1942): 161–75.

Buckingham, Joseph T. *Specimens of Newspaper Literature.* Boston: C. C. Little and J. Brown, 1850.

Chamberlin, Bill F. "Freedom of Expression in Eighteenth-Century Connecticut: Unanswered Questions," in *Newsletters to Newspapers: Eighteenth-Century Journalism,* edited by Donovan H. Bond and W. Reynolds McLeod. Morgantown: School of Journalism, West Virginia University, 1977, 247–62.

Cullen, Maurice R. "Middle-Class Democracy and the Press in Colonial America." *Journalism Quarterly* 46 (1969): 531–35.

Cutler, Charles L. *Connecticut's Revolutionary Press.* Chester, Conn.: Pequot Press, 1975.

Davidson, Philip. *Propaganda in the American Revolution, 1763–1783.* Chapel Hill: University of North Carolina Press, 1941.

Emery, Edwin, and Michael Emery. *The Press and America: An Interpretive History of the Mass Media,* 6th ed. Englewood Cliffs, N.J.: Prentice-Hall, 1988.

Giddens, P. H. "Maryland and the Stamp Act Controversy." *Maryland Historical Magazine* 27 (1932): 79–98.

Griffith, Louis Turner, and John Erwin Talmadge, *Georgia Journalism, 1763–1950.* Athens: University of Georgia Press, 1951.

Harlan, Robert D. "David Hall and the Stamp Act." *Papers of the Bibliographical Society of America* 61 (1967): 13–37.

Harrison, John M. "The War of Words: The Role of Our First Editorial Writers in Making a Revolution," in *Newsletters to Newspapers: Eighteenth-Century Journalism,* edited by Donovan H. Bond and W. Reynolds McLeod. Morgantown: School of Journalism, West Virginia University, 1977, 207–17.

Hart, Jim A. *The Developing Views on the News: Editorial Syndrome, 1500–1800.* Carbondale: Southern Illinois University Press, 1970.

Henry, Susan. "Margaret Draper, Colonial Printer Who Challenged the Patriots." *Journalism History* 1 (1974): 141–44.

Hudson, Frederic. *Journalism in the United States, from 1690 to 1872.* New York: Harper and Brothers, 1873.

Jones, Robert W. *Journalism in the United States.* New York: E. P. Dutton and Company, 1947.

Kobre, Sidney. *Development of American Journalism.* Dubuque, Iowa: W. C. Brown Company, 1969.

———. "The Revolutionary Colonial Press—A Social Interpretation," *Journalism Quarterly* 20 (1943): 193–204.

Langford, Paul. "British Correspondence in the Colonial Press, 1763–1775: A Study in Anglo-American Misunderstanding Before the American Revolution," in *The Press and the American Revolution,* edited by Bernard Bailyn and John B. Hench. Worcester, Mass.: American Antiquarian Society, 1980, 273–313.

Lee, Alfred McClung. "Dunlap and Claypoole: Printers and News Merchants of the Revolution." *Journalism Quarterly* 11 (1934): 160–78.

Lee, James Melvin. *History of American Journalism.* Boston: Houghton Mifflin, 1923.

Leonard, Thomas C. *The Power of the Press: The Birth of American Political Reporting.* New York: Oxford University Press, 1986.

Lorenz, Alfred L. *Hugh Gaine: A Colonial Printer-Editor's Odyssey to Loyalism.* Carbondale: Southern Illinois University Press, 1972.

Morgan, Edmund S., and Helen M. Morgan. *The Stamp Act Crisis: Prologue to Revolution.* Chapel Hill, N.C.: Published for the Institute of Early American History and Culture at Williamsburg, Va., by the University of North Carolina Press, 1953.

Morris, Richard B. *The Era of the American Revolution.* New York: Columbia University Press, 1939.

Mott, Frank Luther. *American Journalism: A History, 1690–1960,* 3rd ed. New York: Macmillan, 1962.

———. "The Newspaper Coverage of Lexington and Concord." *New England Quarterly* 16 (December 1944): 489–505.

Ours, Robert M. "James Rivington: Another Viewpoint," in *Newsletters to Newspapers: Eighteenth-Century Journalism,* edited by Donovan H. Bond and W. Reynolds McLeod. Morgantown: School of Journalism, West Virginia University, 1977, 219–33.

Pomerantz, Sidney I. "The Patriot Newspaper and the American Revolution," in *The Era of the American Revolution,* edited by Richard B. Morris. New York: Columbia University Press, 1939, 305–31.

Potter, Janice, and Robert M. Calhoon, "The Character and Coherence of the Loyalist Press," in *The Press and the American Revolution,* edited by Bernard Bailyn and John B. Hench. Worcester, Mass.: American Antiquarian Society, 1980, 229–72.

Ramsay, David. *The History of the American Revolution.* Philadelphia: R. Aitken, 1789.

Rutland, Robert A. *The Newsmongers: Journalism in the Life of the Nation, 1690–1972.* New York: The Dial Press, 1973.

Schlesinger, Arthur M., Sr. "Colonial Newspapers and the Stamp Act." *New England Quarterly* 8 (1935): 63–83.

———. *Prelude to Independence: The Newspaper War on Great Britain, 1764–1776.* New York: Alfred Knopf, 1958.

Schneider, Norma. "Clementina Rind: 'Editor, Daughter, Mother, Wife.'" *Journalism History* 1 (1974): 137–40.

Silver, Rollo G. "Aprons Instead of Uniforms: The Practice of Printing, 1776–1787." *Proceedings of the American Antiquarian Society* 87 (1977): 111–94.

———. "Government Printing in Massachusetts, 1751–1801." *Studies in Bibliography* 16 (1963): 161–200.

Steirer, William F. "Riding 'Everyman's Hobby Horse': Journalism in Philadelphia, 1764–1794," in *Newsletters to Newspapers: Eighteenth-Century Journalism,* edited by Donovan H. Bond and W. Reynolds McLeod. Morgantown: School of Journalism, West Virginia University, 1977, 263–75.

———. "A Study in Prudence: Philadelphia's Revolutionary Journalists." *Journalism History* 3 (1976): 16–19.

Teeter, Dwight L. "John Dunlap: The Political Economy of a Printer's Success." *Journalism Quarterly* 52 (1975): 3–8, 55.

Thomas, C. M. "The Publication of Newspapers During the American Revolution." *Journalism Quarterly* 9 (1932): 358–73.

Thomas, Isaiah. *The History of Printing in America.* Worcester, Mass.: Isaiah Thomas, Jr., 1810; reprint, Barre, Mass.: Imprint Society, 1970.

Walett, Francis G. "The Impact of the Stamp Act on the Colonial Press," in *Newsletters to Newspapers: Eighteenth-Century Journalism,* edited by Donovan H. Bond and W. Reynolds McLeod. Morgantown: School of Journalism, West Virginia University, 1977, 157–69.

Weir, Robert M. "The Role of the Newspaper Press in the Southern Colonies on the Eve of the Revolution: An Interpretation," in *The Press and the American Revolution,* edited by Bernard Bailyn and John B. Hench. Worcester, Mass.: American Antiquarian Society, 1980, 99–150.

Wood, Gordon S. "The Democratization of Mind in the American Revolution," in *Leadership in the American Revolution,* edited by Don Higginbotham, Library of Congress Symposia on the American Revolution. Washington, D. C.: Library of Congress, 1974, 63–89.

# INDEX